International Political Economy Series

Series Editor: **Timothy M. Shaw**, Visiting
Boston, USA and Emeritus Professor, Univ

The global political economy is in flux as
organization and governance. The IPE sei
analysis and structure over the last three decades. It has always ――
tion on the global South. Now the South increasingly challenges the North as the
centre of development, also reflected in a growing number of submissions and
publications on indebted Eurozone economies in Southern Europe.

An indispensable resource for scholars and researchers, the series examines
a variety of capitalisms and connections by focusing on emerging economies,
companies and sectors, debates and policies. It informs diverse policy communi-
ties as the established trans-Atlantic North declines and 'the rest', especially the
BRICS, rise.

Titles include:

Eirikur Bergmann
ICELAND AND THE INTERNATIONAL FINANCIAL CRISIS
Boom, Bust and Recovery

Yildiz Atasoy (*editor*)
GLOBAL ECONOMIC CRISIS AND THE POLITICS OF DIVERSITY

Gabriel Siles-Brügge
CONSTRUCTING EUROPEAN UNION TRADE POLICY
A Global Idea of Europe

Jewellord Singh and France Bourgouin (*editors*)
RESOURCE GOVERNANCE AND DEVELOPMENTAL STATES IN THE GLOBAL
SOUTH
Critical International Political Economy Perspectives

Tan Tai Yong and Md Mizanur Rahman (*editors*)
DIASPORA ENGAGEMENT AND DEVELOPMENT IN SOUTH ASIA

Leila Simona Talani, Alexander Clarkson and Ramon Pachedo Pardo (*editors*)
DIRTY CITIES
Towards a Political Economy of the Underground in Global Cities

Matthew Louis Bishop
THE POLITICAL ECONOMY OF CARIBBEAN DEVELOPMENT

Xiaoming Huang (*editor*)
MODERN ECONOMIC DEVELOPMENT IN JAPAN AND CHINA
Developmentalism, Capitalism and the World Economic System

Bonnie K. Campbell (*editor*)
MODES OF GOVERNANCE AND REVENUE FLOWS IN AFRICAN MINING

Gopinath Pillai (*editor*)
THE POLITICAL ECONOMY OF SOUTH ASIAN DIASPORA
Patterns of Socio-Economic Influence

Rachel K. Brickner (*editor*)
MIGRATION, GLOBALIZATION AND THE STATE

Juanita Elias and Samanthi Gunawardana (*editors*)
THE GLOBAL POLITICAL ECONOMY OF THE HOUSEHOLD IN ASIA

Tony Heron
PATHWAYS FROM PREFERENTIAL TRADE
The Politics of Trade Adjustment in Africa, the Caribbean and Pacific

David J. Hornsby
RISK REGULATION, SCIENCE AND INTERESTS IN TRANSATLANTIC TRADE
CONFLICTS

Yang Jiang
CHINA'S POLICYMAKING FOR REGIONAL ECONOMIC COOPERATION

Martin Geiger, Antoine Pécoud (*editors*)
DISCIPLINING THE TRANSNATIONAL MOBILITY OF PEOPLE

Michael Breen
THE POLITICS OF IMF LENDING

Laura Carsten Mahrenbach
THE TRADE POLICY OF EMERGING POWERS
Strategic Choices of Brazil and India

Vassilis K. Fouskas and Constantine Dimoulas
GREECE, FINANCIALIZATION AND THE EU
The Political Economy of Debt and Destruction

Hany Besada and Shannon Kindornay (*editors*)
MULTILATERAL DEVELOPMENT COOPERATION IN A CHANGING GLOBAL
ORDER

Caroline Kuzemko
THE ENERGY- SECURITY CLIMATE NEXUS
Institutional Change in Britain and Beyond

Hans Löfgren and Owain David Williams (*editors*)
THE NEW POLITICAL ECONOMY OF PHARMACEUTICALS
Production, Innnovation and TRIPS in the Global South

Timothy Cadman (*editor*)
CLIMATE CHANGE AND GLOBAL POLICY REGIMES
Towards Institutional Legitimacy

Ian Hudson, Mark Hudson and Mara Fridell
FAIR TRADE, SUSTAINABILITY AND SOCIAL CHANGE

International Political Economy Series

Series Standing Order ISBN 978–0–333–71708–0   hardcover
Series Standing Order ISBN 978–0–333–71110–1   paperback

You can receive future titles in this series as they are published by placing a standing order. Please contact your bookseller or, in case of difficulty, write to us at the address below with your name and address, the title of the series and one of the ISBNs quoted above.

Customer Services Department, Macmillan Distribution Ltd, Houndmills, Basingstoke, Hampshire RG21 6XS, England.

Iceland and the International Financial Crisis

Boom, Bust and Recovery

Eirikur Bergmann

Centre of European Studies, Bifröst University, Iceland

First published 2014 by
PALGRAVE MACMILLAN

Palgrave Macmillan in the UK is an imprint of Macmillan Publishers Limited,
registered in England, company number 785998, of Houndmills, Basingstoke,
Hampshire RG21 6XS.

Palgrave Macmillan in the US is a division of St Martin's Press LLC,
175 Fifth Avenue, New York, NY 10010.

Palgrave Macmillan is the global academic imprint of the above companies
and has companies and representatives throughout the world.

Palgrave® and Macmillan® are registered trademarks in the United States,
the United Kingdom, Europe and other countries

ISBN 978-1-349-46152-3   ISBN 978-1-137-33200-4 (eBook)
DOI 10.1057/9781137332004

A catalogue record for this book is available from the British Library.

A catalog record for this book is available from the Library of Congress.

Transferred to Digital Printing in 2013

To my children,
Sólrún Rós, Einar Sigurður, Hrafnhildur and Ægir Bergmann,
who are amongst the generation inheriting Iceland

Contents

Part II   Boom and Bust

Part III   Revolution and Recovery

Preface

The collapse of the Icelandic banks in October 2008 not only delivered a serious blow to the Icelandic economy but also led to a prolonged political crisis. It was simultaneously a crisis in capitalism and a crisis of national identity – later simply referred to as *The Crash*. I was amongst many others involved in thinking through questions of the Icelandic crisis and its recovery, in both an economic and a political dimension. After I had published a few pieces in the British *Guardian* my office was flooded with foreign journalists, many of whom had preconceived ideas about the events in Iceland. It was difficult not to engage in this unprecedented situation. I was, for example, among the founders of the so-called *InDefence* group established in mid-October 2008 to protest against the British government's implementation of anti-terrorist legislation to freeze Icelandic assets in the UK. In 2011 I served on Iceland's elected Constitutional Council, which had the task of drafting a new constitution for the young republic. I have endeavoured not to allow this and other involvements to cloud my judgement when writing this book. In fact, I believe that these experiences have provided me with a good, perhaps even a unique, perspective on explaining the crisis to a wider audience and warning other nations of some of the mistakes that were made prior to, during and after the crisis, which should serve as a lesson to them.

Though I am solely responsible for its content, many have influenced the writing of this book. First I would like to thank my collaborators in the *Imagined Recovery* Project, Dr Claes Belfrage at Liverpool University and Dr David Berry at the University of Sussex. Some of the concepts used and phrases found in the text, mainly in Chapter 2, were developed within the project. Our continuous discussions during the past few years not only allowed me to clarify my thinking on events surrounding The Crash but also opened my eyes to many new avenues explored further in this book. Some of the thinking concerning the impact of post-colonialism, mainly explored in Chapter 1, was initially developed for a project analysing microstates on the periphery of Europe, led by Drs Rebecca Adler-Nissen and Ulrik Pram Gad at Copenhagen University. Chapter 3 contains information relating to Iceland's foreign relations that I developed for a project, now under the heading of *Distant Voices*, first led by Professor Claudia Ramos at the Fernando Pessoa University in Portugal and later by Dr Lise Rye at NTNU in Norway.

I would also specially like to thank two of my colleagues at Bifröst University, Drs Magnús Árni Magnússon and Njörður Sigurjónsson, with whom I share an office, for fruitful discussions throughout the writing process. The text has also benefited from the constructive criticism of anonymous reviewers and from various readers, who also will remain anonymous. Palgrave Macmillan's editors and staff have been stimulating to work with. I would specially like to thank editor of the International Political Economy Series, Professor Timothy Shaw, for his relentless encouragement and insightful comments, as well as Christina Brian and Amanda McGrath for all their support throughout the process. I also thank the Association of Icelandic Non-Fiction Writers, *Hagþenkir*, for its important support.

Last, and perhaps most importantly, I would like to thank my friends and family for tolerating me during some of the more trying periods of the drafting of the book. Special thanks are due to my partner in life, Aino Freyja Järvelä, and to our children, Sólrún Rós Eiríksdóttir, Einar Sigurður Eiríksson, Hrafnhildur Eiríksdóttir and Ægir Bergmann Eiríksson – to whom this book is dedicated.

List of Abbreviations

ASI	Icelandic Confederation of Labour
Benelux	Belgium, Netherlands, Luxembourg
CB	Central Bank
CC	Constitutional Council
CDS	Credit Default Swap
CEO	Chief Executive Officer
CFP	Common Fisheries Policy
CM	Civil Movement
DKK	The Danish Krona
ECB	European Central Bank
EFTA	European Free Trade Association
EEA	European Economic Area
EMU	European Monetary Union
ERM II	European Exchange Rate Mechanism II
ESA	EFTA Surveillance Authority
EU	European Union
FBA	Icelandic Investment Bank
Fed	US Federal Reserve
FME	Icelandic Financial Supervisory Authority
FSA	Financial Supervisory Authority
FT	*The Financial Times*
FX	Foreign Exchange
G20	The Group of Twenty Industrial States
GATT	General Agreement on Tariffs and Trade
GDP	Gross Domestic Product
ICEX	Icelandic Stock Exchange
IMF	International Monetary Fund
INTICE	Icelandic Companies Project
IP	Independence Party
IPE	International Political Economy
ISK	Icelandic Króna
ITQ	Individual Tradable Quota
KFW	German Reconstruction Credit Institute
LGM	Left Green Movement
LIBOR	London Interbank Offered Rate

LÍU	Association of Fishing Vessel Owners
MBA	Masters of Business Administration
NASDAQ	National Association of Securities Dealers Automated Quotations system
NATO	North Atlantic Treaty Organization
OPEC	Organization of Petroleum Exporting Countries
PA	People's Alliance
PM	Prime Minister
PP	Progressive Party
PR	Public Relations
SA	Confederation of Icelandic Employers
SDA	Social Democratic Alliance
SDP	Social Democratic Party
SIC	Special Investigation Commission
WaMu	Washington Mutual
WL	Women's List
UN	United Nations

Introduction – Boom, Bust and Recovery

In autumn 2008 Iceland became the poster child of the global Credit Crunch when our three international banks came tumbling down within a single week, amounting to one of the world's greatest national financial crises. The tiny Nordic country was reported as being a rogue state defaulting on its obligations. In the years leading up to the Crash, Iceland had been trumpeted in world business media as an economic miracle. Its new breed of Viking Capitalists had become rock stars of the global finance-driven economy. Now their action was testing the very foundations of Europe's financial system. A domino effect threatened. Half a decade later, Iceland was, however, already well on the road to recovery, with greater growth and less unemployment than most European states.

This was a financial tsunami without precedent. Iceland also responded significantly differently to the troubles than most other states, allowing its financial system to default rather than throwing good money after bad. In addition, the left-wing government, parachuted in on the canopy of the so-called Pots and Pans revolution, refused to implement strict austerity. The Icelandic case thus provides interesting lessons for the wider world. In this book I will explain the exceptional case of Iceland's fantastical boom, bust and relatively rapid recovery after the Crash. I will provide a clear introduction to the particular case of Iceland both historically and financially, and explain the lessons for the wider EU crisis and for over-reaching economies that over-rely on financial markets.

The Crash illustrated an inherited vulnerability in the economy, deeply rooted in the very smallness the Viking *outvasion* was meant to cure. Cooper and Shaw (2009) maintain that Iceland provides a pertinent example of a small state where vulnerability and resilience became closely intertwined; that its unconventional financial behaviour brought short-term gains but also exposed us to massive long-term problems. These are among some of the characteristics of the Icelandic economy I will explore in this book.

There were a lot of misconceptions about the Icelandic crisis. The then British Prime Minister Gordon Brown, for example, announced to the world on live TV that Iceland was bankrupt, had defaulted on its sovereign debt and was in effect a failed state. Radical forces in southern Europe, on the other hand, told a glorifying story of militant Icelandic revolutionaries taking to the streets and overthrowing a corrupt government before categorically refusing to pay the bankers' debts. In many articles the Spanish daily *El Pais* told a tale of the triumphant proletariat taking power, ousting the elite and then writing its own constitution. In Britain the *Guardian* wrote about a feminist revolution: women cleaning the house after the boys had wrecked the place in mad partying. In America the *New York Times* claimed that Iceland was the first to prosecute and punish its politicians. In his book *Boomerang* Michael Lewis talked about an angry mob roaming the streets of Reykjavik blowing up the Viking Capitalists' luxury cars. After the 2013 parliamentary election the world media, on the other hand, wrongly reported that the old guard was back in power. There seemed to be endless myths about the crisis and the great Icelandic revolution, which I will in this book try to unravel and correct.

The Crash

It was all very dramatic. Clearly something was going very wrong. The global banking giant Lehman Brothers had recently gone into administration in America, sending a shockwave throughout the international financial system. Our government had been travelling the world desperately shopping for money to bail out out the overblown financial system, which had grown way out of control in the preceding years – amounting to almost ten times the country's GDP. But there were no takers. No one was willing to give us more cash. Not even our Nordic neighbours. When we came begging they told us rather to go to the IMF. At first our government felt that to do so would be humiliating, implying that we had failed in our historical quest to be recognized by our neighbours as an independent and fully functioning modern nation state – which is the core of Iceland's national postcolonial identity. Our leaders seemed to think that the IMF was only for failed third-world countries. Instead we sent representatives to Moscow to squeeze some money out of the Russians – or rather to put pressure on the West to step in.

This, however, contradicted all traditional alliances. Since independence in 1944, Iceland has been committed to Western co-operation, both as a founding member of NATO in 1949 and as a participant in the EU Internal Market after entering into the European Economic Area in 1994. We are also a fully participating member of the EU border control scheme, Schengen. Our strongest allies have always been the Nordic states, the UK, the rest of Western Europe and, for a while, America. There was a US military base here until just two years prior to the Crash. Iceland's self-image emphasizes independence but is also tied to Western Europe: we like to think of ourselves as the small Atlantic state that links Europe and America. So it really was a major psychological U-turn for most Icelanders to suddenly turn to the East for help – all the way to Moscow, of all places! To make matters worse, our delegates returned empty handed from Russia.

Running out of time, Iceland found itself without friends in the world. Apart from our tiny neighbour, the Faroe Islands, who sent over enough for us to buy a few vital necessities, no one stepped up to help us. However, this lack of loan opportunities later proved to be a blessing in disguise, as I will explain.

On Monday 6 October 2008 Prime Minister Geir Haarde addressed the nation on television. Apart from the traditional annual New Year's Eve address, this is something our PM never does. We were all watching, gathered round TV sets and computer screens in our workplace, in cafés and at home on that misty afternoon. It was not just that this sophisticated and usually perfectly composed man seemed shaken but that he concluded his unique address by asking God to bless Iceland. This is when we knew we were in serious trouble. Iceland is quite secular. Unlike American politicians, Icelandic politicians never refer to God in public – at least not without cracking a joke.

Before dawn the following morning our first bank fell, the second on the day after that. Then British Prime Minister Gordon Brown invoked the UK Anti-Terrorism Act (passed after '9/11' in 2001) to freeze all Icelandic assets in the UK. That act killed of our last and largest bank still standing, Kaupthing. This had devastating consequences not only for the whole Icelandic economy, but also for the hundreds of thousands of UK citizens who had entrusted our banks with their savings. In only three days all of the Iceland's three international banks, amounting to 85 per cent of the country's financial system, came tumbling down one after the other; first Landsbanki, then Glitnir and finally Kaupthing – after our Central Bank had just handed Kaupthing the rest of our foreign currency reserve in a desperate attempt to save our last financial institution. Iceland is one of the smallest countries in the world and borders on being a micro-state with just over 300,000 inhabitants. However, this experience ranks third in the history of the world's greatest bankruptcies (Halldórsson & Zoega, 2010).

At a stroke, the stock exchange and the entire equity market was virtually wiped out, the tiny currency, the Icelandic króna, tanked, spurring rampant inflation, which in the following weeks and months ate up most people's savings, property values dropped by more than a third and unemployment reached levels never seen before in the life of the young republic. We didn't know what to do. Most remained paralysed, some took to the streets in angry protest while a few more constructively minded people instantly formed new associations aimed to resurrect and reform the stricken nation. Bailing out the domestic operations of the banks alone caused the national debt to shoot from 23 per cent of GDP in 2007 to 78 per cent in 2009 (Central Bank of Iceland, 2010). The addition of other costs brought the debt level to well over 100 per cent of GDP.

Iceland had few good options. The IMF would not consider our loan application until we had settled our dispute with the UK and Dutch governments over the Icesave deposits accounts, which the fallen Landsbanki had set up in those countries, leaving many of their citizens without access to their money. Even though our government steadfastly argued that we weren't legally at fault and that the nation would fulfil all its legal obligations regarding Icesave, the IMF wouldn't budge. It was being pressured by the UK and Dutch governments, backed by the whole EU apparatus. This was a staring contest we could not afford to drag out.

In the Western media Iceland was reported as being a failed state: our government had defaulted on its legal obligations, and we were virtually doomed – falling into an economic 'abyss' with all imports 'blocked'. (An illuminating example of the fall from grace came in the midst of the havoc when the Japanese unilaterally and without any explanation cancelled a planned concert tour of the Icelandic Symphony Orchestra in Tokyo and other Japanese cities.) As I will discuss in the following chapter, being recognized as a partner in Western culture speaks to the inner core of Iceland's postcolonial national identity. This misreporting thus hurt our self-image. Many friends abroad called asking if we were OK, if we still had food and shelter. They sounded convinced that we had all lost our jobs, and offered to help. This was, however, not the case. Despite what was written in the world's tabloids, we still went to work every day, received our salaries, paid our bills and gathered in the pubs in the evenings. Finally, the IMF came through with a loan package and a programme backed by our Nordic neighbours and Poland. As I will explain, the dispute over Icesave soon contributed in a dramatic way to Iceland's postcolonial identity. Fuelled by harsh nationalistic rhetoric the dispute subsequently turned into the most serious international conflict Iceland had entered into since the Cod Wars with the British in the 1970s.

Iceland's reputation abroad was in tatters. We were caught in a perfect media storm, with disaster stories blazing across the world. In an article titled 'Iceland's next saga: The wounded tiger's tale' the *Globe and Mail*, for example, dramatically reported a 'sudden spasm of depopulation as Icelanders prepare to flee' (Hart, 2008). Even the very name of the country gained specific connotations, linked with crisis, bankers' excess, reckless business dealings and economic disaster. Iceland's economic collapse was unprecedented. Leaders in crisis-ridden countries kept insisting that whatever problem they might face in these troubled times, at least they were not as bad as Iceland. Others thought that Iceland was only the canary in the coalmine; that more countries were on the same trajectory to economic devastation. The *Guardian*'s David Teather wrote that Iceland was 'seen as a warning for the rest of the world' (Teather, 2008). In Ireland a popular joke asked, 'What is the difference between Ireland and Iceland?' Answer: 'One letter and six months.' Another joke asked, 'What is the Capital of Iceland?' Answer: 'About five euros.' Similarly, in the UK, the *Financial Times* wrote about *Reykjavik-on-Thames* (Murphy, 2008a). Furthermore, independence movements in neighbouring states like Scotland lost a role model.

Iceland and Ireland provide an interesting comparison. Both developed relatively late in the 20th century and both grew an unsustainable financial sector around the turn of the century, which had over-extended itself and would burst with devastating effect. The Irish banks loaned far too much to property developers, provoking a massive housing bubble, while Iceland's expansion abroad grew unsustainable and drawing back high risk capital against high interest. Economist and Nobel laureate Paul Krugman demonstrates that both countries had run into a bind by being just like the US, 'only more so' – both had 'jumped with both feet into the brave new world of unsupervised global markets' (Krugman, 2009). The two countries were, however, on each side of the EU fence, which might have determined their very different responses: Ireland bailing out banks and providing a blanket guarantee for all liabilities while the Icelandic banks were taken into administration. (For more on the Irish case, see Kirby, 2010.)

The blame game

Internally, the blame game started instantly in the aftermath of what generally is simply referred to as The Crash (*Hrunið*) (Jóhannesson, 2009). Our usually calm and sleepily safe society was ripped apart in internal conflict. The left-wing opposition blamed the neoliberal establishment, including the Central Bank; the governor of the Central Bank blamed the risk-seeking bankers; the bankers blamed the government; and the Prime Minister attributed the whole dreadful sequence of events to external forces, mainly the international Credit Crunch. This lack of any sense of responsibility angered the public to the extent that they took to the streets in greater numbers than ever before.

At the turn of the century, Iceland's three main sectoral banks had been privatized and each passed into the ownership of a nouveau-rich clan. By vigorously enforcing its deregulation policy the laissez-faire government had created a monster it couldn't control: the Icelandic Viking Capitalist was born. In an effort to gain international recognition the new Icelandic business Vikings headed for the high streets around Europe with their pockets full of borrowed money – literally storming the global financial market with the savings of generations of hard-working Icelanders. It seemed that Iceland's historical journey towards modernity was finally complete. The new business elite were heroically branded outvasion Vikings (*Útrásarvíkingur*), referring to Iceland's Golden Age of the settlement society in the 9th and 10th centuries, when Icelanders were still free, before falling prey to foreign oppression.

In linking the new outvasion Vikings with this particular memory of the past, based on a collective myth created during Iceland's struggle for independence from Denmark in the 19th century, the discourse on the economic boom was framed and explained through collective nationalistic sentiments, which spoke directly to the people's postcolonial political identity. I maintain that the enthusiastic behaviour of the outvasion Vikings and the widespread, almost cheerleading acceptance of their endeavours at home must be explained in relation to Iceland's history and through its postcolonial national identity. This is similar to, for example, what Foukas and Dimoulas claim is true of the crisis in Greece: that a historical and geopolitical analysis is vital to understand economic developments (Foukas & Dimoulas, 2013). Linking acquisitions of foreign companies with the masculine image of the Viking explorers implied that the Icelandic businessmen had unique natural characteristics, which helped them get ahead in international business.

The extensive growth of the economy was thus in a way intertwined with a notion of a starting point of a new area for Iceland.

Many seemingly irresponsible actions of the business Vikings were legitimized and made sense of through this nationalistic discourse. The Viking heritage is aggressive and masculine. Accordingly it was in a kind of a testosterone-driven pissing contest that Icelandic CEOs, fresh out of business school, took over established companies in fields they couldn't even pronounce. The fast decision-making and risk-seeking behaviour of this new breed was celebrated by our President as well as in the business media around the world, boosting the already overblown egos of these young alpha-males. Within one short decade this traditional Nordic welfare state economy was transferred into one of deregulated bonanza capitalism. This occurred also without much criticism in the academic debate, which rather welcomed the change.

When the clouds started to gather on the horizon in early 2006, all criticism against what we had grown accustomed to calling the *Icelandic economic miracle* was dismissed as ill-intentioned whining by envious foreigners, as it violated our established postcolonial self-image. Any voice of caution and classical wisdom was thus dismissed as old-fashioned. In an opinion-oppressed political environment the regulation industry, for example, was mocked by politicians and the business elite alike. Throwing nationalism into the mix of inexperience, the Icelandic government responded to foreign criticism to the poor state of our economy by launching a defensive PR campaign in London, New York and Copenhagen. Then came The Crash. Russian-style privatization and rapid deregulation had led to exponential growth of the financial sector. Fuelled by nationalistic rhetoric Iceland had gone in less than a decade from a resource-based local economy, dependent on fishing and geo-thermal energy, to a global financial giant.

When the dust had settled we saw that it was an evil mix of greed, incompetence, nepotism, nationalism, youthful risk addiction and a kind of collective superiority complex which had led to the fall of the whole Icelandic financial sector in October 2008. As I will explain in the following chapter, this development can perhaps best be explained through postcolonial analysis.

The Pots and Pans revolution

The across the centre government, led by the hegemonic right-wing Independence Party (IP) in coalition with the junior Social Democratic Alliance (SDA), was ousted in a series of largely non-violent popular protests in January 2009, which is most commonly referred to as the *Pots and Pans revolution (Búsáhaldabyltingin)*. It was the first government to collapse after the international financial crisis hit. Peaceful protests had started in October 2008. Frustration grew, first with the lack of any sense of responsibility, then with the lack of effective action to ease the perceived economic pain most people felt, and finally with the sense that all the political elite were incompetent. Its failure to meet foreign pressure forcefully enough in the Icesave dispute added to this notion of incompetence.

Initially the government tried to dismiss the protesters as frustrated wannabe politicians and disillusioned youngsters who did not understand the complexity of the situation. But when our grandmothers put down their knitting needles, strapped their boots on and took to the streets shouting for an election we saw that the disgust was almost universal. Without much organization or central planning the public surrounded the Parliament building when it resumed after the Christmas recess on 20 January. The protestors put forward a clear demand for an early election. Ignoring them, the ministers and parliamentarians tried to sit out the protest, hiding inside the old building in central Reykjavik. This time it didn't work. The protests grew and the people kept warm by burning torches in front of the building. They were going nowhere. The Parliament remained under siege well into this dark night in Iceland's history, and the vigil resumed the following morning.

This was the first time in Icelandic history that a young anarchist might have expected to meet his grandmother in the crowd demonstrating against the government and drumming with her kitchen knife on pots and pans. The Icelandic public feared that their country had virtually been stolen by a globetrotting business elite that had spent more time rubbing shoulders with international high society than giving back to the society that had enabled them to enjoy this privileged lifestyle. Ashamed at having allowed this monstrous Viking business culture to grow beyond control, ordinary Icelanders were determined to take their country back.

We now understand that the Icelandic finance-dominated growth model collapsed under its own weight. Perhaps much as in Ireland. As Pedar Kirby (2010: 4) explains, though Ireland's recession surely mirrors external developments, the particular causes of its crisis were 'decisively local in origin' as the economy had grown unsustainable. The same is true of Iceland, as I will explain in Chapters 4, 5 and 6 in Part II. In the following chapter I will offer an additional explanation and demonstrate how the constitution of Iceland's postcolonial national identity, which emphasizes formal self-authority as well as a desire to be recognized as a partner in Western culture, prevented us from acknowledging the systemic faults in the set-up of our economic and political structure. Here is another interesting parallel with Ireland, which, having belonged to the UK, was keen on demonstrating its new-found economic prosperity in order to emphasize its independence (Fagan, 2003). Furthermore, both were gripped by fear of the grim days of the past returning.

On 1 February 2009 the ousted government was replaced by a fragile left-wing caretaker government led by the SDA in coalition with the Left Green Movement (LGM), which leans much further to the left. This was a minority government backed by a new leadership within the Progressive Party (PP), which had until 2007 served as junior partner in coalitions with the IP. A well known activist for social reform, the Social Affairs minister Jóhanna Sigurðardóttir, who had belonged to the far left of the SDA, became Iceland's first female Prime Minister (and the first openly gay PM in the world). The government promised to clean up its act and abandon corrupt practices with a more professional and transparent decision-making process. Subsequently, the three politically appointed governors of the Central Bank were replaced by a single professional governor (Már Guðmundsson, who nevertheless had affiliations with the SDA) and the director and board of the Financial Supervisory Authority were sacked. After gaining a majority in the following parliamentary elections, in spring 2009, the new government initiated a number of policies and programmes aimed at replacing the collapsed neoliberal growth model with a resurrected Nordic welfare society. The election results showed a massive swing to the left. For the first time in the young republic's history, a pure left-wing majority coalition was formed. Many interpreted the result as a powerful shift away from the Viking Capitalism that appeared to have left the country in economic ruin. Four years later the pendulum shifted back in the April 2013 parliament election, resulting in right of centre government resuming power again, as I discuss further.

Instead of implementing strict austerity, the left-wing post crisis government responded to The Crash with more broad-based measures aimed at protecting the welfare and purchasing power of the lower income groups, thus phasing in fiscal consolidation over a number of years with borrowing from abroad and raising taxes as well as cutting spending. The Nobel Prize-winning economist Joseph Stiglitz has claimed that economic inequality was stifling economic recovery in the US. His main argument is that the middle class had become 'too weak to support the consumer spending that has historically driven our economic growth' (Stiglitz, 2013). Paul Krugman disputed the claim as unfounded. While agreeing that inequality was politically unfortunate, he added: 'economics is not a morality play' (Krugman, 2013). This debate between the two American Nobel Prize-winning economists over the impact of inequality on recovery is interesting for the Icelandic case as the main effort of the left-wing government was indeed to prevent inequality growing with the progressing crisis.

Recovery and new critical order

The Crash was followed by a severe economic, social and political crisis. Key government institutions and the political class stood accused of having sponsored the economic rise and collapse. However devastating, this collapse also provided opportunities, as crisis in capitalism can open up our imagination to alternative 'economic imaginaries' (Jessop, 2004). The constitutional revision process was, for example, an integral part of the 'imagined recovery' of Iceland from this profound crisis. Indeed, the crisis did open up the public debate, with a flood of suggestions for recovery measures pouring through almost all outlets for public discussion; in the media, in open forum meetings and on the internet. New associations were being formed that challenged the ruling class and the whole political system. Serious discussions followed on creating a new Icelandic republic, French style – in data-science lingo, updating the system to Iceland 2.0.

Among major government initiatives was the imposition of tougher regulations on the financial industry. The new office of Special Prosecutor was established to investigate criminal activities in the financial sector leading up to The Crash, and Parliament appointed a Special Investigation Research Commission (a 'truth committee'), which was to analyse events and eventually proposed to Parliament that a hitherto dormant clause in the constitution relating to the prosecution of government ministers should be used to hold political leaders accountable. The former Prime Minister was indeed prosecuted before this special court and sentenced to punishment. But as I will explain, this was in effect only a slap on the wrist; he never saw a jail cell. The fact that his political opponents singled out only Haarde for trial further undermined the whole exercise.

An agreement was struck with the UK and Dutch governments with regard to the Icesave deposit accounts. This was mainly so that Iceland could regain access to international financial markets and to allow the IMF to be brought in to stabilize the economy, not least through the introduction of capital controls and the co-funding of a loan package with the Nordic and Polish governments. The agreement, however, proved a hard sell to the general public. In an extraordinary move the President refused to pass the bill, referring it to a referendum, in which it was rejected by a large majority, spurring one of the greatest international disputes Iceland had ever fought. In early 2013, the EFTA Court ruled on the case, vindicating Iceland of wrongdoing and dismissing the claim of the British and Dutch authorities, which, with the backing of the EU, had insisted that Iceland was responsible for the Icesave deposits. After the ruling Iceland's relationship with the outside world normalized again.

Iceland is the smallest currency area in world. An application for EU membership was made in order to create a more stable framework around the economy together with the aim of fast-tracking the country into the Eurozone as a way out of currency controls and to gain access to a credible currency. Soon after the initial shock had died down, the accession negotiation process foundered on the rocks of nationalistic rhetoric, resulting in widespread opposition to membership, even beyond previous levels. After the spring 2013 election, the new right of centre government, led by the PP, decided to freeze the negotiations.

Together with a complete overhaul of the Constitution these previously mentioned measures were instigated to not only resurrect but rather to establish a reformed base of the Icelandic society and marked a paradigm shift from the collapsed neoliberal model. In addition to these major governmental initiatives the whole party system, which traditionally consisted of four main political parties, was challenged by emerging political parties and an ever-increasing pressure to renew the leadership of the established ones. Symbolic of this was the election of a comedian, Jón Gnarr, as Mayor of Reykjavik.

Interestingly, all of these initiatives, both the ones instigated by the government and those emerging from grassroots measures, were subsequently highly politicized in a radical 'new critical order' emerging from the crisis, contesting most initiatives for what constitutes 'recovery'. The emergence of 'critical orders' following crises is not unusual historically, but the existence of a sustained one in which imagined recoveries can take form and stabilize in an advanced capitalist economy is. By studying the process of these previously mentioned proposed reforms I will analyse this critical order, which has lodged deeply on the micro level of Icelandic everyday life and is in direct opposition to reparative moves.

Half a decade after The Crash, most economic indicators pointed to the rapid recovery of Iceland's economy, perhaps supporting Stiglitz's contention mentioned above. The currency had stabilized, though it was still locked behind capital controls; GDP was growing again and predicted soon to be up to its pre-crisis level; unemployment was amongst the lowest in Europe, below 5 per cent; and perhaps most importantly, opinion polls indicated as early as 2010 that Icelanders were becoming more positive in their economic outlook (Conway, 2010). Still, and despite the benefits of its longstanding opposition to the previously hegemonic Independence Party, delegitimizing a capitalist 'rise from the ruins' proved a hard sell for the post-crisis left-wing coalition government, which lost heavily in the spring 2013 parliamentary elections, when the IP and PP again won the majority they had so often enjoyed in the pre-crisis period. PP leader Sigmundur Davíð Gunnlaugsson, whose popularity had risen during the campaign against the agreements with the British and the Dutch on Icesave, replaced Sigurðardóttir as Prime Minister. The failure of the challenger, Þóra Arnórsdóttir, who had stood against President Ólafur Ragnar Grímsson in the 2012 presidential election, running on a ticket marking the end of crisis politics and a renewed unification of Icelanders, was another example of a rejected proposal for reform.

Outline and analysis

This book tells the story of Iceland's incredible boom and bust and provides a distinction between the *imagined* and *real* recovery after The Crash. Its principal novelty is to apply postcolonial analysis, which more is commonly used to explain cultural and political identities and their effect on bilateral foreign relations in newly independent states, on the development of Iceland's economy leading up to The Crash. The same model can also help to explain Iceland's response to external forces in its aftermath as well as the efforts towards recovery and indeed recognition abroad. This approach fits into Critical International Political Economy, which departs from orthodox IPE (with its emphasis on empirical research) by applying ontological enquiry to historical evolution (Shields, Bruff & Macartney, 2011).

The book is structured into nine chapters in three parts in addition to this introduction and final conclusions. I start the analysis by framing my postcolonial theoretical model within critical IPE, based on a post-structural approach. Through it I explain Iceland's political and economic history and analyse its national identity emerging out of the independence struggle in the 19th and early 20th centuries. A collective myth of Iceland's history was created to construct a cultural-political identity, which emphasizes formal sovereignty as well as the desire to be recognized as a partner in the Western world. Icelandic politics were subsequently dominated by a nationalistic discourse, which later was the driving force behind the Viking-like endeavours of Icelandic businessmen in Western Europe.

In Chapter 2 I provide an overview of the country's economic history, which is marked by repeated cycles of boom and bust. In the 20th century, Iceland moved from being amongst the poorest economies and most backward societies in Europe to becoming one of the most modern and prosperous in the world. Access to investment during and in the wake of WWII allowed the rapid growth of a resource-based economy around fishing and geo-thermal energy, until the creation of the finance-based Viking economy towards the end of the millennium.

Chapter 3 deals with Iceland's foreign relations, which are linked with its economic development and also dictated by its postcolonial national identity. This has, for example, resulted in Iceland's peculiar position in European integration, insofar as it participates in the EU Single Market through the EEA without being a formal member of the EU. In this chapter I explain Iceland's often strained relationship with its neighbours, which can be traced to its postcolonial identity.

These three background chapters in Part I, titled 'Rise and Shine', provide a basis for an understanding of the boom and bust of the Icelandic economy after the turn of the millennium, which I will turn to next. In Part II, titled 'Boom and Bust', also divided into three chapters, I analyse the rise of the so-called Icelandic economic miracle and explain its dramatic downfall.

Chapter 4 discusses the emergence of Iceland's neoliberal, finance-driven economy, which was taking shape around the turn of the century. I map the widespread outvasion of the Viking Capitalists, when Iceland was hailed as an economic miracle by the world's media, and explain how the incredible boom of the finance-driven Viking Capitalist economy was fuelled by a deeply rooted nationalistic rhetoric.

By 2006 we were living on borrowed time, as discussed in Chapter 5, which deals with the so-called Geyser Crisis and the build-up to the banking crash of October 2008. After a near-death experience in the mini crisis of 2006, the Icelandic Viking Capitalists threw off all chains and blew even more hot air into the economy – until finally falling off the financial cliff. Liquidity dried up abroad and Iceland was pushed out of international financial markets.

The Crash of 2008 not only destroyed Iceland's economic well-being but also brought with it a profound crisis of identity. While navigating through extraordinary turmoil on international markets, Iceland was also fending off hostile action by the British authorities. External forces thus significantly contributed to the level of crisis. Still, Iceland's finance-driven economy collapsed under its own weight. In Chapter 6 I discuss the catastrophic events of October 2008.

In Part III, headed 'Revolution and Recovery', I explain the events surrounding the Pots and Pans revolution and analyse Iceland's economic recovery and political restructuring after The Crash, including the constitutional revision process.

The across-the-centre grand coalition of the Independence Party and the Social Democratic Alliance was ousted after a series of protests known as the Pots and Pans revolution. Frustrated by the government's lack of accountability and seeming weakness in representing Iceland's interests against the UK and Dutch governments in the Icesave dispute, the public took to the streets in larger numbers than ever before. In Chapter 7 I discuss these unprecedented events and the considerable effect of the Icesave dispute.

In Chapters 8 and 9 I analyse Iceland's economic recovery and political reform. Five years after suffering one of the most profound economic crises of any developed country, Iceland was performing much better than expected, with modest growth and lower unemployment than elsewhere in Europe.

As discussed in Chapter 9, political reform was, however, caught in a new critical order, which was directly opposed to proposed reparative moves. Initially, for example, the constitutional reform process was seen as a healing process but gradually this too was politicized, eventually falling into traditional trenches of Icelandic party politics.

Relevant conclusions are drawn and discussed at the end of each chapter. Short overall conclusions follow in a separate, final chapter that discusses the lessons of the Icelandic financial crisis. Each of the three parts – and indeed each chapter in the book – is structured in such a way that it can be read independently. Some repetition is unavoidable to ensure the independence of each chapter. Those only interested in the story of the Icelandic Crash itself can, for example, skip over the three chapters in Part I, which provide the background and lay a theoretical basis for the following discussion. I recommend, however, reading the chapters in order.

Part I
Rise and Shine

1
Birth of a Nation – A Postcolonical Project

Iceland was settled in 874[1] by Norwegian explorers, allegedly fleeing tyranny and the increased tax burden of King Harald. According to historical tales a small society descended from Irish clergy had by then already died out. Half a century later, the Icelandic state was formed with the establishment of the *Alþingi* in 930. The *Alþingi* was a parliamentary court held in a rocky gorge where the European and American tectonic plates meet. The cliffs created a natural loudspeaker so that all attendees could hear the voice of the person occupying the podium. The site, located inland in the south of Iceland, was in accordance with its function named *Þingvellir*, meaning 'parliamentary fields'. After troubled times of fierce battles between the main noble families, Iceland entered into a union with the King of Norway by an agreement that is now referred to as the Old Treaty. The importance of the *Alþingi* gradually diminished but it wasn't formally cancelled until the year 1800.

The end of the first millennium saw increased clashes between Christianity and the old pagan religion. The matter was referred to the sage Þorgrímur Ljósvetingagoði, who, after a period of reflection, ruled on a compromise in the year 1000: that Icelanders should publicly convert to Christianity but still be allowed to continue worshiping their pagan gods in private. When Norway fell under Danish rule in 1380, Iceland was brought in line with it. Copenhagen did not, however, gain complete control over the country until Icelanders were forced to accept the absolute power of the Danish king in 1662. From then on, the *Alþingi* was only occasionally convened and solely in the capacity of a local court, having been stripped of its legislative powers. When absolutism was finally ended in Denmark in 1848, after a lengthy struggle for democratic reform, born out of the Enlightenment, Icelanders started to fight for their independence, and the notion of a separate Icelandic nation was born.

The first step towards independence was taken in 1844, when the *Alþingi* was 'resurrected' as an advisory parliamentary body in Reykjavik. A new democratic constitution came into force in Denmark in 1849 and, after ending Iceland's domestically elected Constitutional Assembly (*Þjóðfundurinn*) by force in 1951 and unilaterally deciding to keep control over the country in the Position Law's (*Stöðulögin*) of 1871, the Danish king finally handed Icelanders their own constitution in 1874. Iceland was granted home rule in 1904, but with very limited executive powers. More importantly, sovereignty was won in 1918, which included full internal independence and for the most part external control within a personal union with the Danish monarch as head of state. Full independence was to follow in 1944 – against the will of Denmark, when it was still under Nazi occupation (for more, see Karlsson, 2000).

Most students of Icelandic politics acknowledge the importance of the independence struggle in the development of its contemporary political identity. In this chapter I will explain how the myth of Iceland's history was used to construct a cultural-political identity that emphasizes formal sovereignty as well as a desire to be recognized as a partner in the Western world. As I will illustrate, Icelandic politics have been dominated since the end of the 19th century by the nationalist discourse developed during the independence struggle. As will become further evident in Chapter 4, which discusses the boom years, this nationalistic postcolonial political identity was indeed the driving force behind the Viking-like endeavours of Icelandic businessmen in Western Europe around the turn of the millennium. I therefore maintain that any model developed to study Iceland's political and economic development as well as its foreign relations cannot afford to ignore the extensive influence of the colonial past. This is in line with, for example, Penny Griffin (2011), which frames poststructural analysis within critical International Political Economy, emphasizing the importance of studying historical links of exploitation, domination and force – for example in postcolonial relations.

Postcolonial theories emphasize the importance of analysing the impact of colonial contact on contemporary politics and the cultural legacy of colonialism, and thus critically explore the link between the past and the present – which I claim is central to an understanding of the development of Iceland's politics and economy. It is through that relationship that Iceland's postcolonial national identity was created. It is therefore not a question of a temporary situation fading out over time after the country had gained independence, but rather an established and regularly reconstructed political culture, still ongoing in contemporary politics.

The independence struggle

In the realm of contemporary Icelandic politics, the legacy of the more than a century-long independence struggle in the 19th and early 20th century (1830–1944) is still very present. The publication of the journal *Ármann á Alþingi*, edited by Baldvin Einarsson, in Copenhagen in 1830 can be viewed as the starting point of the struggle. Further journals promoting Iceland's autonomy followed, written by groups of Icelandic intellectuals in Copenhagen. The journal *Fjölnir* (1835–1847), edited by a group of romantic nationalists, and *Ný félagsrit* (1841–1873), led by Iceland's independence hero Jón Sigurðsson, were the most influential.

The struggle was fought with legal argumentation rather than with arms; that is, with words rather than violence, thus emphasizing rhetoric over force. It was led by a small group of Icelandic intellectuals in Copenhagen, who, by referring to Iceland's history of independent Vikings, developed a national myth that served as a justification for their emphasis on sovereignty and independence. The term *myth* is here used in the sense that Iceland's history was creatively interpreted to fit the claim for self-rule. According to the myth, Iceland is a unique nation and it is the duty of all Icelanders to actively guard its sovereignty and independence. History professor Guðmundur Hálfdanarson (2001: 96) explains how Iceland's independence hero Jón Sigurðsson has since become the symbolic father of all Icelanders.

Icelandic historian Jón Sigurðsson (1811–1879), living in Copenhagen, gradually emerged as the leader of the struggle and has since become Iceland's national hero. Out of the myth interpreting the history of Iceland's settlement republic (930–1262) he was instrumental in formulating the claim that Icelanders had a natural right, as a separate nation with a unique language, to declare its self-rule. Sigurðsson became President of the Icelandic Literary Society in Copenhagen and later President of the resurrected *Alþingi*. Even though he was never President of Iceland, he is still referred to as 'President Jón' (*Jón forseti*). Iceland's national day is on his birthday, 17 June. Historian Páll Björnsson (2010) documents that all camps in Icelandic politics – conservatives, communists, nationalists and liberals alike – refer to Sigurðsson to advance and indeed to legitimize their arguments in contemporary politics.

Iceland's political identity, carved out in the independence struggle, is based on a fundamental belief in *formal* sovereignty, which still dictates our foreign relations to a great extent. Growing from a population of around 60,000 inhabitants in the mid-19th century to 330,000 at present, Iceland borders on being a microstate. However, as is evident from the following discourse analysis, even though its smallness surely puts limits on its administrative capacity to operate a fully functioning modern independent state, no alternative is ever voiced in Icelandic political discourse. To propose otherwise would be considered blasphemy, which no politician would dare be accused of.

Counting as a separate nation was instrumental to the demand of creating the Icelandic nation state. Young as the nation is, Icelanders can to a greater extent than perhaps most other social groups claim to constitute a nation. As an island located far out in the Atlantic Ocean Iceland is isolated from other countries. Icelanders speak their own language and are of the same ethnicity and most accept traditional Christian values. Most Icelanders, furthermore, have a similar understanding of their history and are united in valuing their literary heritage.

The colonial heritage

Only a handful of scholars, mainly those analysing Icelandic cultural relations, have studied the importance of the country's colonial past. Anthropology Professor Kristín Loftsdóttir (2011), for example, analysed how the colonial experience was instrumental in shaping our national identity, which was formulated in close dialogue with European colonial identity. Since then it had been 'constantly remanufactured through various discourses and praxis' (Loftsdóttir, 2011). By studying the representations of the Viking image in Icelandic rhetoric Ann-Sofie Nielsen Germaud (2010) examines the importance of the colonial past in Iceland's contemporary discourse. She concludes that the Viking notion is a central but changeable element in the modern collective Icelandic self-image. Referring to Claude Lévi-Stauss's division of societies according to their 'hot' or 'cold' relationship with the past, Nielsen Germaud categorizes Iceland as a clearly 'hot society' 'where history is an internalized generation that helps to contextualize the future through historically based cultural memory' (Nielsen Germaud, 2010). The discursive representation of the past is indeed continually present in Icelandic politics. Accordingly, it can be argued that the contemporary political condition in Iceland is very much a result of its historical relationship with neighbouring countries.

Evidence for this was, for example, found in Prime Minister Gunnlaugsson's first address to the nation, on Iceland's national day, on 17 June 2013, in which he discussed Iceland's 'No' vote in the referendum on the Icesave agreement. Referring to the Viking heritage, he explained that precisely because they were descended from Vikings, Icelanders were independently minded and would thus not surrender to foreign authority (Gunnlaugsson, 2013).

This is in line with Andreas Huyssen's (2001) claim that a framework for understanding the present is built through remembering past events, where the past even constitutes the source of understanding for complex global interrelations in the present. Importantly, he points out that this involves a successful marketing of these collective memories. The constant and continuous remembrance of the past thus provides a framework and context for an understanding of the present. Anthony Smith (1993) explains how collective memories in relation to a colonial past can even be contradictory and inconsistent.

Along these lines, Loftsdóttir (2010) stresses that the Icelandic case indeed indicates how relationships and identities of the late 19th- and early 20th-century colonial/imperial world are remembered in a particular way, and thus continue to haunt the present. She explains how contemporary interpretations of the state of the economy stand in a dynamic relationship with a notion of its past. Interestingly, however, despite many scholars' reference to the importance of the postcolonial relationship when analysing Iceland's political identity, no wide-ranging study has until now been made on how it has affected the development of our political economy and foreign relations.

The colonial past is also vividly present in contemporary popular culture, as can be found in Björk's song 'Declare Independence', which she dedicated to Greenland and the Faroe Island and also performed in Tibet. In an interview with *The Australian* she explained how being a colony of Norway and Denmark had left its mark on her nation's psyche, bringing, for example, 'lack of confidence' and 'mistrust of foreigners' (quoted in Westwood, 2008).

The national myth

Iceland's national myth, which developed in the independence struggle, creates a Golden Age starting with the settlement in the year 874, peaking after the state-like formulation in 930 and ending when Iceland fell under foreign rule with the Old Treaty with Norway in 1262. Further deterioration occurs when falling under Danish rule in 1380 and with introduction of Absolutism in 1662. Several texts were later influential in reaffirming this myth. Jón Jónsson Aðils (1869–1920), who in 1911 became Iceland's first history professor, described the society of the Golden Age as superior to all others and its unique and pure language as the key to its soul. He claimed that Icelanders not only had enjoyed the highest standard of living but that their culture was so rich that it 'only compares to ancient Greece during the highest period of civilization' (Jónsson Aðils, 1903).

According to the myth, Icelandic society started to deteriorate after the country entered into the Old Treaty. A period of humiliation followed after it fell under Danish rule. But Jónsson Aðils and his followers explain that, however weak and humiliated the people may have been, the Icelandic national spirit never died, and at last, in the early 19th century, courageous and wise men finally rose up and reclaimed the nation's own worth and lifted the national spirit by fighting for its independence. As Nielsen Germaud (2011) explains, the myth creates a U-shaped curve of history, whose two peaks – in the distant past and at the end of the story – represent autonomy and the avoidance of external influence.

Importantly for future development, the purity of the nation and language is emphasized. Jónsson Aðils expressed the hope that Icelanders would in the future have the opportunity to demonstrate to other nations their importance in world culture, thus articulating Icelanders' desire to be recognized as equals by their powerful neighbouring states.

This myth was kept alive throughout the 20th century, for example, in schoolbooks. One was written by Jónas Jónsson frá Hriflu, an educator who later became the leader of the Progressive Party and one of the most influential figures in Icelandic politics and culture. According to his textbook, read by all elementary students for decades, Iceland's economic prosperity is directly attributed to its gaining independence from Denmark. Icelanders are furthermore pictured as the finest 'selection' of Norwegians, descendants of the strong and independent-minded farmers who fled the oppression of King Harald to protect their freedom. He then claims that this noble breed of Norway's finest social class was through the centuries shaped by the harshness of the natural surroundings, creating the unique Icelandic nation, which compares to no other. Historian Guðmundur Finnbogason (1925) further claimed that the harsh Icelandic environment had through the centuries weeded out the weakest and thus even increased the quality of the population. As I will explain further in Chapter 4, this is the myth our President was tapping into in the boom years when explaining how Icelanders were all but destined for greatness in the new global economy.

Kristín Loftsdóttir claims that these ethnocentric images need to be understood in the context of Iceland's marginal position in Europe at the time, 'as a poor subject nation with a population of less than a quarter of a million in search of national independence' (Loftsdóttir, 2011). This is also in line with philosopher Frantz Fanon's (1963) claim that nationalism in colonized countries might seem more aggressive as its liberation movements use it to separate themselves from its colonizers by emphasizing their distinctiveness. Interestingly, however, in the Icelandic case, the independence struggle not only expressed the desire to be different but also the desire to be recognized as a partner in Western culture.

Iceland's independence movement clearly drew its ideas from international trends at the time, most importantly the Enlightenment and Romanticism. However, when the policy for sovereignty and later full independence – Icelandic nationalism – was being developed, its creators looked back a thousand years, to the settlement republic, for arguments to justify their claim rather than to current international development (Hermannsson, 2005: 83). The emphasis was on drawing an unbroken link to the Golden Age rather than on linking the independence struggle with international ideological developments of the time. Iceland's path to modernization and progress was therefore seen through its own unique past rather than with reference to international trends (Hermannsson, 2005: 252, 292). Illustrative of this trend is the naming of Iceland's new Parliament in Reykjavik in 1844 after the *Alþingi*. The old parliamentary court in *Þingvellir* (parliamentary fields) had become the holy site of the Icelandic nation, in which it is forever recreated through collective memory.

In his landmark study, Guðmundur Hálfdanarson (2001: 36–39) explains how this sense of nationalism was stronger than in most other European states at the time, being based on a historical conviction that justified the full formal sovereignty and independence of the nation. The nation became almost a concrete natural fact in the Icelandic mind. A free and sovereign Icelandic nation became an integral part of the self-image of the nation. Icelandic nationalism was thus created on the basis of a romantic notion of a natural and pure, or at least special, separate nation. This notion became a vital force in the independence struggle.

The Icelandic History Association has repeatedly tried to correct this myth – without much success. For example, it announced that an official report on Iceland's image in 2008 (which I will discuss further in Chapter 4) was in stark contrast to contemporary historical research. Still, the myth was constantly reconstructed and easily survived The

Crash. In his book on Iceland's economic collapse the former Chief Economist of Kaupthing Bank, turned Lecturer in Economics after The Crash, Ásgeir Jónsson (2009) starts his analysis by reproducing the myth of the Golden Age in a long introductory chapter, where he explains how Iceland was built by free-spirited Norwegians who were fleeing oppression in Norway and finding freedom in Iceland. Then Iceland lost its autonomy, falling into poverty and a dormant mode of existence under foreign rule. Working his way through the myth, Jónsson describes how economic prosperity emerged with independence. He goes on to branding the boom years between 1997 and 2007 Iceland's 'Golden Decade'. For another example of this national myth in contemporary discourse we can turn to former TV journalist Elin Hirst, announcing her parliamentary candidates for the IP leading up to the 2013 election: 'Iceland is a small nation that has in a miraculously short time risen from being the poorest state in Europe to being one of the richest in the world, precisely because it finally got to control its own affairs' (Hirst, 2012).

Equal partner

Equally importantly, the external struggle for sovereignty was also fuelled by a wish for external recognition as being an equal partner with the other states of Europe. Political scientist Birgir Hermannsson (2005: 125–127) documents that Iceland's struggle for independence was not only an effort to gain authority over its own affairs but also a vehicle for the promotion of modernization in a country that had been one of the poorest and most backward in Europe for centuries. Formally Iceland was not a colony of Denmark but rather a dependency, or a 'bi-land' as it was called in Denmark. The position of the Icelanders in the 19th century was ambiguous, as Loftsdóttir (2010) explains: they were generally not represented as complete 'savages', but neither as fully belonging among 'civilised' peoples. Nineteenth-century travel books depict Icelanders as uncivilized, dirty and lacy while also characterizing the population with romantic fulfilment.

Frustration with this depiction was, for example, reflected in the protest of Icelandic students in 1905 against being portrayed as colonial subjects in a Danish colonial exhibition in Copenhagen – as they did not want to be associated with colonized people from Greenland and Africa. This illustrates the internal wish of being distinguished from other subjugated or colonized peoples. Despite being a dependency of Denmark, Iceland situated itself within imperial Europe when speaking of the exploration and colonization of the world. This can be seen in 19th-century textbooks (Loftsdóttir, 2010). The objection to being associated with other colonies in the Danish colonial exhibition was not with the inhumanity of the exercise but rather of being displayed on the wrong side, thus revealing their anxieties of being classified with colonized people. Being recognized within white Western culture was central for Icelanders in the context of finding their place in the hierarchy of civilized peoples (Nielsen Germaud, 2010).

This struggle for external recognition has ever since been reflected in both internal and external discussions. Icelanders are still preoccupied with the image of the country internationally. Anthropologists Gísli Pálsson and Paul Durrenberger (1992: 313), for example, claim that the primary task amongst Icelanders writing on external relations is not so much to understand others but to be understood *by* them.

The Vikings

The use of Viking imagery illustrates this preoccupation quite well. As I will explain further when analysing the boom years, the internal celebration of the endeavours of Iceland's businessmen abroad, usually referred to as Iceland's *outvasion*, is a reflection of the striving for recognition as a partner in Western culture. The term outvasion (*útrás*) means the opposite of the word '*innrás*', invasion, but also plays on an old word, literally meaning 'release of tension'. With the sudden flocking of Icelandic businessmen abroad around the turn of the second millennium, the word outvasion took on a new meaning: the acquisition of companies abroad (Magnússon, 2011). Accordingly, the businessmen themselves were positively referred to as Outvasion Vikings (*útrásarvíkingar*). The whole idea behind the outvasion concept was indeed fuelled by its symbolic meaning of marking Iceland's complete entry into modernity.

This digs deep into the myth of the Viking past in emphasizing masculine qualities and the narrative of world explorers. Contrary to its significance in many other places, the Viking image is positive in Icelandic discourse, where it symbolizes Iceland's Golden Age – representing a time of political autonomy and cultural greatness. Viking imagery appears, for example, in myths, images, sagas and legends and has been significant in Iceland's feuds and negotiations with neighbours where they represent the characteristics of the collective. In both contemporary Icelandic culture and external national branding, Viking imagery is very present. It can be found on statues in public spaces as well as on consumer products like beer cans and sports scarves.

Many businessmen played on the Viking symbols. Leading Viking Capitalist Jón Ásgeir Jóhannesson (Glitnir, Iceland frozen food, Baugur, Hamlays, Magasin du Nord), for example, named his yacht *The Viking* and decorated the entrance hall of his London office with a three-metre high statue of the earliest known world explorer in Iceland, Leifur Eiríksson (who lived around 1000 AD and allegedly sailed to America 500 years before Columbus). Björgólfur Thor Björgólfsson (Landsbanki, Straumur, West Ham United) played on old Nordic mythology in the logo of his company Novator. One of the leading Viking Capitalists, Hannes Smárason, explained how foreign acquisitions could be traced to the energy of the Viking spirit (Schram, 2009).

Leading members of the more benign cultural outvasion nourished the same notion. In an interview with the *Guardian* in March 2008, bassist Georg Holm of the famous band Sigur Ros was quoted: 'Like all Icelanders, we are intensely proud of our mighty homeland in the far North Atlantic', adding that it was 'in our Viking blood to want to conquer nations and peoples' (quoted in Hooper, 2008).

I maintain that these positive connotations of the outvasion concept and the widespread internal acceptance of the endeavours of the Viking Capitalists can only be fully understood in connection with a particular memory of the past and speaks to the fear of being perceived by others as lacking modernity. The outvasion notion thus digs into the wider discourse on national identity that revolves around living in a harsh environment and surviving through centuries of hardship, as articulated by our President. When explaining the unique characteristics of the Icelandic businessmen, he listed 13 qualities, one of which was a 'heritage of discovery and exploration fostered by the medieval Viking sagas' (Grímsson, 2005).

In Chapter 4 I will discuss further how nationalistic rhetoric was used to make sense of the economic boom. This perhaps wishful thinking that Iceland was making its final entry into modernity through the outvasion revolves around the interplay between desires and anxieties within Iceland's national identity. Loftsdóttir (2012) maintains that these anxieties have been part of Iceland's national discourse for a long time and are 'interconnected with the desire to gain recognition from the more powerful European nation states'. Interestingly, but correspondingly, the nationalistic discourse only intensified with the country's greater involvement in the global economy, with increased focus on the image of the Viking Capitalists. National images were recycled, renegotiated and even reformulated in a highly globalized context, as Loftsdóttir (2012) explains: 'stressing the complex interplay between the notions "global" and "local"'. Investment overseas and increased participation in global markets is thus seen as a continuation of the independence struggle.

Ever lasting struggle

When studying Iceland's nation-building, it can be seen that the fragility of the nation is always present. The notion of constant threat to its very existence can, for example, been found in the writings of parliamentarian Bjarni Jónsson at the beginning of the 20th century. After claiming that the nation as such is the core of their spiritual life he insists that all 'good Icelanders' should do their utmost to 'protect and promote their nationality' (quoted in Bjarnason, 2013: 21). Otherwise, Icelanders ran the risk of 'vanishing in the vast ocean of nations.' To prevent such devastation, Icelanders had to nourish their cultural heritage and indeed 'prove both to themselves and to others that they are a living nation.' In 1907, the largest newspaper in Reykjavik similarly wrote that Icelanders must be proactive in showing others that on the island lives a 'separated and remarkable cultural nation [...] this we must strive to become recognised for throughout the educated word' (quoted in 'Ísland fyrir Íslendinga', 1907).

The success of this struggle – for external recognition as a fully functioning modern state deeply rooted in Western culture – was threatened when the crisis hit in autumn 2008. Further anxiety was felt after misreporting in the international media after The Crash, speaking directly to the longstanding fear of misrecognition by foreigners. Iceland's economic relationship with others is interpreted through a romantic nationalistic discourse; thus, the meaning of the crisis cannot be reduced to a purely economic level. To understand the real meaning of the crisis in Iceland its impact on identity and Iceland's position in the world has to be taken into account.

It should be stressed here that Iceland's national myth is not unique. Indeed, many nations base their nationhood on similar kinds of myth creation. This is what Anthony D. Smith (1993) calls the 'Cult of a Golden Age': the fact that national leaders often refer to a Golden Age in time of hardship to reinforce a sense of community. What is, however, interesting is that after Iceland had gained full independence the independence struggle did not end. Rather, a new one started: the ever-lasting independence struggle. And a new political idea was born: the notion that the fight for independence is a constant struggle and that it will never end (Bergmann, 2011a). Accordingly, it is the collective duty of all

Icelanders to guard the country's independence. In his landmark study on Icelandic politics, including the Icelandic political identity, political science professor Ólafur Ragnar Grímsson (1978), later President of Iceland, claimed that this common understanding of Icelandic nationalism, created in the independence struggle, had since become one of the most important ideas in Icelandic political discourse.

Conclusion

Iceland's postcolonial national identity brings forward a dual insistence, as has been demonstrated: on being formally sovereign as well as on being recognised as an equal partner in Europe. This has developed into what can be termed the Icelandic Postcolonial Project. The dual insistence has also developed into a divide in Icelandic politics between *isolationists* and *internationalists*. One side emphasizes independence while the other expresses a wish to be a fully functioning modern economy on an equal footing with other participants in Western culture. While one part of the national identify pulls Iceland away from others, by emphasizing its uniqueness, the other part is pushing us into participating in the global economy to further Iceland's prosperity. However, as a small state, bordering even on being defined as a microstate, Iceland struggles with both claims.

These two sides of Iceland's national identify are often at odds, creating a tension regarding its direction that is debated in internal political discussions. It is precisely within these boundaries where Iceland's postcolonial sovereignty games are played – as I will discuss further in Chapter 3, which deals with Iceland's foreign relations. This defining struggle can be identified throughout the development of the economy, with an emphasis on diversification directing the resource-based economy towards an unsustainable, finance-driven Viking economy around the turn of the millennium. The effect of the postcolonial identity is perhaps most evident in Iceland's foreign relations, bringing it, through the EEA agreement, into the European Single Market without its enjoying the institutional protection of formal membership when the crisis hit. Furthermore, as analysed later in this book, the postcolonial national identity also defined Iceland's response to the crisis after it hit the country severely in autumn 2008. The same forces were also at play in the discourse on Iceland's recovery after The Crash.

2
Coming of Age – Economic History

By exploiting the fish stocks surrounding the country, Iceland was in the 20th century pulled from being one of the poorest and most backward societies in Europe to becoming one of the richest countries in the world. The economy was based on selling fish to the British – we provided them with cod for their 'fish and chips'. Being based on fishing, Iceland's economy is characterized by continuous boom and bust cycles. The crisis of 2008 might have been more profound than others, but this sort of volatility in the economy is nothing uncommon for Icelanders.

Until the mid-19th century Iceland was isolated and remained at medieval level with little or no growth. There were no towns to speak of. Most people worked for food and lodging on family run farms in the countryside. There was hardly any functional monetary or other sort of financial system. Rather, Iceland was like a still picture from the Middle Ages – a frozen society. A small number of farmers produced traditional food products and the Danish monarch monopolized all foreign trade. In 1855 the Danish Crown finally liberalized external trade, which allowed the relatively late emergence of capitalism. Alongside the independence struggle Icelanders campaigned for freedom in foreign trade but after the liberalization of external trade we still kept tight controls on domestic trade. Workers, for example, were until the late 19th century forced to work on farms in certain regions and were banned from seeking more lucrative jobs elsewhere or in other sectors, such as in the new fishing towns around the coast (for more, see Gunnarsson, 1987).

Iceland's approach to foreign trade can be explained by the still ongoing tension between those who advocated caution in foreign relations and promoted a self-sufficient economy and those who campaigned for openness to foreign markets and strove for participation in international trade co-operation. This tension between *isolationists* and *internationalists* still characterizes Iceland's postcolonial national identity and stems directly from the previously described dilemma of the independence struggle: to be at once independent from foreign authority but still recognized as a prosperous modern economy on an equal footing with other Western states.

Early fragile finanicalization

The rise and fall of Íslandsbanki (Iceland's Bank) in early 20th century can serve as an interesting parallel to the events leading up to the crisis in the early 21st century. In many ways the establishment of Íslandsbanki in 1904 marks the start of the boom and bust cycle which Iceland's economy has been marked by ever since. The joint-stock venture bank was created by the *Alþingi* and sponsored by the Danish Crown. The bank was, however, privately owned by Danish investors. Not so uncommonly for the tide of the time, this private foreign bank served simultaneously as Iceland's central bank and the country's only commercial bank. This was considered acceptable as Iceland was still a part of the Danish Kingdom and the bank was, like almost all other central banks of the time, to base the worth of its notes on the international gold standard and could therefore not print money of its own accord. Establishment of this first real financial institution had revolutionary effects for the small and weak enterprises in the country, which for centuries had been starved of foreign cash. Throughout the 19th century Iceland had been served by the domestic Landsbanki (National bank of Iceland) and a few savings and loans institutions, which did not have access to foreign funding (Baldvinsdóttir, 1998).

Access to foreign investment capital was pivotal for the rapid economic growth in the 20th century. This country, which in economic terms had been dormant for centuries, was now wide awake. The large-scale emigration to America that had started in the mid-19th century finally slowed and gradually reversed in the early 20th century (Bjarnason, 2013). Fuelled by the nationalistic sentiments of the independence struggle, this relatively backward society was thirsting for rapid modernization. Íslandsbanki mainly invested in the fisheries sector, which in the coming years increased foreign revenues many times over. Motor trawlers were bought to catch more fish than before and processing facilities were built, further increasing the value of the catch. The British were demanding fresh cod for their 'fish and chips' and the Spanish seemed to need an endless supply of salted fish for their *bacalao*. Business was booming. The bank furthermore offered deposit accounts to a population that had until then mostly kept their modest savings at home. This led to initial small-scale money multiplication and indeed primitive financialization of the society. Industrialization of the economy soon emerged and for 16 years after Ísalndsbanki was founded in 1904 Iceland enjoyed steady growth with greater prosperity than before (for more, see Jónsson, 2009).

With increased liberalization, Iceland's late-emerging capitalism came to centre on a regime of extensive accumulation of absolute surplus value extraction through the expansion of the fishing sector. Facilitated by a very basic technological upgrade (basic trawler vessels and fish processing equipment), this expansion took place on the basis of large numbers of workers seeking wage-labour in coastal towns and away from quasi-peonage agricultural labour relations in the countryside. In 1900 most of the population worked in agriculture. In the first decades of the 20th century, however, people flocked from the agricultural countryside to the fishing towns. Reykjavik emerged as the new economic hub. Its population grew from 10 per cent of the national total in 1900 to 40 per cent in 1930. This development was to continue, as now, in the 21st century, two-thirds of Iceland's population live in the greater Reykjavik area.

With this early financialization came the formation of a bourgeoisie of merchants and entrepreneurs, which would come to revolve around 14 families, popularly known as 'The Octopus', and wage-labourers around an industrialization, monetization, entrepreneurship and productivity (Árnason, 1991). Closely linked to the Independence Party The Octopus dominated many branches of the economy, including fishing, imports, petrol distribution, shipping and insurance, and held a monopoly on much of the country's business with the American army base. Trade unions emerged after the turn of the century. However, the political arm of the labour movement, the Social Democratic Party (SDP), was small by Scandinavian standards and was dominated by a social-liberal faction, which accepted individualism and the pursuit of wealth (Kristjánsson, 1977). Yet, wage-labour, the basic technological upgrade and infrastructural development needed funding. The accumulation strategy pointed to the institutionalization of a credit system.

This primitive financial system, instituted in the first years of the last century, was, however, very vulnerable, which is perhaps best illustrated by the fact that a single bankruptcy of a fishing company in 1914 almost killed off Íslandsbanki when it lost more than quarter of its equity. Paradoxically, the bank was saved when food prices on international markets hiked on the outbreak of World War I. By the end of the war the stock price of the bank had doubled (Jónsson, 2009). Another effect of WWI was the suspension of the gold standard, which resulted in central banks being freed to print money. Íslandsbanki exploited this new monetary regime by spewing new cash into the economy. After WWI, pressure to devalue the Icelandic króna (ISK) thus started to build, accompanying increased inflation – which Iceland has been infested with ever since. Prices quadrupled and outstanding banknote issues increased sevenfold (Baldvinsdóttir, 1998). Still the government insisted on keeping the peg with the Danish krona (DKK) as both currencies were at the time considered legal tender in Iceland. By 1920, however, it was impossible to keep the ISK trading at par with the DKK – thus the saga of the constant devaluation of the ISK started. By 2012, the ISK had fallen by almost 100 per cent against the DKK.

The creation of Íslandsbanki, this mediating mechanism in the mode of regulation, led to the trans-nationalization of Icelandic capital accumulation and could have laid the foundations of a more intensive regime of accumulation. Indeed, Íslandsbanki's ability to ensure the steady inflow of investment capital presented the key legitimate test of this new historical block's capacity to routinize this regime of accumulation. Trouble started for Íslandsbanki, however, when Europe entered into recession in 1920 and fish prices fell sharply on international markets. The bank was bailed out through government involvement with emergency loans from Denmark and the UK. The ability of the bank to operate as a credible central bank was subsequently questioned. Many suspected Íslandsbanki, a *foreign* bank, of serving *external* interests, mainly its Danish shareholders (Jónsson, 2009). Based on national sentiments this spurred increasing discussion on establishing domestic financial services, which would be focused on serving only the interest of this newly established sovereign state. Icelanders had tasted the benefits of investment banking for economic growth. Now they wanted their own public bank, Landsbanki, to take over central banking operations from the private, foreign-owned Íslandsbanki. This was not only to protect the country's economic interests but also to nourish the nationalistic sentiments developing in the independence struggle. Independence from the Danish Kingdom had become a hegemonic element of the Icelandic societal paradigm (Bergmann, 2011a). Ridding Iceland of foreign economic interest was therefore seen as a vital part of protecting the sovereign status that had only recently been won. Íslandsbanki had negotiated note-issuing rights until 1933. Now it had become the victim of Icelandic nationalism. In the early 1920s, the Icelandic authorities decided to gradually shift money-issuing rights to its own Landsbanki, with exclusive rights to print the national currency from 1928. By 1933, Íslandsbanki was to repurchase all its outstanding note issues.

Rather as happened after The Crash of 2008, the private, foreign-owned Íslandsbanki was in the late 1920s left to fend for itself under a drastically altered situation, at least partly created by domestic government decisions. The bank had to either massively shrink its balance sheet or find a new funding base. Íslandsbanki suffered further blows when the Great Depression of 1929 hit, when, for example, two fishing companies that amounted to a significant share of the bank's loan book went bankrupt. To add insult to injury Landsbanki refused to extend a bill it had bought from Íslandsbanki, which spurred a run on its deposits. The *Alþingi* then forced the issue, categorically refusing to bail out the foreign bank. Íslandsbanki did not have the means to withstand this twofold blow: the international depression and unfavourable domestic government decisions. This marked the end of international banking in Iceland for centuries. After gaining sovereignty in 1918, Iceland lost access to international financial markets after nationalizing banking services. Following the fall of Íslandsbanki the government nationalized the operation and opened Útvegsbankinn, a joint-stock Fisheries Bank of Iceland.

Just as Íslandsbanki was bailed out by government intervention in 1920, Landsbanki found itself in trouble a decade later when the effects of the Great Depression started to bite. In 1931, the Icelandic government agreed on the Landsbanki petition to introduce capital controls – which remained in force until 1994, when Iceland entered into the EEA agreement. It is often claimed that history is destined to repeat itself – that year, 1994, then marked the prelude to the next banking bubble, which burst in October 2008.

Further sectoral banking institutions were introduced after the Great Depression. Búnaðarbankinn, the public agricultural bank, established in 1930, was sponsored by the Progressive Party (PP), which was the political arm of the Co-operative Movement. Three private banks also emerged. Iðnaðarbankinn, the Bank of Industries, opened its doors in 1953; Verslunarbankinn, the Bank of Commerce, was founded in 1961; and Alþýðubankinn, the People's Bank, was established in 1971 – partly sponsored by the Social Democratic Party. These banks represented the interests of competing sectors of the economy, each claiming to represent progress, albeit through innovation in agricultural production and the promotion of industrialization. Iceland subsequently became overbanked as the rival banks competed by opening more and more branches around the country. Key outcomes were a degree of isolationism and a slowing of industrialization and diversification. In 1988, the three private sectoral banks acquired Útvegsbankinn and emerged as a new Íslandsbanki.

Party of four

Iceland's political party system was taking shape in the early 20th century. Ever since, the system has consisted of four main but shifting parties (for more, see Kristinsson, 2006). Despite repeated attempts, efforts to break up this party of four have thus far failed. The right-of-centre Independence Party (IP) (*Sjálfstæðisflokkurinn*) emerged as the largest political party and indeed the country's hegemonic power. The bourgeois conservative party was able to simultaneously tap into the heritage of the independence struggle and promote liberal economic policies. It is closely linked with the Confederation of Icelandic Employers (SA), including the Association of Fishing Vessel Owners (LÍÚ). Since its creation in 1929 the IP has been in government for most of the 20th century and the period leading up to The Crash of 2008, usually in coalition with either the PP or the SDP/SDA. The agricultural Progressive Party (PP) (*Framsóknarflokkurinn*) occupied the centre of Icelandic politics and was often able to increase its importance by forming coalitions with both left and right.

The left wing in Icelandic politics was weakened by frequent fragmentation in 20th century. The Social Democratic Party (SDP) (*Alþýðuflokkuirnn*) was established in 1916 as the political wing of the labour movement (ASI) (*Alþýðusamband Íslands*). In 1930, a communist group split from the party, marking a continued fragmentation in the coming decades. In the latter half of the century the People's Alliance (PA) (*Alþýðubandalagið*) emerged as the united home of those on the left of the SDP. The splinter was mainly a cause of foreign policy issues, and the classical divide in Icelandic politics between *internationalists* and *isolationists* ran straight down the spine of the left. While the SDP promoted participation in international organizations like NATO and the European integration project, the PA was more rooted in the heritage of the independence struggle and concerned with protecting Iceland's sovereignty against Western forces. Indeed, it was a peculiarity of Icelandic socialists in the early 20th century that they were far more nationalistic than similar parties in other European countries (Kristjánsdóttir, 2008). This split has remained ever since.

Attempts at uniting the left continued throughout the century. The latest serious attempt was made around the turn of the millennium with the merger of the SDP and the PA together with two satellite parties into the Social Democratic Alliance (SDA) (*Samfylkingin*). In effect, however, that attempt was foiled by the establishment of the Left Green Movement (LGM) (*Vinstri Hreyfingin – grænt framboð*), which was almost instantly able to fill the space to the left of the SDA that the PA had previously occupied.

In addition to these four main parties, a fifth and sometimes also sixth parties have temporarily occupied up to 15 per cent of the seats in Parliament. The longest surviving of these extra parties was the Women's List (*Kvennalistinn*), which was represented in Parliament between 1983 and 1999, until it merged with others into the SDA.

Through most of the 20th century, the Icelandic economy was split between the main ruling parties, the IP and PP. It was heavily controlled by regulations, governmental licensing, and import and export controls. This was branded 'the rule of halves.[1] Most private firms were closely tied to the IP through the Employers Association and the powerful Co-operative Movement was in effect the business branch of the Progressive Party. The Co-operative Movement controlled companies in most fields of the economy and was for a while, because of its centrist organization, the most influential in the economy. The rule of halves was partially broken when the Co-operative Movement collapsed in 1992.

Rich in fish

For centuries Icelanders had been isolated from the tumult of the world. During the Second World War, however, Iceland became geostratically important which brought increased foreign attention. We were rushed to instant modernization after the British Navy landed at Reykjavik in 1940. The war brought much needed work for a starving workforce and a massive inflow of foreign cash when US troops took over this isolated northern outpost of the war in 1941. Buoyed by foreign cash, the economy instantly took off, which in turn provided us with enough confidence to push for complete independence from Denmark in 1944.

All of a sudden Iceland also found itself in a vital geostrategic position, between the superpowers of the world, which it was able to exploit throughout the Cold War to advance its economy. Despite economically benefiting from the war, Iceland received a massive aid package from the US Marshall Aid Plan. It became a founding member of NATO, joined the UN and was viewed as an important player in world politics during the Cold War. America became Iceland's new best friend with a bilateral defence agreement in 1951 and the opening up of the US market for Icelandic seafood products. The US was allocated land for a military base in Keflavik on the Reykjanes Peninsula close to Reykjavik in exchange for defending Iceland against any foreign threat (Ingimundarson, 1996). In a way, Iceland became a client state of the US. Backed by its new ally in the West, Iceland was then able modernize its economy quite rapidly. In its first decade, the military base accounted for up to 20 per cent of the country's foreign exchange earnings.

The new ally in the West served Iceland well during the so-called Cod Wars (not to be confused with the Cold War) with the British. The dispute was fought in several rounds of confrontation in the 1950s and the 1970s. Iceland had in gradual steps unilaterally expanded its exclusive fishing zone to 200 nautical miles. The first confrontation occurred in 1958 when Iceland moved the zone from 4 to 12 miles. Foreign trawlers, mainly British, which had for decades been fishing close to Iceland's shores, were not happy with the move. Initially they ignored the decision of this insignificant, newly independent state and simply continued with their fishing. After repeated incidents of ramming between Icelandic patrol vessels and warships of the Royal British Navy, which had been called in to protect the British fishing trawlers, an agreement was reached. The British agreed to move out of the 12-mile zone in exchange for the Icelandic government's agreement to refer any further expansion to the International Court of Justice in The Hague (Jóhannesson, 2006).

The second confrontation broke out in 1972, when Iceland unilaterally announced an expansion to 50 nautical miles. The fisheries minister of the new left-wing government, Lúðvík Jósepsson (PA), justified his decision to abandon the previous agreement of the right-wing government with the UK on the grounds that Iceland not only had the right but was indeed obligated to protect its economic independence (Jósepsson, 1973). Despite Iceland's decision, British trawlers kept on fishing within the 50-mile zone. Our small coastguard responded by cutting the fishing nets from behind the British trawlers with specially designed scissors, which were attached to the patrol ships. Again the British Royal Navy sailed into Iceland's waters to protect their trawlers, escalating the dispute. Again repeated ramming of Icelandic ships and British tugboats, warships and trawlers occurred. It served Iceland's interests that this confrontation between two NATO states at the height of the Cold War was thought to weaken the organization. Its Secretary General, Joseph Luns, was subsequently able to broker an agreement whereby the fishing of British trawlers within Iceland's 50-mile zone was limited to a small area.

A few years later, the hardest-fought confrontation of the three Cod Wars broke out when Iceland announced an expansion to 200 miles in 1975. As before, the British trawlers refused to leave. The Icelandic coastguard thus resumed cutting their fishing nets, separating the trawlers from their catch. The British Navy could of course have sunk the entire Icelandic coastguard in a single battle and thus allowed their trawlers to continue bringing back home cod for British fish and chips. In total the British Navy deployed 22 frigates, 7 supply ships, 9 tugboats and 3 support ships to protect its fishing boats within 200 miles of Iceland's coastline. The Icelandic coastguard, on the other hand, consisted of just four patrol vessels and two lightly armed trawlers (Jóhannesson, 2006).

The UK's massive military might was met with Iceland's new geostrategic importance in the Cold War. By threatening to leave NATO and close its military base in Keflavik, thus opening up the North-West Atlantic to the Soviets, the Icelandic government was able to exploit its newly established Washington connection to put pressure on Westminster. Backed by US diplomacy Iceland was able in 1976 to drive British trawlers out of the 200-mile fishing zone. Later, US Secretary of State Henry Kissinger described Iceland's behaviour as arrogant and its use of its geostrategic position as the 'tyranny of the tiny'. UK fishing towns like Hull and Grimsby were subsequently left in economic ruin. Only in 2012, 35 years later, did the British government compensate for their loss, with an apology and a thousand-pound donation to each of the 2,500 fishermen who lost their livelihood (Drainey, 2012).

In Icelandic political discourse the Cod Wars are viewed as a continuation of Iceland's eternal independence struggle, this time as a fight for its economic independence against a foreign authority that had for more than a century exploited its natural resources. The captains of the patrol vessels became national heroes and have been household names ever since. The goal was to gain control over the fishing resources surrounding the country. Since independence, the fishing industry has been the most important sector of the economy and the foundation of Iceland's economic independence. Because of this importance a characteristics of an postcolonial relationship developed between Iceland and the UK during the Cod Wars, which in 2008 was to reappear in the dispute over the Icesave deposit accounts.

Emergence of a historic block

Extensive accumulation based on the fisheries sector thus continued to characterize the Icelandic political economy during the decades immediately after independence from Denmark in 1944. Like its Nordic neighbours (see Katzenstein, 1985) Iceland sought economic progress during this period through a heavily export-dependent regime of accumulation based on its rich but narrow range of natural resources by generating growth through the accumulation of foreign exchange. In the wake of the Cod Wars the fast growing fishing companies renewed their fleet, buying many new high-tech trawlers. Fisheries became the engine room of Iceland's economy, generating the bulk of the country's foreign income and ensuring rapid growth throughout the 20th century. Around them a prosperous support industry developed.

Iceland's size and remoteness nevertheless reduced its structural capacity to pursue the type of accumulation strategies aimed at industrialization and diversification that had been adopted by the other Nordic countries (Mjøset, 1987). Instead, the Icelandic regime of accumulation continued to focus on the expansion of the workforce, mainly through feminization and urbanization. Throughout the second half of the 20th century, labour force participation was amongst the highest in Europe, with an unemployment rate averaging around 2 per cent. At the same time, the value of the fishing industry was increasing through the expansion of fishing limits and the trawler fleet. These structural limitations also translated into, and were reinforced by, the skills base, state bureaucracy and infrastructure, as well as exclusion from value chains, limited incentives for foreign direct investment and a tendency towards monopolistic or oligopolistic ownership structures (Jónsson, 1991). Despite food and staple goods being relatively disadvantaged under the General Agreement on Tariffs and Trade (GATT), fungible fish products generated high profits. Continuity of demand was also ensured by the large NATO base in Keflavik.

Thanks to the vast expansion of the exclusive fishing zone during the Cod Wars, the fishing sector grew, which accelerated foreign income. Foreign currency was now flowing into the country, causing increased inflation, in the range of 30 to 50 per cent annually. Indeed, fishing provided the only export industry of importance, constituting roughly 90 per cent of all merchandise exports in the early 1960s, and became the engine of the Icelandic growth model, which grew annually by around 4 per cent on average for the rest of the century. However, the profit generated was hugely affected by unpredictable fluctuations in the annual size of harvests. Translated into labour market relations, Iceland's insertion into the world economy played into the hands of fisheries capital. Soon the government's economic policy was being dictated by the interest of the fishing industry, which demanded protection against its volatility. Subsequently, monetary policy came to serve the interest of the sector, which generated the country's foreign income. The exchange rate was tuned to the export needs of the fisheries, with repeated devaluation of the króna, which often spurred inflation. The population in effect came to live on a share-of-the-catch income (Jónsson, 2009: 37). Economic development thus suffered from a 'Dutch disease' as most public decisions were skewed in favour of the fishing industry.

Paradoxically, although the labour movement had grown large during the early stage of capitalism and did, for instance, engage in collective wage bargaining and successfully defend full employment, it was fragmented and its interests were ineffectively channelled into parliamentary politics. Indeed, the labour movement never succeeded in establishing common ground with employers, which could serve as the foundation for relatively peaceful labour relations, as, for example, in Sweden. Emerging partly in response to the political weakness of industrial capital, the Independence Party took advantage of this fragmentation by representing itself as defending the interests of industry more broadly, for example by infiltrating the ASI and by influencing its various organizations through interlocking networks of kinship and ownership (Baldvinsdóttir, 1998).

The IP combined demands for a laissez-faire economy, in opposition to socialism and co-operatives, with demands for law and order often couched in nationalist discourse. To disguise its class allegiances, the party claimed to harmoniously represent all classes, captured discursively by its slogan 'class with class' (*stétt með stétt*) and practically by its commitment to full employment through highly accommodating monetary policies (Kristjánsson, 1977). As a consequence of this paradox, the labour movement was never able to push for any compromise-based incomes policy, which could have enabled the reinvestment of profits into labour and technology to ensure social protection and competitiveness. Iceland's construction of a comprehensive and universalist welfare state unfolded at best unevenly during the period and was able neither to provide effective wage protection against the effects of small annual harvests, nor to reduce inequality (Ólafsson, 2005; Mjøset, 1987). In no policy area, apart from in health policy and education, could it be seen as redistributive.

The destabilization of international monetary relations and price levels in the late 1960s put significant external pressure on national economies. Food prices surged and hence the prices of and profits from the sale of Icelandic fish products. In accordance with the inflationary procyclicality of the Icelandic growth model, the resulting profit surge was not effectively channelled into productive investments, thus preventing excessive inflationary pressure, but was rather used to offset growing (albeit not internationally deviating) wage demands. This became a fundamental problem for the growth model once demand stagnated and fishing stocks collapsed in the 1970s. Governments from across the political spectrum were troubled in dealing with this inherent weakness in the growth model.

Social Democratic participation in government contributed to the introduction of wage indexation, which resulted in wages partly following profit rates. Although labour market conflict was avoided, public indebtedness and inflation kept on growing. With the subsequent OPEC oil shock in 1973, stagflationary pressures in the world economy drove both government and justificatory regime into disarray as demand for fish products slumped. Profit rates fell, public indebtedness grew and inflation once again shot up. The government responded to demands from fisheries capital to defend profit rates by dropping wage indexation and repeatedly devaluing the króna to strengthen the distribution of income transfers towards the fisheries sector (Mjøset, 1987). The government, however, failed to reverse the accommodating monetary policies, with public indebtedness and inflation shooting up as a consequence in the 1970s. As the subsequent (uneven) resumption of growth in the economy, benefitting the fisheries sector in particular, was understood to come on the back of unfair income transfers, an unprecedented wave of strikes hit the country, lasting from 1974 to 1977. Radical dissent against this *rentier* capitalism (Gylfason, 2006) as well as the societal paradigm underpinning it resulted in unprecedented support for the SDP and the more radical leftist People's Alliance in the 1978 elections.

Inflation had been upsetting the economy throughout most of the century and causing great difficulties. During the inflationary period of the 1970s and 1980s real interest rates were kept negative as the nominal rate was kept below a fixed ceiling. Loans were thus tantamount to gifts, which the government-controlled banks handed out to those the ruling class deemed worthy. This implicit subsidy to favourable business was financed by an inflation tax on deposits and other monetary assets. Consequently, saving fell and deposit instalments shrank (Halldórsson & Zoega, 2010). This was an unsustainable financial system. As a part of a broad-based economic reform this led the government in 1979 to introduce an innovative mechanism of inflation indexation on bank loans, which soon became standard in bank lending. Housing loan borrowers were to pay a fixed real interest rate but hikes in inflation would be accumulated on top of the nominal interest rate onto the principal, which as a result would grow with inflation throughout the maturity of the loan. As a result, the lion's share of bank loans in the system would gradually become immune to changes in short-term policy rates, the main monetary tool of the Central Bank. The equity of households, however, became immensely sensitive to inflation, in effect turning almost the entire population into venture capitalists. This practice severely punished the ordinary person in The Crash of 2008, when the currency tanked, spurring rampant inflation and dumping many households into negative equity.

ITQ and neoliberal modernization

In the midst of crisis of the late 1970s, Iceland entered a moment of selection between competing economic models. Within the IP a generational shift was occurring and young neoliberals rose through the ranks around the journal *The Locomotive* (Eimreiðin). Inspired by the libertarian and monetarist currents of the time, their articulation of a neoliberal economic imaginary to substantially modernize the failing growth model and justificatory regime became increasingly influential in the Icelandic economy. Influenced by neoliberal economists like Friedrich von Hayek, Milton Friedman and James M. Buchanan, who all visited the country in the 1980s, Icelandic capital accumulation was to be re-co-ordinated according to financial market norms and values. Interestingly, this is when neoliberal financialization also started in Greece (Foukas & Dimoulas, 2013) and in Ireland (Kirby, 2010), which were to compare to Iceland in the contemporary financial crisis.

With the old regime undermined, the young neoliberals sought to introduce a largely new set of tests to support a neoliberal accumulation strategy. IP governments after the 1983 elections were significantly influenced by the Locomotive Group's ideas, and set out first and foremost to fight inflation through raising interest rates and weakening special interests, particularly labour. Devaluing the króna as a regulatory mechanism was now deemed unacceptable. Strong private property rights had to be introduced as they were argued to provide incentives for efficient market behaviour, which in turn would bring about fair outcomes. Central to the formulation of this accumulation strategy was the neoliberal modernization of the fisheries sector through the introduction of the regulatory system of Individual Transferable Quota (ITQ).

After the Cod Wars the fishing industry had grown rapidly with ever increasing numbers of fishing vessels and the introduction of technological advancements in fishing. Initially, this led to greater value for export but gradually also to massive overfishing. By the late 1980s it was clear that the catch had to be restricted. The right-of-centre government decided to introduce a quota system based on dividing the total allowable catch between fish vessel owners and the transfer of fishing rights on the free market. The government simply decided to hand the fishing rights to those fishing vessel owners who had utilized the stock in the few previous years – turning others away empty handed and instantly creating massive equity for those lucky enough to have been fishing in Icelandic waters in the relevant years. All of a sudden, they could freely trade the fishing rights, though formally not their private property. This decision was founded on the idea that fishing rights 'should be developed as far as possible into a system of private property rights' (Gissurarson, 2000).

While the shift to the Viking finance-dominated regime of accumulation was not made until the subsequent period, as I will discuss in Chapter 4, the introduction of the ITQ system was crucial to the emergence of this regime. This came through a series of shock-therapy reforms between 1977 and 1991. Controversially, by turning uncaught fish and their 'production' into property based on historical catch levels, the very right to produce and all its derivatives were made tradable. At the same time as it was intended to do away with overfishing, this was supposed to incentivize optimal efficiency in the fisheries sector. This was perfectly in line with the neoliberal economic imaginary of breaking the boom-and-bust nature of the fisheries cycle by engineering productive efficiency in the fisheries sector through market mechanisms. While open in the abstract (Gissurarson, 2000), the ITQ system came to be designed so as to institutionalize the market power of the 'giants' in the Icelandic fisheries sector, further creating opportunities for fisheries capital to separate ownership from actual fishing through the construction of a leasing system.

Opposition to the ITQ system grew and generated a number of trials of strength. First, the market mechanisms, including that of a lease system, set in motion by the ITQ system were criticized for fundamentally transforming the power distribution in production relations to the benefit of fisheries capital. Equal wage formation across the fisheries sector was fundamentally undermined as wages became increasingly determined by market prices of different fish, size of annual catch, trade quotas and oil prices. A key counter criticism here was that the inflationary production relations of old required a shake-up as labour power in the old growth regime had led to constant wage pressures across the sector with uncontrolled expansion of production and eventual overfishing as outcomes.

Second, the distribution of quotas on the basis of catch history was criticized. This related to the principle of distribution, which allocated quotas to vessel owners rather than to fishermen. Fishing rights, it was argued, were 'traditionally the birth right of all Icelanders, but would now be inherited by the holders' descendants like any other privately owned item' (Helgason & Palsson, 1997). Third, there was the criticism of fisheries capital for its blind pursuit of profit. Specifically, to seek to profit from the commodification of a natural resource, not least such a central one as fish, was deemed immoral. However, partly mitigating these criticisms was the SDP's insistence upon the insertion of the first article in the Fisheries Management Act, stating that the fish stocks are 'the common property' of the Icelandic nation (Gissurarson, 2000).

Introducing ITQ did not instantly correct the long lasing over fishing, leading to a collapse of the cod stock in 1989, which resulted in a serious blow to the economy. The government responded by devaluating the króna while freezing salaries, which led inflation to shoot up and purchasing power to plunge. Once again the economy had fallen into recession after overheating. In an attempt at promoting stability in this crisis-ridden economy, the left-of-centre government led by the PP was in early 1990 able to negotiate a historic neo-corporatist agreement with most labour market stakeholders, including all major employers and labour unions (Macheda, 2012). This 'National Consensus Agreement' (*Þjóðarsáttin*) ended bitter labour market disputes, which were marked by unrest and frequent strikes. The main aim was to break the vicious cycle of wage increases eaten up by inflation. The agreement laid a new foundation for a long-lasting peace in the labour market and paved the way for the economy to take off a few years later.

Conclusion

Throughout the 20th century, Iceland's economy was characteristic by continuous cycles of boom and bust. It was connected with international financial markets at the beginning of the century by the establishment of Íslandsbanki. The inflow of foreign cash had a revolutionary effect, leading to fast industrialization and the creation of a modernized economy based on fishing. Iceland's economy was thus based on a fragile model of monosectoral production. With the collapse of the old Íslandsbanki, Iceland's financial system was nationalized and in effect moved out of international markets with the introduction of capital controls in 1931. There was thus no banking tradition to speak of when international financial markets opened again in 1994, more than 60 years later.

Despite the inflow of foreign currency, mainly into the fisheries sector, Icelandic society and the rest of the economy remained relatively isolated until the landing of the British and American militaries during the Second World War. The war rushed Iceland into modernization and pushed us into a strategic position in the Cold War, which we were able exploit to advance the economy.

The volatility of the fishing industry, resulting in ongoing cycles of boom and bust, spurred in the latter half of the 20th century a strive for diversification – which is often lacking in small states that are more reliant on trade than larger states (for more, see Cooper & Shaw, 2009). With the utilization of natural resources such as waterfalls and geothermal energy, power production was taking off and it eventually emerged as another significant pillar of the economy. The first aluminium smelters were built in the 1960s. By the end of the century, Iceland produced 4 per cent of the world's aluminium. Tourism was also growing, by nearly 7 per cent a year, and gradually emerging as the third pillar of Iceland's economy. By the end of 20th century, Iceland's economy had thus been transformed. Within a single century Iceland had been turned from a poor, backward, medieval society into one of the most vibrant and prosperous economies in the world. In 1904 our purchasing power was similar to that of Ghana today. By the end of the century we had surpassed Denmark, growing by an average of 2.6 per cent a year throughout the century (Halldórsson & Zoega, 2010).

Icelanders had modernized faster than perhaps any other people. Through internationalization and diversification we had jumped to the top of the international ranking of the fastest growing economies.

Our troubles from previous recessions were over, our natural resources were generating steady foreign income and many new sectors of the economy were taking off. Our government was furthermore all but debt free and pension funds were filled to the brim with steady injections of cash. All this had led to the international financial market considering us to be of the highest creditworthiness. Nevertheless, the massive but unsustainable financialization of the first decade of the 21st century was yet to come.

3
The Independent State – Foreign Relations

Since gaining full independence in 1944, Iceland has been struggling to find its proper place in the world. In this chapter I analyse how post-imperialism shapes Iceland's foreign relations. As described in Chapter 1, Iceland's national identity created a dilemma between emphasis on self-rule and thus isolationism in foreign relations on the one hand and participation in international relations in order to support its claim for recognition as a European partner on the other. As I will illustrate, the legacy of the independence struggle still directs the discourse Icelandic politicians use in the debate on foreign relations. A strong emphasis on sovereignty has become the foundation on which Icelandic politics rests. Participation in European Union supra-national institutions, for example, falls rather outside the framework of Icelandic political discourse, which highlights Iceland's sovereignty and stresses an everlasting independence struggle.

Leading up to The Crash, pressure to adopt the euro to replace the small and volatile Icelandic króna had, however, been building. The oversized Icelandic banks were operating in a market that included 500 million people but with a currency and a Central Bank that was backed up by only roughly 330,000 inhabitants. Still, rather than proposing full membership of the EU and the EMU, many politicians started to entertain the idea that Iceland might unilaterally adopt the euro without membership of the EU. That approach fits in with the current relationship Iceland has with the European integration process, namely participating actively but not being a formal part of EU institutions, with the apparent loss of formal sovereignty that entails.

Until the collapse of the banking system, Iceland was in no hurry to join the EU and seemed quite happy with its de facto membership through the European Economic Area (EEA) agreement, which brought it into the Single European Market without representation in EU institutions. The collapse of the currency alongside with the financial system, however, created a new urgency for the government to apply for EU membership. The lure of the euro was splitting the population down the usual political line: between *internationalists* and *isolationists*. Iceland was the last of the fully functioning sovereign states in Western Europe to apply for membership of the European Union. It took a complete meltdown of the whole banking industry to bring the question of possible EU membership back onto the political agenda. Even though Iceland was facing its biggest recession in modern times, the EU debate was fiercely fought. In fact, it shook the whole political landscape. On the surface, the debate revolved around two main factors: the benefits of the euro and the inconvenience of the Common Fisheries Policy (CFP). Under the surface, however, lay good old nationalism. Not in the classical sense, but rather a special understanding of Iceland's sovereignty as discussed in Chapter 1.

Three pillars

Iceland's foreign relations are supported by three main pillars: the European pillar, the Atlantic pillar and the rest-of-the-world pillar (Bergmann, 2007). The European pillar is by far the most important and contains most of the country's major trade agreements and the vital foreign links that underpin the economy, such as its membership in the European Free Trade Association (EFTA) and the EEA Agreement. Iceland is also a member of the Council of Europe and is firmly rooted within the heritage of Nordic co-operation. Here we can also mention the close bilateral trade and cultural relationship with the UK. Ever since the Treaty of Rome was signed in 1957 Icelanders have debated their place in Europe. Directly resulting from the heritage of the independence struggle, debates on foreign relations have become more acrimonious than almost any other political disputes in the country (Ingimundarson, 1996; Bergmann, 2011a). Iceland joined EFTA in 1970, a decade after it was established, and entered with its EFTA partners into the EEA in 1994, which resulted in its becoming a kind of de facto member of the EU.

The Atlantic pillar is the second most important and comprises the founding membership of NATO in 1949 and the defence agreement with the US since 1951, which resulted in a close bilateral relationship with Washington on foreign policy matters. Icelanders were unified in the independence struggle, with more than 90 per cent of the electorate agreeing to full independence in a national referendum in 1944 – ending the 600-year-long relationship with Denmark while the latter was still under Nazi occupation. This feeling of unity was shattered only a few years later when a fierce debate on membership of NATO arose and culminated in violent riots in front of the Parliament building.

While Iceland mostly relied on the European pillar to underpin its economy, it relied much more heavily on the Atlantic pillar for its strategic security. After the US government decided to close its army base in Keflavik in 2006, the Atlantic pillar, however, became less important than before, giving more weight to the European co-operation in foreign and security policy matters in addition to the economic co-operation. The third pillar consists of foreign relations with the rest of the world, for example through the United Nations and the World Trade Organization.

Political science professor Baldur Thorhallsson (2009) maintains that since 1990 Iceland has become more active and more ambitious in international co-operation, no longer focusing only on bilateral relationships but also fostering more complex multilateral relationships. Still, although such a shift may indeed have taken place, Iceland was not prepared to join the EU, resulting in a more ambiguous position in foreign relations when the crisis hit.

Outside in Europe

Mainly on the grounds of guarding its sovereignty, after having struggled for independence from Denmark for more than a century, Iceland has remained outside the European Union. Independence and formal sovereignty are then almost synonymous with *democracy* in Icelandic public debate.

Economically, however, Iceland feels the same need as other European states to participate in European co-operation, which can explain its membership in the European Economic Area agreement (EEA). The agreement has brought Iceland into the Single European Market, but at a cost: Iceland has de facto agreed to adopt the EU's legislation within the boundaries of the agreement, and thus to a transfer of decision making and domestic governmental power to the EU. Through the EEA Iceland adopts three-quarters of EU laws (Europautredningen, 2012) and close to one-fifth of all laws passed in the Icelandic parliament derives from the EU – which is a higher percentage than in many EU member state (Bergmann, 2011b).

This dilemma, between economic interests on the one hand and a belief in the sovereignty of the Icelandic nation, and thus democracy, on the other has created something of a rift between the emphasis on the free and sovereign democratic nation and the reality Iceland is faced with in the EEA co-operation.

Only after the collapse of the country's entire financial system in 2008 did the new left-wing government apply for EU membership, in July 2009 – the very last of the Nordic five. This was in many ways a response to the fundamental systemic flaw in the economic set-up Iceland found itself in being an active participant in the European internal market but without the collective back-up that would come from being a full and formal member of the EU's institutions and political machinery: Iceland had become a participant in a vast legal framework without due democratic representation. In some respects, Iceland's financial crisis threw it out of its comfort zone and forced it to face the flawed situation it found itself in within the European integration process. However, soon after the initial shock had calmed, opposition to membership rose again, even beyond previous levels. Opinion polls indicated increased opposition to the accession negotiations, more than two-thirds of Icelanders saying that they would refuse membership in a referendum (Samtök Iðnaðarins, 2013). This allowed the new right-of-centre coalition to freeze the negotiations after the April 2013 parliamentary elections.

Challenges

To understand the approach to Europe it is important to note that even though Iceland formally remained outside the EU it was still an active participant in European integration. In fact, Iceland was in some ways more deeply involved in the European integration process than some of the EU's official members. To name a few examples, Denmark had many formal opt-outs from the EU treaties that Iceland was subject to through the EEA, and the EU's border regulation was applied in Iceland through the Schengen agreement, while the UK and Ireland were exempted from that part of EU co-operation (Adler-Nissen, 2008).

The EEA has facilitated the active Europeanization of Iceland, bringing it into the Single Market in return for its agreement to adopt the regulatory framework of the European Union. The agreement calls for the constant revision and update of Icelandic law to ensure that the country is in line with European laws and regulations (for more, see Bergmann, 2011b). We are thus very deeply involved in the European project and excluded from very few areas. In certain matters, such as those relating to the environment, transport and food hygiene, the vast majority of the legislation passed in the Icelandic parliament is initiated through the EEA. Furthermore, the border between what is considered part of the Single Market (and therefore what is considered EEA-relevant) and other aspects of EU legislation is becoming increasingly blurred.

The agreement does not, however, provide access to the EU's institutions and decision-making processes. It also does not cover the Common Agricultural Policy and regional cohesion policies and, perhaps most importantly for Iceland, it does not include the Common Fisheries Policy. We do not participate in the EU's trade policy, monetary policy, tax regimes or foreign affairs, nor many of the EU's internal policies, including judiciary affairs that fall outside the Schengen and Dublin Agreements.

The EEA has facilitated the transformation of the Icelandic economy, which has not only grown rapidly but also become more diversified and internationalized. However, despite the obvious economic benefits, the EEA Agreement has also presented grave challenges to the tiny economy and, more importantly, to our cherished democracy.

Despite Iceland's, Norway's and Liechtenstein's formal equality in the institutional framework, it has always been clear that the EU is the dominant partner. As a result, the automatic implementation of EU legislation is rarely discussed in the *Alþingi* as the EFTA's cannot refuse EU legislation without threatening the whole arrangement. Vetoing EU legislation could lead to dismissal from the EEA Agreement, not only for the individual state, but also for its two other EEA EFTA partners. Often referred to as the *nuclear bomb clause*, the formal veto right might be effective, but perhaps not to anyone's benefit if it was used.

Entering the Single European Market altered the composition of the Icelandic economy, for example by opening up the international financial market. It also, however, created a new vulnerability, which became evident in the 2008 financial crisis. After privatization and extensive deregulation, the Icelandic banks grew rapidly on European markets and well beyond our capability to bail them out when the crisis hit, as will be discussed further in the following chapters. The Depositors' Guarantee Fund, set up on the basis of a European directive, never had enough funding to cover a systemic collapse and no help came from the European institutions, which Iceland was not part of. This *neither-in-nor-out* arrangement – with one foot in on the Single European Market, with all the obligations that entailed, and the other foot outside the EU institutions, and therefore without access to back-up from, for example, the European Central Bank – proved to be flawed when the country was faced with a crisis of this magnitude.

The emphasis on formal sovereignty but active practical participation in the European market had left us without the safety net that the euro and other institutional mechanisms bring to EU members. So when the international financial crisis hit Iceland, not only did the country's oversized banks come crashing down, but the króna instantly went in to free-fall, with devastating effects on the general public.

Even though the EEA is dynamic, it does not respond to the operational and institutional changes of the EU. Since the 1992 Maastricht Treaty, various political shifts and institutional turns have altered the EU, meaning that the political and legal environment in which the EEA operates has changed dramatically. With only Iceland, Liechtenstein and Norway representing EFTA, while the EU has grown to 28 Member States with a total of around 500 million inhabitants, the influence of the EFTA countries within the EEA has diminished significantly. Icelandic officials working in the field are convinced that the EEA is becoming decreasingly important to the EU and has thus been relegated to a status lower than it enjoyed previously.

Compensating for smallness

Although it has grown from a population of around 60,000 in the mid-19th century to roughly 330,000 at present, Iceland still borders on being a microstate. As a result, Iceland can operate only a much smaller administration than most of its counterparts within EFTA and the EU. Only roughly a hundred diplomats are working in the entire Foreign Service. Because of this systemic lack of resources, Iceland has been forced to focus much more actively on specific policy areas (Thorhallsson, 2000).

Smallness compels external co-operation (Cooper & Shaw, 2009). To compensate for its smallness Iceland relies on close co-operation with its neighbours and even outsources some of its state duties (for example, strategic security) to Washington and part of its legislation to Brussels through the EEA. In this regard, the foreign services of neighbouring states, especially the other Nordics and most frequently Denmark and Norway, become a strategic source of information and assistance. This is a strategic game by a small administration to gain access to information and background analysis that requires greater manpower than Iceland has to call on.

Iceland's forced relationship with Norway in the EEA, which are to harmonize their position so that they speak with one voice within the EEA, is not always happy. Senior diplomats in Iceland's Foreign Service claim that their Norwegian counterparts seem to forget on occasion that they are in a binding agreement with two smaller partners (Bergmann, 2011b). Norway, as the largest EEA power within EFTA, tends to operate alone on issues that are of concern to all three of them. The two countries have often operated quite different European policies. It is claimed that, since the Norwegian people have twice refused to accede to the EU, the Norwegian government is very concerned with proving itself to be 'a good European'. Iceland, on the other hand, has never felt the need to gain that kind of approval in Brussels. As a result, the Icelandic government feels that Norway is keen to give in to the demands of the EU, rather than sticking firmly to the principles of the EEA Agreement and, indeed, the EFTA Convention (Bergmann, 2011b).

The relationship between Iceland and Norway in the EEA can perhaps be compared to an arranged marriage between distant cousins. This is not a relationship entered into on the basis of true love; there is, instead, an uneven balance of power and ongoing and unresolved tensions between the two parties, which are exacerbated by the obligation to make it work.

Iceland's sense of sovereignty

Rationalist International Relations (IR) scholars have explained Iceland's hesitance to join the EU mainly in terms of the interests of the fishing sector, which claims that the EU Fisheries Policy contradicts Iceland's economic interest (Ingebritsen, 2000). This can, however, be questioned by referring to the fact that until the profound economic collapse of 2008 a majority never materialized in Parliament to put the fishing hypothesis to the test in accession negotiations with the EU. Those parliamentarians otherwise in favour of seeking membership if the fisheries issue could be solved should then have been willing to test that in accession negotiations, to see if their concern might be met with adequate opt-outs. Until The Crash of 2008, they were, however, never willing to do that. Combined with the increased opposition the accession negotiations have faced in the wake of the crisis this indicates that other factors might have contributed to Iceland's anti-EU policy. I thus maintain that problems over the fishing issue is not solely an economic argument but indeed a pivotal part of Iceland's post-independence identity. The rationalist approach underestimates the importance of Iceland's strong national identity, created in the independence struggle. Instead, I argue that to fully understand Iceland's relationship with the EU and its hesitant position with regard to the European integration process, it is necessary to analyse its historical relations, the legacy of its colonial past and the rhetoric of the independence struggle – which is still central to the Icelandic political discourse.

As established in Chapter 1, most students of Icelandic politics do acknowledge the importance of the independence struggle on the development of Iceland's political identity. Still, the importance of its post-imperial identity has largely been overlooked in established scholarship on Iceland's EU relations. Kristinsson (2006), for example, only mentions in passing that 'the word independence strikes a key note in Icelandic political rhetoric' before returning to fishing and demographic factors when explaining Iceland's EU relations. The interest-based rationalist approach neglects the political effect of Iceland's postcolonial identity and the strong emphasis on formal sovereignty that was created in the independence struggle. I maintain that within the parameters of Iceland's national identity, EU membership is seen to threaten our sovereignty and thus the cherished democracy which Icelanders claim can be traced back to the parliamentary court of the settlement society in the year 930: the *Alþingi*.

To study the impact of national identity on European integration policies we can turn to Lene Hansen's and Ole Wæver's (2002) post-structuralist framework. They show that to understand what room for manoeuvre governments have in foreign policy it is necessary to study national identities and their impact, for example by analysing domestic political discourse. It is thus helpful to analyse the conceptual constellation of the 'nation' in studying whether, and how, the idea of participation in European integration can fit within the boundaries of a nation's political discourse.

The framework claims that when the idea of 'Europe' threatens the idea of the 'nation' within the domestic debate it becomes difficult to promote further participation in European integration. Thus, the idea of the Icelandic nation and its sovereignty and how that idea fits with Iceland being an integral part of the supra-national European integration process, are as important as – if not more important than – the interests of the leading economic sector, fishing, when studying the relationship the nation has with Europe. Similarly, Iver B. Neumann (2002) finds that the core concept in Norway's relationship with Europe is that of 'the people' (*folket*), which is tied to national patriotism. The

European project is, however, seen as being tied to bureaucracy and the elite and thereby in opposition to the people. This is significantly contrary to Iceland as a distinction between the ordinary public and an elite is not present in the debate. The Icelandic concept corresponding to *folket* is *þjóðin*, which incorporates both the common population and the elite.

According to this model, it is therefore not the personal conviction of the participants that is most important, but rather the discourse they apply in the political debate to put their arguments forward – in other words, how they manoeuvre within the domestic language games made possible and necessary by the concept of sovereignty under postcolonial conditions. To understand Iceland's foreign policy and its policy on Europe it is therefore necessary to frame the analysis within the historical context and map how our nation and state-building, which emerged out of the independence struggle, impact on the foreign policy of the present. A historical account is thus needed to provide an understanding of the framework to which contemporary political discourse must relate if it is to make sense. In the following section I thus examine whether and how politicians try to fit participation in European integration with the Icelandic nation's political discourse, which can be difficult to facilitate. However, in order to uphold itself as a modern Nordic welfare state, Iceland has an economic need to participate in the EU's Internal Market, resulting in the EEA Agreement.

The discourses on Europe

In this section I analyse the rhetoric politicians use when debating participation in European integration, focusing on its effect on Iceland's internal democracy and external independence. In order to illustrate the continuity of the discourse and how the nationalist rhetoric travels through contemporary politics, I will provide examples from the main debates on Europe; first on EFTA (1970), second on the EEA Agreement (1994) and third on possible EU membership. As will be discussed in the next chapter, the rhetoric used in foreign relations during the boom years leading up to the collapse of the financial system in autumn 2008 also provides interesting insight into the impact of the national identity discourse, including the postcolonial rhetoric and the rhetoric that followed The Crash in connection with the Icesave dispute with the UK and the Dutch government and the involvement of the IMF. The postcolonial emphasis on guarding Iceland's democracy by never surrendering to foreign authority again is most often only an underlying factor in contemporary political discourse, which often makes it difficult to identify specific examples. In time of crisis, however, this rhetoric becomes more explicit, as was evident in the Icesave dispute.

Icelandic politics revolves around a double axis: the traditional left/right axis and an internationalist/isolationist axis structured by the issue of Iceland's sovereignty in relation to NATO and to European co-operation. As described before, the party system consists of four main political parties. The left-of-centre Social Democratic Alliance (SDA) is the only party that has consistently campaigned for EU membership. The right-of-centre Independence Party (IP) supported Iceland's membership of EFTA and the EEA but then turned against EU membership. The leftist Left Green Movement (LGM) has campaigned against further participation in European integration, though recently less aggressively. The small, central Progressive Party (PP) was for a long time split on the European issue and lacked a clearly defined policy; since the recent change in leadership, however, the party has turned ever more vigorously against EU membership.

When debating EFTA membership (1968–1969), Icelandic parliamentarians mostly referred to impact on the economy, as is to be expected considering that EFTA was a purely intergovernmental organization. However, the narrative of the independence struggle and conservative ideas on the nation and its sovereignty were always in the background and formed in effect a base for the economic arguments (Bergmann, 2011a). Parliamentarians referred to what they called the undisputed distinctiveness of the nation and said, for example, that it was 'only natural that our relationship with EFTA will be marked by that distinctiveness'.[1] This understanding of uniqueness and distinctiveness was then used as an argument for the multiple opt-outs and special solutions which Iceland brought to the table when negotiating EFTA accession. Those arguing against further participation in the European integration process feared a loss of identity in such a close relationship with the big nations of Europe. Directly tapping into the national myth, many parliamentarians referred to the Old Treaty of 1262 and the introduction of Absolutism in Denmark in 1662 in their argument against integration with other nations.

In the parliamentary debates leading up to the EEA Agreement (1989–1993) the sovereignty argument had moved to the forefront (Bergmann, 2011a). When referring to economic benefits, EEA advocates emphasized the aims of the independence struggle, progress and modernization, in putting Iceland forward as an equal partner in Europe. Foreign

Minister Hannibalsson (SDP) argued that the EEA would be Iceland's 'passport' to the future and the key to economic prosperity.[2] He referred to Jón Sigurðsson, the hero of the independence struggle, to support his claim that the EEA was a continuation of the independence struggle and would push Iceland further into modernity.

The sovereignty argument was central to the discourse of the No camp, which used it even more systematically and forcefully. They accused the Yes side of being unpatriotic and argued that the EEA threatened Iceland's sovereignty, which would be shifted to undemocratic institutions in Brussels. Thus, Iceland would fall under foreign rule once again. And even though the agreement would bring economic benefits, it should be rejected solely on the ground that it violated Icelanders' 'sense of sovereignty'.[3] Interestingly, however, the meaning of sovereignty, what it consists of, was hardly discussed. A parliamentarian for the PP emphasized the importance of protecting the purity of Iceland's identity and language, protecting it from being contaminated by too intimate foreign relations: 'if we submit [to the EEA] we would of course instantly lose our language, culture and independence in a very short time.'[4] This supports Kristín Loftsdóttir's (2010) claim that Icelanders continued to associate national identity with purity of the nation and its language.

In the debate on possible EU membership at the beginning of the 2000s, the importance of sovereignty was dominant (Bergmann, 2011a). The No side claimed that the EU's fisheries policy was not only contrary to our economic interest but also, as one IP parliamentarian maintained, brought with it 'complete transfer of our nation's sovereignty and authority'.[5] Iceland's national heritage and unique culture was emphasized when debating the EU's fisheries policy. It was argued that Icelanders should continue to develop a competitive society and strong economy on their own, claiming that it would be a retrograde step of great consequence if Iceland were to lose its self-rule through membership of the EU. Iceland would be locked inside an unproductive trade bloc and trapped in an undemocratic bureaucracy. At one point, Prime Minister Davíð Oddsson described the EU as one the most undemocratic bureaucratic monstrosity ever created. On the other side of the left/right axis the leader of the LGM similarly remained firmly within the boundaries of the postcolonial discourse when he said that membership would mean 'diminished independence and sovereignty, loss of distinctiveness'.[6]

Not until after the collapse of the financial system and the ousting of the across-the-centre IP/SDA coalition in the so-called Pots and Pans Revolution of January 2009 did the new left-wing government

(SDA/LGM) apply for EU membership.[7] The Yes side tapped straight into the postcolonial independence discourse by promoting the EU as a way forward to protect and strengthen Iceland's sovereignty rather than as a step away from independence, continually referring to Jón Sigurðsson to advance their argument.

Campaigning against the EU, however, one parliamentarian (IP) remembered Iceland's 65th anniversary of independence: 'We were the poorest nation in Europe after 600 years of co-operation with nations to the south in Europe [– the same ones] we would be joining now.'[8] In line with the national myth, he explained that Iceland's misfortune and humiliation had started after the Old Treaty of 1262, and only with independence were we able to become one of the richest nations in the world. He concluded that with EU membership Iceland would again become a 'depopulated, poor province in a huge European super-state'. A colleague (IP) said that Icelanders should never forget that they were a unique nation, 'tough and hardworking and with a soul that could never been broken by foreigners'. One parliamentarian (PP) claimed that *formal* sovereignty 'makes the nation what she is today'[9]; another (LGM) that Iceland's main independence hero, Jón Sigurðsson, 'would turn in his grave if the EU application went forward'[10]; and yet another (LGM) feared that the will of the nation would diminish after EU membership and concluded that 'he who is glad when forced to obey becomes a slave'.[11]

In all of these debates on advancing further into European integration, the same tropes of the sovereignty argument are constantly applied. When analysing this discourse it becomes evident that the fishing factor, central as it has been, is not only an economic matter but also an integral part of Iceland's sovereignty discourse as developed in the independence struggle. The oft used argument that Iceland cannot join the EU because of the EU's Common Fisheries Policy is therefore not a purely economic argument but a pivotal part of Iceland's assertion of its post-independence identity. Complete control over the fishing zone is a symbol of the free and independent Icelandic nation. By extension, keeping European vessels out of Iceland's fishing zone is framed as part of the everlasting independence struggle.

It is also noteworthy that though the discourse does indeed revolve around protecting Iceland's 'formal' sovereignty, the meaning of sovereignty is hardly discussed. Hermannsson (2005) argues that even though Icelanders agree on the importance of protecting their sovereignty, they have little common understanding of its meaning and therefore refrain from debating it.

The importance of sovereignty claims, based on Iceland's national identity, came thrusting to the forefront in the debate on the EEA and continued through the debates on possible EU membership. After The Crash of 2008 and leading up to the EU application in summer 2009 the debate was on both sides dominated by harsh nationalistic rhetoric, directly stemming from the independence struggle, for example by referring to the uniqueness of the Icelandic nation.

The No side applied this discourse more directly while the Yes side rather linked their economic argument with that part of the sovereignty discourse that speaks to modernization and economic progress, arguing that further integration would promote growth and thus ensure Iceland's economic independence, that gaining free access for Icelandic fish into the Single Market was an indirect continuation of the independence struggle – the EEA thus helping to secure Iceland's economic sovereignty. The No side, on the other hand, claimed that keeping control over the fishing grounds was vital to guarding Iceland's independence.

However, when digging into the discourse around the impact of EU membership on Icelandic fisheries' interests, we see how the fisheries argument is itself fuelled by nationalistic rhetoric. In the independence struggle the *peasant* was a symbol of the independent Icelandic nation, but with the increasing importance of fishing, the *seaman* gradually took over as the representative of the sovereign Icelandic nation state. Icelanders fought the British in the so-called Cod Wars to gain control over their fishing resources around the country and since independence the fishing industry has been the most important sector of the economy and has surely been the foundation of Iceland's economic independence (Hermannsson, 2005). The nation and the seaman are for example intertwined in fishermen's folksongs that represent the patriotic Icelander and have become de facto national anthems. The fish in the sea and the fisherman are in this respect symbols of the independent Icelandic nation. This is especially interesting in this context as, in some cases in the debate, the importance of keeping control over fishing resources is, up to a point at least, also an integral part of the *everlasting independence struggle*. The oft used argument that Iceland cannot join the EU because of the EU's Common Fisheries Policy is therefore not simply an economic argument but also a vital part of Iceland's independence struggle. Complete control over the fishing zone becomes in this way a symbol of the free and independent Icelandic nation.

Conclusion

The colonial experience is still very present in contemporary politics in Iceland, in terms of both rhetoric and praxis. The national myth carved out in the independence struggle laid the foundation on which the republic still rests and set the parameters around its political identity and for its relation to the EU. The postcolonial political identity put the emphasis on formal sovereignty and contained an insistence on being recognized as an equal partner in Europe, rather than a microstate that relies on a larger metropole. Formal independence is seen as a prerequisite for a prosperous modern Iceland that enjoys external recognition. This postcolonial identity still characterizes the rhetoric Icelandic politicians use when debating participation in European integration. It was furthermore very present in the identity politics of the boom years as well as in the debate over the Icesave deposit accounts after The Crash, as will be further discussed. Thus, when claiming that the root of Iceland's Euroscepticism is to be found in economic interests surrounding fishing, rationalist theorists neglect the importance of Iceland's postcolonial identity in contemporary politics, especially when it comes to foreign relations.

Postcolonial analyses have proven helpful in understanding how the colonial experience still frames the discourse of Iceland's political economy. When analysing contemporary political debates it is thus important to take into account its historical context. In fact, our relationship with the EU only makes sense when we take into account its colonial history and its postcolonial national identity, which emphasizes formal sovereignty. For example, when digging into the role that fishing plays in the opposition to the EU, we see how it is fuelled by nationalistic rhetoric. The rhetoric of the independence struggle travels through different avenues in modern politics.

When analysing the debates on Europe, we clearly see an emphasis on modernization and economic progress. Economically, like other people in Europe, Icelanders felt a pressure to participate in the European project, which might explain our membership of the EEA – which brought us into the Single European Market. Through the EEA Iceland agreed to transfer decision-making in significant fields of the economy to the European level.

At the same time, however, other forces were pulling in the opposite direction. The postcolonial political discourse, so deeply rooted in the independence struggle, has had the effect that we have been hesitant to agree to the 'formal' transfer of sovereignty which is implied by full membership of the European Union. In this regard, participation in the EU's supra-national institutions falls outside the framework of established political discourse, which emphasizes a formally sovereign and independent Icelandic nation-state, making it more difficult for Icelandic politicians to argue for full and formal membership of a supra-national organization such as the EU. However, for a brief period after The Crash of 2008, a majority for membership application emerged, resulting in an application in mid-2009. Since then, however, opinion polls have indicated a sharp decline in support, resulting in the new right-of-centre government freezing the accession negotiations after the spring 2013 parliamentary elections.

It is within these boundaries that Icelandic postcolonial sovereignty games are currently played. To uphold a modern Nordic welfare state recognized as an equal partner in Western culture, Iceland feels the need to participate in the Single European Market, thus accepting the EEA. However, formally surrendering to supra-national EU institutions challenges the boundaries of the postcolonial political framework. This can also be described as a dilemma between economic interests and ideas on formal sovereignty – illustrating an interesting rift between practical participation in European integration and ideas of a free and sovereign Icelandic nation.

When Iceland handles this dilemma, the relation to the other Nordic countries plays a significant role. Despite the heavy impact of the past colonial relationship with imperial Denmark and Norway on contemporary political discourse, Iceland is consistently discursively represented without a foreign metropole. The Nordic states are presented as equals but also serve as a point of reference for Iceland in positioning itself in the world. In diplomatic terms, however, Iceland was still very dependent on close co-operation with, and even help from, its Nordic counterparts – and other European states such as Germany. In that regard it is interesting that Iceland was reported to be relying more heavily on Oslo than on Copenhagen; to support the insistence on being recognized as an equal partner, Iceland is keen to distance itself from its most recent metropole. In any case, this dependence on diplomatic assistance from neighbours is somewhat in tension with the emphasis on being capable and self-sufficient.

Iceland's history and sense of nationhood can be traced back to the Middle Ages, while modern Icelandic society has quite a young aspect to it. As a newly independent republic, Iceland has a juvenile side to its identity, which is seen, for example, in its efforts to be noticed in the world – especially by the other Nordics, as became evident in the boom years when our Viking Capitalists bought up everything they could get their inexperienced hands on in Scandinavia and in the UK. The other Nordic capitals, Copenhagen and Stockholm, and even also Oslo and Helsinki, are long established while Reykjavik is still an unfinished project. In that sense, the Icelandic sovereignty project is still in progress.

Part II
Boom and Bust

4
The Nordic Tiger – Imagined Economic Miracle

In the decades straddling the new millennium, Icelanders experienced two consecutive cycles of credit-driven boom and bust. The high-tec industry grew rapidly in the 1990s with, for example, the establishment of numerous internet and bio-tec companies, which emerged as the new vehicle into the future. For a while, the newly established internet company Oz became one of the wealthiest in the country even though we were never really sure of the value of its products. Most of these new companies, constituting what was referred to as Iceland's *new economy*, were, however, washed away when the dot.com bubble burst at the turn of the century and capital inflow ceased. It was not long, however, before the next bubble – the banking bubble, starting in 2003, which proved to be one of the fastest growing in world history.

The Independence Party resumed power in 1991, now headed by the leader of The Locomotive group, Davíð Oddsson. The party was to reign until it was ousted in the Pots and Pans Revolution of January 2009.[1] The banking sector had lagged behind other sectors in economic development. Capital markets were heavily controlled, most banks were state owned and interest rates were often set below inflation, allowing government-appointed bankers to allocate subsidized loans to favourable businesses. Thanks to a neoliberal deregulation strategy, Iceland was in one decade – from Iceland's entry into the Single European Market in the mid-1990s until the privatization of financial institutions in the first years of the 21st century – transformed from being amongst the most heavily regulated and backward banking regimes, shut within its own borders, to being one of the most liberal and international in the world.

Since the collapse of Íslandsbanki in 1930 the króna had been on an adjustable peg and hardly tradable on foreign markets. The exchange rate was set to fit the interests of the fishing industry, with frequent devaluations. A fall in fish catch would be met with depreciation of the króna and thus diminished purchasing power of the population. When the króna was finally allowed to float on the free market in 2001, it had lost more than 99 per cent of its value against the Danish krona since the two were separated in 1920. After only seven years of free floating in international waters (2001–2008) the króna collapsed during the financial crisis and was again tied to an anchor behind capital controls.

Driven by their struggle for modernization Icelanders seemed at the beginning of the new millennium to have found their own unique way to succeed in the world of globalized high finance, buying up banks and established companies around Europe – especially focusing on known landmarks on the high streets of London and Copenhagen. Unemployment was hardly measurable as labour force participation was the highest in the Western world. For a while, Icelanders seemed to be enjoying the fruits of the neoliberal accumulation strategy of privatization and the liberalization of markets, particularly financial markets, operated in the latter half of the 1990s (Gissurarson, 2004).

While economic diversification and higher education were significant elements of this accumulation strategy, for example in the promotion of aluminium, creative and high-tech industries, it centred on the idea of liberating Icelandic capital from the structural constraints of an island economy. The Social Democrats had also been promoting the aggressive internationalization of Icelandic capital. A key move was the attainment of entry into the European internal market by the signing of the European Economic Area agreement, as discussed in the previous chapter. The IP/PP government then, however, sought to prevent the full transnationalization of Icelandic capital by tying it closely to the Icelandic economy through monetarist policies promoting a strong króna. Following the neo-corporatist pacts of the early 1990s, this accumulation strategy also enjoyed the stability provided by a labour movement contingently in support of a monetarist policy paradigm, preventing wage drift and exchange rate fluctuation. As a result, even inflation was brought under control.

The establishment of DeCode Genetics perhaps marks the start of the finanicialization and internationalization of the Icelandic economy. However morally questionable the operation, its founder, Dr Kári Stefánsson, was able to secure support from Prime Minister Davíð Oddsson, his old school mate. Together they tapped into the national myth of Icelanders being a unique breed when claiming that by using the exceptional Icelandic genealogical data in medical research the company would not only generate wealth for all Icelanders but also contribute to curing diseases worldwide. Soon, shares in the company were trading above US$50 on the black market as many Icelanders mortgaged their homes to buy into the genealogical adventure. This fitted the Icelandic identity well, as genealogy had been a favourite pastime in the country for centuries – most of us are obsessed with tracing our ancestries. In mid-2000 the company was listed on the NASDAQ. Its stock prices, however, collapsed when the tech bubble burst the following year, finally bottoming at around only one dollar a share. Ordinary Icelanders had gained and lost a great deal of money. In 2012, the rest of the company was finally sold to foreign investors. The story of DeCode was to repeat itself on a much larger scale in the banking bubble, when the stock market multiplied nine times in value before collapsing in October 2008.

Surely Iceland had been a prime candidate for a banking crisis. Studies on the smaller Nordic banking crisis in the 1990s, for example, show that countries with liberal financial systems are more volatile than those operating stricter banking regulations (Detragiache & Demirgüc-Kunt, 1998). More dramatically, however, this was the first time that a financial system of a modern state had tanked in its entirety. In addition, this was not only a banking crisis but also a currency crisis, a *twin crisis*, in Kaminsky and Reinhardt's (1999) phrase, of broken banks and collapsed currency.

Privatization and deregulation

In the early 1990s, there were few separate banking entities in Iceland. Landsbanki and Búnaðarbanki were both state owned and the new private Íslandsbanki had been formed from four smaller banks – one failed state bank and three sectoral banks – each serving a fraction of the economy. A network of small savings and loan funds with close ties to municipalities existed as well as a range of public-sector investment funds. Many of these had in the preceding years been collected and merged into a united investment fund, the Icelandic Investment Fund – FBA. Another significant element of the financial system was the private investment bank Kaupthing, established in 1982 by eight individuals. The system was fragile, as most banks had suffered losses in the 1989 mini-crisis and lack of capital and equity limited their manoeuvrability. To remain solvent Landsbanki, for example, needed a capital injection from the government in 1993. The entire banking assets of the country were less than a single year's GDP, with equity at just over 7 per cent of GDP. Still, before privatization, considerable public financial assets had been building up within the state banks. The pension system had accumulated substantial wealth and equity was being generated through the fishing quota system.

Access to foreign capital opened up with Iceland's entrance into the Single European Market through the EEA in 1994 and privatization of the financial system started in 1998 when the FBA was sold off. Dramatic events surrounding this initial privatization marked the start of the friction between the new business elite and the IP establishment, which was to heighten in the coming years with growing mutual distrust. Against the will of the government, young Jón Ásgeir Jóhannesson, who was to lead retail conglomerate Baugur Group, was, together with a collection of young investors, able to gain control of the investment bank FBA. The Prime Minister openly voiced his fury over novice investors gaining control of the bank instead of the more established investors who the government was usually in business with. Consequently, the privatization programme of the government was changed. Instead of the state retail banks being sold off to a broad base of investors, as initially planned, to ensure diversified ownership, they would be sold to major shareholders with international backing.

Íslandsbanki merged with the FBA in 2000, increasing the power of the new breed of businessman standing outside the political elite. Kaupthing had also been growing rapidly and was the first to break into international markets, opening an office in Luxembourg in 1998 which financed many of Iceland's first aquisitions abroad. In 2000, Kaupthing went public with an initial offering of shares. The state banks were lagging behind in this development. Partial privatization had, however, already started in 1998, when limited shares in Landsbanki and Búnaðarbanki were sold to the public in a broad-based offering. In 2002, the government finally solicited bids on its remaining shares in the two main banks. However, in contrast to previous bids and contrary to the carefully orchestrated governmental plan for privatization, the controlling shares would be sold in bulk.

After havoc over the privatization process Landsbanki was sold to the third-highest bidder (Jónsson, 2009: 49), the Samson Group, led by father and son Björgólfur Guðmundsson and Björgólfur Thor Björgólfsson. Through various Russian ventures, they and a third colleague had come into money, eventually selling a beer factory in St Petersburg to Heineken for US$400 million. Björgólfur Guðmundsson had been a staunch party man in the IP before leaving the country after bankrupting a container ship company in the mid-1980s, but the Samson Group was still considered to be close with the IP leadership. The then editor of the daily *Morgunblaðið*, which is closely tied to the IP, reported that Prime Minister Oddsson 'considered it necessary that Landsbanki should come into the ownership of people whom the party was at least on speaking terms with' (Gunnarsson, 2004).

It illustrates the closeness of the connection between IP and Landsbanki that the IP's Secretary General, Kjartan Gunnarsson, remained a member of the bank's board, and even became vice-chairman, after the Samson Group had acquired it. Apart from the Samson Group he held the highest individually owned shares in the bank.

The government's shares in Búnaðarbanki were sold to the S-group, named after the initial of *Sambandið*, the fallen Icelandic Co-operative Movement discussed in Chapter 2. The group was in effect a coalition of relatively new investors with close ties to the PP, including former Minister of Commerce and Central Bank governor Finnur Ingólfsson, who had in his previous capacities been instrumental in planning the privatization. Apparently the S-group had presented a fake foreign partner to make their offer seem more favourable and to meet the terms of international backing (Hreinsson, Gunnarsson & Benediktsdóttir, 2010).

The privatization of the two major state banks was reportedly a result of a political bargain between the ruling parties. The chief governmental official of the Privatization Committee, Steingrímur Ari Arason, resigned in protest against the government's involvement in the process, maintaining that the two leaders of the coalition parties, Davíð Oddsson and Halldór Ásgrímsson, had each hand-picked the buyers. The report of Parliament's Special Investigative Commission (SIC) into the events leading up to The Crash states that the bid criteria had been defined and weighted to give the predicted results, that the criteria were fluid and were repeatedly relaxed by political decisions. It states that political objectives gradually became increasingly dominant before the 2003 sale (ibid.). The IP/PP government thus in effect steered the banks into the hands of politically chosen groups of investors with relative inexperience of banking. The groups then formed a temporary alliance to finance the deals through cross-investments.

From this opportunist structure resulted what can be understood as a 'Viking', finance-dominated regime of accumulation. Rapid privatization and market liberalization presented Viking Capitalists with the chance to exploit the informal and networked bureaucracy that had developed during previous accumulation regimes. The goal of the government was to free capital for it to be distributed more broadly through the economy, to promote diversification and to increase growth. One of its main aims was to promote investment by the general public, bringing down interest rates and thus providing people with more favourable loans. Public authorities were, however, still heavily involved in lending through the governmental Housing Financing Fund and the Student Loan Fund.

Rival groups of Viking Capitalists

Three banking conglomerates emerged out of the almost simultaneous privatization, deregulation and internationalization of the Icelandic economy, each entrenched in its own power networks. This sector of the economy was to combine justifications for a Viking, finance-dominated regime of accumulation with criticisms of the monosectoralism and the cronyism associated with preceding periods to form a new historic bloc deeply embedded in Icelandic society and translating particular interests into a recognized general interest (Overbeek, 2004). Respecting neither traditional power networks nor the rules of the game, the Viking faction challenged the 'Octopus' faction head on, both through such criticism and through, frequently hostile, takeovers of key units of 'Octopus' conglomerates. Indeed, the emergence of the Viking faction of capital and the government's promotion of a finance-dominated accumulation regime led to intra-class conflict. Yet, more widely, the growth of the financial sector was welcomed as it fitted in neatly with the wider aim of diversifying the economy and breaking the boom-and-bust cycle of previous periods and the exchange rate volatility it translated into, which had been hurting other sectors.

The new breed of bankers was mostly led by men in their thirties, many of whom had studied together in the Business Department at the University of Iceland in Reykjavik before leaving for MBA studies in Europe and America. The older generation of cautious bankers, who prior to privatization had mainly been tied to domestic operations under heavy regulations, was swiftly brushed aside when the young guns broke free of past constrains and stormed international markets. As a result, no institutional memory, tradition or knowledge of international banking was left in the system when the financial bubble started to build. The fate of the old Íslandsbanki in the 1930s, which had left Iceland closed behind capital controls for over half a century, was no longer deemed relevant in the modern banking world. The three rival groups each developed their own identity, which is interesting to explore.

Búnaðarbanki/Kaupthing

When Búnaðarbanki was privatized in January 2003, the rapidly growing young investment fund Kaupthing was emerging as the boldest investment bank in the country. Its management consisted of dedicated youngsters led by the slightly older Sigurður Einarsson, who later came to dominate Iceland's largest bank. The cronies of the PP who acquired Búnaðarbanki had no experience of banking and were thus vulnerable when Kaupthing came asking about a possible merger. The Kaupthing clan gradually gained control of the united entity, which was initially named KB Bank. Pension funds invested heavily in the bank, leading initially to broad ownership with little control over the management, which was free to operate at will.

More broadly, involving pension funds in the financing of the banking system also served the purpose of linking the potentially destabilizing labour movement with the interests of the market world. Rendering the labour movements contingent support necessary was its co-management of Iceland's substantial occupational pension funds, whose investment strategies had come under pressure to embrace portfolio investment strategies to satisfy demands for high returns as wage-growth ground to a halt.

The banking sector was becoming a forum for overblown egos. The management of Búnaðarbanki had revolved around Sigurjón Árnason, who was believed to be brilliant with numbers but, unlike Einarsson, a micro manager. Árnason would not bow to Einarsson and moved with his whole crew over to Landsbanki before Einarsson brought in his tight-knit cult of followers. A few years later, when Einarsson and his team of managers had gained complete control over the merged bank, he changed the name of the united entity back to Kaupthing. In the following years the management of the bank was able to steer controlling shares of the bank into the hands of investors in and around the Exista holding company. The main owners were tight with the S-group, which still held a large stake in the bank. Exista grew out of Bakkavör, which with the help of Einarsson and his team in Kaupthing had become the leading producer of prepared food in the UK.

Each year Kaupthing had more than doubled in size. It had been upgraded from a small, unrated domestic investment bank to a universal retail bank with A2 rating on international markets. Kaupthing's main emphasis was on fast growth through foreign acquisitions. The aggressive culture of high-risk, fast decision making and hard partying that had developed in Kaupthing when it was a small, robust investment fund in the 1990s spilled over into what was to become Iceland's largest commercial bank (for more, see Thorvaldsson, 2011).

Landsbanki (and Straumur)

The return of Björgólfur Guðmundsson to Icelandic business was considered the comeback of the century. After years in exile he not only acquired Landsbanki, which he believed had killed off this shipping company Hafskip in 1985, but also bought his former main rival, Eimskip, which in 1914 had been partly funded by Icelandic settlers in America in order to link Iceland with the outside world. Eimskip became all but sacred in Iceland as it was believed to be instrumental in its independence. Guðmundsson went on to buy into many of the country's most important companies, including its largest publishing house, which was also the power base of Icelandic culture as it controlled much of the country's literary heritage. Dressed in his trademark pin-striped suits he came to be Iceland's greatest philanthropist, loved by the public, and was for a while perhaps more influential in the island's cultural life than even the Minister of Culture, who in effect was downgraded to second fiddle in many opening ceremonies.

The Samson Group portrayed a much more sophisticated façade than the other business groups. To most Icelanders, Björgólfur Guðmundsson was the soft face of the Samson Group, which controlled Landsbanki. His son Björgólfur Thor Björgólfsson was, however, the primus motor in most of their business ventures. Through his investment company Novator he controlled their foreign investments from his spacious office on Park Lane in London. In their portfolio were phone companies in Eastern Europe, international drug companies and businesses around the world. When his father bought Premier League football club West Ham United in East London, his son saw it as a well deserved trophy investment, though perhaps a rather pricey toy for his elderly father to enjoy in his senior years. In many of his international investments, Björgólfur Thor bypassed Landsbanki and instead used investment bank Straumur-Burðarás. Landsbanki had acquired Straumur investment fund from Íslandsbanki. Burðarás had held Eimskip's extensive investments, which the shipping company had accumulated to a sizable sum over the decades. Björgólfur Thor was able to merge the two and turned the result into an aggressive investment bank. In 2007, Björgólfur Thor was ranked in *Forbes* magazine among the richest people in the world, with an estimated net worth of US$3.5 billion[2]. The sophisticated face of Landsbanki was, however, misleading. After Árnason and his team were brought in from Búnaðarbanki, the bank became almost as aggressive as Kaupthing in its operations, first mostly domestically but soon also abroad.

Íslandsbanki/Glitnir

The third group seeking to entrench itself within the emerging accumulation regime revolved around Jón Ásgeir Jóhannesson and his retail conglomerate Baugur. Jóhannesson and his colleagues had manoeuvred themselves into the FBA against the will of the government. Their control was, however, diminished when the investment bank merged with retail bank Íslandsbanki, owned by Iceland's established old money, the so-called network of wholesalers. Jóhannesson was a street-smart businessman of the roughest sort who viewed himself as an outsider in the Icelandic world of business. He had left high school to establish Iceland's first low-budget supermarket, Bónus, together with his father. When Hagkaup, the giant retail company they challenged when entering the market, moved to acquire Bónus to get them out of the way, he quickly reversed the deal through leverage acquisition. This became the blueprint for his dealings around the world. With his wild long hair and dressed in tight black jeans he portrayed the persona of a rock star rather than a businessman or a refined banker.

Íslandsbanki was the smallest of the three and the last to embark on the voyage abroad, which became known as the Icelandic Viking outvasion. The bank was managed by the young and vibrant Bjarni Ármannsson, who had left Kaupthing to become CEO of the FBA. After the merger he had to use all his diplomatic skills to manoeuvre through its boardroom, where a fierce power struggle was raging. The old guard of Iceland's cautious wholesalers was under siege by the rough crowd around Jón Ásgeir Jóhannesson. Ármansson identified Norway as the bank's main market for growth and changed its name to Glitnir, after the ancient Norse god of law and justice.

After exhausting other domestic lending opportunities, having burst through his lending limits in Kaupthing and Landsbanki, Jóhannesson started buying into Glitnir. Foreign banks like Deutsche Bank, HBOS and Royal Bank of Scotland had lent large sums of money to his group but Jóhannesson seemed to have an insatiable appetite for cash and thus set his sights on acquiring Glitnir. In 2007, the rough crowd finally gained control over the bank when Jóhannesson's business partner, Hannes Smárason, came into a third of the shares through his holding company

FL-Group, which later was renamed Stoðir. Amongst his main acquisitions was a controlling stake in AMR Corp, the parent company of American Airlines. Strapped to a golden parachute, Ármannsson was pushed out and a young subordinate from the London office, Lárus Welding, took control. After fast retuning the bank was instantly turned from being the most cautious of the three to perhaps the most aggressive.

Official expansion policy

The expansion of the banking sector was not entirely self-driven. It was also a result of government policies to broaden the base of the economy. In 2001, one of the main political advisors of the IP leadership, Professor Hannes H. Gissurarson, published a book entitled *How Can Iceland Become the Richest Country in the World?*[3] In it he outlined policies of privatization, capital liberalization and low taxation in accordance with tax havens like Jersey, Isle of Man, Cayman Islands and the British Virgin Islands. He argued that in combination with new banking secrecy laws, Iceland would through these measures be able to develop a competitive edge in the financial industry on a world scale (Gissurarson, 2001). In a piece in the *Wall Street Journal*, headled *A Miracle on Iceland*, Gissurarson (2004) claimed that Mr Oddsson's implementation of neoliberal policies in line with Milton Friedman's and Fredrik Von Hayek's thinking had led Iceland to become 'one of the world's most prosperous countries'. In 2006, a government-appointed committee, analysing whether Iceland should become an international financial hub, reached similar conclusions (Prime Ministers Office, 2006). The committee was led by Kaupthing's Einarsson.

Leveraged expansion abroad

After economic restructuring, the three banks all headed for international markets through the newly opened gates of the European Economic Area. With fast growth and increased foreign equity their borrowing became easier and cheaper as interest rates fell on the international market. Each of the banks bought into foreign markets. In 2000, Landsbanki acquired the small but long established Heritable Bank in London and Íslandsbanki-FBA gained control over two tiny banks in Copenhagen and London. Kaupthing was, however, the most aggressive. While still an investment fund it opened offices in Luxembourg in 1998, followed by small brokerages in New York, Stockholm and Copenhagen. By 2004, Kaupthing had mustered enough clout to buy Denmark's third-largest bank, the conservative FIH Bank, which specialized in lending to small and medium-size firms. The acquisition, which more than doubled Kaupthing's balance sheet, was mainly financed by the largest offering to date on the Icelandic stock exchange, amounting to 4 per cent of the country's GDP. To fund aggressive economic expansion, overseas investment capital was increasingly mobilized on the rapidly growing ICEX stock market, which had become the popular symbol for the success of Iceland's Viking Capitalism. A swath of the population was turning into venture capitalists. After acquiring the respectable Singer & Friedlander bank in London, established in 1907, as well as operations in the Isle of Man in the following year, Kaupthing was able to offer its customers wholesale funded services for large-scale investments.

This marked Iceland's entry into the big league of European banking. The others followed suit, opening brokerages in Luxembourg and snatching up financial firms in Scandinavia and the UK. Glitnir, for example, acquired two regional banks in Norway: Kredidbanken and BN.

The state became virtually debt free, which provided the Icelandic banks with better ratings, perhaps on assumption that the state would back them up if they entered troubled waters. Bond issuance on the European market became a fruitful source of funding in the early years. After winning triple-A ratings, the newly privatized Icelandic banks found a world full of cheap cash. Established German banks were amongst those most willing to lend money to the Icelandic Viking Capitalists, which in turn were, after decades of capital controls, eager to get their hands on as much foreign currency as they could grab. Indeed, this was a perfect match. The Icelandic banks did not seem to be much bothered about the quality of their equity. Fuelled by foreign funding, Icelandic firms were thus able to flock en masse onto international markets, opening subsidiaries and buying up foreign firms through leveraged acquisitions.

With easy access to foreign money and lowered equity constrains at home, the banks were enthusiastic to expand their lending. Interestingly, however, during the years of massive growth in the banking sector, fierce rivalry developed between the groups, with growing animosity and mutual accusations of wrongdoing. As a result, they seldom worked together on deals. The owners of the banks and related business partners were, however, still able to exploit the situation and draw massive amounts from this seemingly endless flow of cash. In all of the three banks the owners became the largest groups of borrowers, with almost unlimited access to their vaults. Through wide-ranging investments the three main blocs came to dominate the small Icelandic economy, controlling, for example, insurance companies, oil companies and media groups. In only a few years, the owners in effect turned these universal commercial banks into their private investment funds.

Procyclical policies

As has been described here, Iceland experienced an incredible boom in the first years of the new millennium – which would, however, collapse dramatically in autumn 2008. It will be the task of scholars for decades to come to analyse what really happened and how these events could have occurred (see, for example, Matthiasson, 2008). In addition to large-scale privatization, the sudden opening of European markets and cheap foreign loans there were other domestic policy factors that played a significant role. With the 1990 labour market Consensus Agreement, inflation, which had devastated Iceland's economy for decades, had finally been brought down. In 2001, a new monetary policy was introduced whereby the regime of a fixed exchange rate, which had proved extremely hard to maintain, was abandoned and the króna allowed to float freely, though anchored to a target inflation rate of 2.5 per cent (with 1.5 per cent fluctuation margin), which the Central Bank was to keep to.

While neo-corporatism and the introduction of the Individual Tradable Quota (ITQ) system in fisheries had dramatically reshaped societal paradigms in a market world direction, the social regulation of a finance-dominated regime of accumulation required further efforts. One particularly influential such effort was the continuous promotion and protection of home ownership. Iceland has a very strong tradition of home ownership, which is deeply embedded in the Icelandic culture of independence. In the wake of the 2003 election, the government kept an election promise of the PP and further increased the general maximum loan of the public Housing Financing Fund from around 65 per cent of market value to 90 per cent. The move significantly shrank the retail banks' lucrative market in topping up the equity gap, which many new homebuyers needed to bridge. Subsequently, the banks entered the housing market with all guns blazing, not only providing full financing on housing but also offering better terms than the government housing fund. Parliament commissioned an investigative commission to look into the Public Housing Fund, which concluded that it had been moved from a social vehicle into a market-orientated financial firm in aggressive competition with the banks, but still operating with public backing (Flyering, Heiðarsson & Stefánsson, 2013). As a result, house prices skyrocketed, doubling from 2004 to 2007 and thus forcing up inflation once again. This added to the suffering of the general public as housing loans were indexed to the consumer price index, which in turn further strengthened commitment to monetarist policies.

Another contributing factor to the fantastical boom was the government-initiated investment in numerous public power plants. This was in accordance with a long-standing wish to utilize the country's geothermal energy in order to both expand and diversify the economy. The largest of these was the aluminium smelter in Reyðarfjörður in the east of Iceland, which called for gigantic construction of river dams and massive industrial buildings. The PP drew most of its support from the countryside, which had for decades been gradually depopulating as people were flocking to the capital. This threatened not only the PP's existence but also the entire Icelandic project as our identity is partly based on the importance of populating the whole country and on the deeply rooted notion inherited from the independence struggle of the free and virtuous farmer. In an attempt to reverse the trend, the government teamed up with local municipalities and global aluminium companies to finance the biggest investment project since the settlement – as luck would have it located in the old home constituency of the leader of the PP. In just a few years, Iceland's aluminium production tripled, adding almost 5 per cent to economic growth.

While the PP was freely allowed to inflate the economy in order to fulfil their extensive election promises, the IP leadership, the coalition's senior partner, was busy pushing through the tax cut programme carved out by the neoliberal Locomotive group. Money was flowing into the state's coffers in unprecedented amounts. In 2002, corporate tax was lowered from 30 to 18 per cent and in 2008 to 15 per cent. In 2003, property tax was brought down from 1.2 to 0.6 per cent and it was abolished altogether in 2006. In 2004, the rate for the highest income tax bracket was lowered as well as that for the general income bracket. In each of 2005, 2006 and 2007, income tax was lowered by 1 per cent. In 2007, value added tax on selected items was brought from 17 per cent down to 7. Despite these extensive tax cuts, revenues were still on the rise, allowing the government to both increase public spending and pay all its foreign debts.

Already in 2004, Iceland ranked ninth on the world index of Economic Freedom. It had moved up from 53rd place in 1975. Neoliberal scholars like Arthur Laffer were referring to Iceland as a model tax regime (Laffer, Moore & Williams, 2007).

The government's stated objective was to maintain economic stability and reduce economic fluctuation, thus controlling the seemingly endless boom and bust cycle. However, while the Central Bank was by law mandated to keep to the set inflation target, the government's fiscal policy was pulling in the opposite direction, creating a constant tension between the two main areas of economic policy. Against their stated aims, Icelandic governments from the mid-1990s ran an entirely procyclical fiscal policy (Nielsson & Torfason, 2012).

Perhaps each of these policy projects of the government might have been achievable in separation but when they were executed simultaneously the collective effect was to inflate the economy so drastically that it would eventually spin out of control. Prime Minister Davíð Oddsson dismissed most voices of caution. He claimed, for example, that economists were as a class far too pessimistic; according to them, tax cuts were inadvisable both in times of growth and in times of decline (quoted in Jónsson, 2000). After a disagreement with the National Institute of Economic Analysis (Þjóðhagsstofnun), he abolished the institution in 2002 and moved economic analysis to the Statistics Bureau, which answered directly to the Prime Ministers Office.

Another aspect relates to Iceland's participation in the European Internal Market, which, for example, required Iceland to adopt EU regulations in the financial sector. EU directives stipulate a free flow of capital within a common framework, which members are to honour. Within the framework, however, each Member State is free to implement stricter rules in accordance with local conditions. Iceland never laid down any such rules to limit its credit institutions. In fact it stuck to the bare minimum of such regulation.

On the contrary, the government was eager to advance the country's competitiveness abroad without violating the minimum requirements of the EEA agreement. To this end, financial firms' liberty to invest in non-financial businesses, to extend credit to directors, to invest in real estate companies, to lend money to buy own shares and to open for ownership in other credit institutions was increased. Similarly and with the same aim, the government reduced restrictions on the operating structure of securities companies.

To counter the massive credit demand, bringing with it inflationary pressure, after the króna had been floated in 2001, the Central Bank had no option but to increase its base rate, which was thus kept very high throughout the boom years. In the five years leading up to The Crash, the Central Bank frequently raised its interest rate, which rose in steps from 5.3 per cent to 15.5 per cent. Paradoxically, the government's Housing Financing Fund was at the same time lowering interest rates in fierce competition with the banks.

The transition capacity of setting domestic interest rates to control credit demand was, however, limited, as two-thirds of loans were at a fixed interest rate but indexed to the consumer price index where inflation would accumulate on top of the principal of the loan, which would thus be mostly pushed to the back end of it. Borrowers were thus more sensitive to long-term real interest rates than short-term nominal rates. Raising nominal interest rates, however, served to inflate the value of the króna on money markets, giving our small currency the appearance of strength and providing Icelandic banks with easy and cheap access to foreign capital. The impact of hiking interest rates was further undermined as many borrowers, amounting to one-sixth of the market, shunned the high-interest króna and instead took out loans in foreign currencies with nominal interest rates set to the international level. Turning a blind eye to the risk most new corporate loans were in this form. And the general public did not seem to comprehend the exchange rate risks of borrowing in foreign currency. These FX-linked loans were to hit us on the head when the currency tanked.

For some reason, the Central Bank did nothing to make wholesale borrowing on the international market more costly. Indeed, nothing at all was done to control the ever-increasing liquidity flowing over the riverbanks of Iceland's economy. The bank never even considered, for example, extending holdings in foreign assets to counter the demand created by this relaxed fiscal policy. On the contrary and to the surprise of many, the bank even reduced reserve requirements in 2003. In addition, as late as spring 2008, when the crisis was already raging, the bank abandoned its reserve requirements on deposits collected in foreign branches of the Icelandic banks. As a result of these measures the entire system was short of foreign cash when the crisis hit.

Defining the hiking of interest rates as its only available tool against inflation, the Central Bank did little to limit the growth of the banking sector, which was expanding beyond the capacity of the state to control it. The Icelandic Financial Supervisory Authority (FME) also remained weak and was never equipped with enough capacity to be able to catch up with the growth of the financial system. In 2006, a total staff of only 45 was to supervise three banks, each of which was among the 300 largest banks in the world. Furthermore, the FME never even considered it their task to curb the unsustainable growth of the banks. This was in line with the government's policy of supporting the internationalization and growth of the banks and indeed to keep them domiciled in Iceland even though their size had outgrown the capacity of the Central Bank to back them up and the FME to control them.

Another side-effect of the high base rate was that it attracted hot money from abroad. The interest rate offered in Iceland was gradually becoming amongst the highest attainable in the world. Demand was building for foreign issue bonds in Icelandic króna among investors who wanted to exploit the sizable interest rate differential. Among those issuing the so-called glacier bonds were the European Investment Bank and the German KFW. They would use Icelandic banks to swap their króna back to foreign currency. The Central Bank seemed to have no control over the inflow of money brought over through the carry trade by investors who borrowed against it in low-yielding currencies and pocketing the difference, these also included ordinary investors such as 'Belgian dentists' and 'Japanese housewives', as commentators for some reason often referred to them (Jóhannesson, 2009: 263). In fact, the Central Bank never even tried to control the liquidity in the financial system.

Due to the small size of the economy the Icelandic exchange rate is all the more sensitive to capital movements. Still, many foreign investors did not seem to be bothered by the incredibly high value of this tiny nation's currency; despite the fact that interest rate parity clearly indicated it was due to depreciate significantly. In the lead-up to The Crash, these glacier bonds amounted to almost 40 per cent of the country's GDP. These are closely monitored, high-risk investments. Traders thus tend to abandon their stakes fast when the climate changes against their interest. Still, The Crash took many by surprise, and they found themselves instantly locked within the Icelandic króna regime behind capital controls.

Spinning out of control

Iceland belonged to a group of states that experienced a net inflow of capital in the first years of the new millennium; they also included Estonia, Germany, Greece, Ireland, Italy, Latvia, Lithuania, Portugal, Spain and the UK. Many of these were amongst the most severely hit countries in the coming crisis, that is the PIIGS (Portugal, Ireland, Italy, Greece and Spain). Iceland was in many respects, however, in a league of its own. The inflow into Iceland was greater and more rapid than elsewhere. The banking sector grew much faster, labour market participation was higher, unemployment was virtually non-existent and GDP per capita grew well beyond other capital inflow states to become the highest in Europe, second only to the US on the world index. By 2005, there were ever more visible signs of serious overheating. Fuelled by foreign capital, the three banks grew exponentially, from amounting to just over one year's GDP in 2000 to almost ten times the country's annual GDP when the system collapsed. The most rapid growth was in the last few years. In 2005 alone, the three banks took out €15 billion worth of new debt, which was significantly higher than the country's GDP. In the same year, the banks reported a 40 per cent return on equity while the European average was 15 per cent. Between 2004 and The Crash of 2008, the banks had been able to issue bonds amounting to almost €50 billion, four times the GDP of the country (Benediktsdóttir, Danielsson & Zoega, 2011). The primitive stock market also expanded massively, with many new listings. Breaking the world record, the stock market multiplied nine times over from the low of 2001 to the peak in 2007, when around 70 per cent of its value was in the financial sector (Halldórsson & Zoega, 2010).

Credit-driven consumption and investment led to a sustained current account deficit, averaging just below 15 per cent a year between 2003 and 2007. In this period, GDP grew by 6.4 per cent a year. Illustrative of the excess is that in 2007 more luxury Range Rovers were sold in Iceland than in Denmark and Sweden combined. The money supply increased by up to half a year and housing prices doubled in only a few years, while the rise in real wages lagged behind. Iceland was clearly living well beyond its means. Credit expanded beyond most people's imagination. Corporate firms and ordinary households alike tripled their real exposure. Foreign liabilities rose from 75 per cent of GDP to almost 500 per cent and domestic liabilities went from 60 per cent to around 270 per cent. Despite being unsustainable, the capital inflow was driving the whole economy with both asset prices and the currency rising way beyond their underlying values, promoting both imports at bargain price and investment in the bloated economy. Still the government took no measures to increase savings. On the contrary, this seeming strength lured many into taking on mortgages and consumer debt, particularly car loans, denominated in foreign currency, to finance the spending bonanza of the 2000s.

The inflow of money also distorted the composition of the economy, for example expanding the construction industry well beyond the capacity of the labour force. Increased demand led to a rapid inflow of foreign workers, growing to almost 10 per cent of the work force before The Crash of 2008. Most foreign workers came from Eastern Europe after these had entered the EU. Many brought their families over. In just a few years, Iceland went from being a highly homogeneous society to becoming significantly multicultural. Many Icelanders welcomed the change but xenophobia also grew in public discourse, coming to the surface of Icelandic politics when the so-called Liberal Party (which in fact was anything but liberal in its policies) campaigned actively against immigration and multiculturalism while nourishing the nationalist sentiment always underlying Icelandic political discourse.

Iceland is a small country with limited human resources. The financial sector was thus sucking talent from other branches of the economy, which as a result suffered a constant brain drain, depriving many creative industry innovations of the oxygen they needed to take off. Not many could compete with the banks, which were offering new recruits fresh out of college higher salaries than their parents could even have dreamed of. The banks were indeed sponsoring the financialization of the entire society.

Mother of all shopping sprees

Iceland was not only a recipient of money. Our Viking Capitalists exploited the situation and utilized the newly privatized banks to embark on one of the greatest shopping sprees in world history, buying up businesses and investing their borrowed cash around the world. The simultaneous leveraged *outvasion* of Icelandic companies was also caused by fierce internal competition between the groups of Viking Capitalists. Jón Ásgeir Jóhannesson bought up many of the main retail companies in London and Copenhagen, including House of Fraser, Hamley's, Karen Miller and Iceland frozen food stores, to name just a few. Within his portfolio were companies running more than 3,800 stores and employing 65,000 people. For a while, the company owned a large proportion of the UK's high street stores.

Icelandic investors acquired airlines on both side of the Atlantic and held stakes in the travel industry around the world. The Kaupthing clan was focusing on financial firms and insurance companies throughout Scandinavia. Björgólfur Thor became a real live business tycoon in the newly liberal Eastern Europe, acquiring many newly privatized firms, such as phone and drug companies, while his father rubbed shoulders with international high society in his private chairman's lounge at West Ham stadium in East London.

All the groups established real estate holding companies, acquiring many landmark buildings in neighbouring capitals. Often, they would compete against each other for the same assets and, because of their constant rivalry and mutual animosity, on occasion entered into fiercely fought bidding wars. Many of the main acquisitions in 2006, 2007 and 2008 were far greater than most Icelanders could comprehend. Even these paled into insignificance when compared with some of the planned endeavours, which were halted only by The Crash. Amongst them were Askar Capital's plans to build a high-rise neighbourhood in Macau and even a complete high-tech town in India.

Being children of the Icelandic postcolonial national identity, discussed in Chapter 1, many Viking Capitalists were focused on Copenhagen, Iceland's old colonial capital. London was always the main hub of their ventures but acquisitions in Copenhagen were hailed in the Icelandic media – and by the Viking Capitalists themselves – as the greatest conquests. Before the boom, Icelandic business ventures in Copenhagen were mostly limited to a few pizza parlours, inner neighbourhood cafes and side-street bars. In only a few years, Icelandic businessmen had acquired the two largest and most majestic Danish downtown department stores (Magasin Du Nord and Illum), the country's second-largest airline (Sterling) and its most prestigious hotel (D'Angleterre), and their real estate companies not only held large shares of the main shopping streets but also many key government buildings. Many of these can be considered trophy investments rather than coldly calculated business deals, each acquisition perhaps a statement by the former poor colony that it had now grown up and should be taken seriously on the world stage. In addition, Icelanders established their own Danish newspaper (*Nyhedsavisen*), which became one of the most widely distributed in the country. They also ran their own chains of fashion boutiques, restaurants and delegate food stores. Icelanders living in Copenhagen were for a while able to spend their money almost solely with Icelandic-held companies, which would fulfil most of their daily needs.

Before the boom, Iceland had for centuries been an egalitarian society with no super-rich people. The income of the old wholesaler class was perhaps a few times higher than that of their employees on the shop floor. In the new millennium, however, high salaries in the banking sector were causing the upper class to lose touch with ordinary Icelanders. Prices in Reykjavik were rising beyond the means of many locals as the nouveau-riche behaviour of the Viking Capitalists ripped apart the fabric of society. On Friday afternoons, Reykjavik airport would be filled with the private jets of the Viking Capitalists returning home just in time for their bookings at the trendy new Reykjavik restaurants. Internationally celebrated artists performed at their parties. Elton John came to sing at Kaupthing's Ólafur Ólafsson's 50th birthday party and American rapper 50 Cent performed at Björgólfur Thor's 40th birthday party in Jamaica – to which guests from Iceland had been brought in his rented Boeing 747. For his annual parties for Icelanders in London, Ármann Þorvaldsson, the CEO of Kaupthing Singer and Friedlander, hired famous bands like Duran Duran. Once, he introduced Tom Jones on stage and sang with him the legend's hit song *Delilah*. Reports of racing Ferraris in Monte Carlo, partying with high society on private yachts in Florida and in the Mediterranean and even eating gold risotto at business dinners filled the news. The Icelandic businessmen were, however, enjoying the limelight and the ego-nourishing attention of the international media, which hailed them as a new breed of business geniuses. The business sections of the world's most prestigious newspapers celebrated their fast decision making as a fresh and admirable style of doing business. Jón Ásgeir Jóhannesson, for example, stemmed the overflow of tedious information and became famous for his 'one-page' management style and distaste for bureaucracy.

Foreign acquisitions were the buzzword of the day and this new style of business was affecting the whole society. Even small-time businessmen, owners of dry-cleaning shops and car service centres, would leverage themselves to open up subsidiaries abroad just to be part of the game. Those left behind and operating only in Iceland were thought to have been relegated to a second league.

Nourishing the superiority complex

The seemingly reckless behaviour of the Viking Capitalists cannot be solely attributed to their own individual characteristics. To galvanize the coherence and credibility of this emerging Viking Capitalist historic bloc, the Icelandic authorities in effect blessed their operations. In this respect the political, intellectual and moral leadership of President Ólafur Ragnar Grímsson cannot be overestimated. His speeches around the world at the time of the millennium, steeped as they were in the nationalist discourse, gave valuable credibility to the Viking faction of capital both in Iceland and internationally. Already at the turn of the millennium, he was predicting 'that the features of the new global economy are such as to allow us Icelanders to prosper as never before and give our global partners access to a highly rewarding co-operation' (Grímsson, 2000). He explained that creativity was the backbone of the Icelandic heritage, 'creativity which centuries ago produced the Icelandic sagas and the Edda Poems, unique literary achievements in medieval Europe [...] is clearly what confers a competitive edge in the modern global economy and will do so even more in the knowledge-based industries and services of the 21st century' (ibid.).

Kristín Loftsdóttir (2011) points out that Icelanders have long emphasized the purity of their ethnic origin, 'combined with grand narratives of how they gained independence and became one of the richest nations in the world.' Tapping directly into the national myth, the President didn't hesitate to explain Iceland's postcolonial success in terms of the unique origin of the nation, thus linking the present with the past. He went on to explain how Icelandic creativity manifests itself not only in literature and the arts but also in the running of modern companies. 'Thousands of companies all over the country demonstrate the fascinating combination of entrepreneurship and creativity which is so uniquely Icelandic' (Grímsson, 2000). He proclaimed that in the new global economy, Icelanders' spirit of exploration and the Icelandic heritage of creativity gave the nation unique opportunities to prosper as never before. Thanks to this, Iceland was becoming 'one of the most interesting modern societies on earth, a society that is using technology to achieve one of the highest living standards in the world' (ibid.). He concluded his millennium speech in Los Angeles by saying that it was in 'this spirit that we have come to Los Angeles to share with you [the people of America] the excitement of our future' (ibid.).

With the growing success of Viking Capitalism, the President's nationalistic rhetoric amplified. In a speech at the Walbrook Club in London a few years later, he started off by linking the success of the Icelandic businessmen to the Cod Wars between Iceland and the UK and reminded his audience that Iceland was the 'only nation on earth to defeat the British Navy, not once but three times' (Grímsson, 2005). He said that with this unique track record in mind, 'it is no wonder that young entrepreneurial Vikings have arrived in London full of confidence and ready to take on the world!' (ibid.). When explaining Iceland's success he enthused in typical nationalist discourse that Icelandic 'business culture, our approach, our way of thinking and our behaviour patterns, rooted in our traditions and national identity', had through 'unique qualities given [our] businesses a competitive edge, enabling us to win where others either failed or did not dare to enter. Our entrepreneurs have thus been able to move faster and more effectively, to be more original and more flexible, more reliable but also more daring than many others' (ibid.).

Though the President perhaps went further than most, his narratives were widely echoed during the boom years. Tapping into the national myth deriving from the independence struggle, a report on the image of Iceland commissioned by the Prime Minister's office in 2008 attributed this perceived success to 'unique characteristics' of the Icelandic nation 'which separate Icelanders from other nations' (Prime Ministers Office,

2008). This uniqueness of the Icelandic nation was said to stem from the fact that the people lived in harmony with harsh nature, which had created a special natural force within the Icelandic nation. The report concluded that on this basis the core of Iceland's image should be 'power, freedom and peace' (ibid.). Here the internationalization of Iceland's economy is indeed interpreted through a romantic nationalist discourse. A report on the future of Iceland commissioned by the Icelandic Chamber of Commerce in 2006 echoed the writings of Jón Jónsson Aðils a century earlier in placing Iceland at the peak of civilization when it suggested that Iceland should 'no longer compare itself with the other Nordic states, as we overreach them in most fields' (Icelandic Chamber of Commerce, 2006). In 2007, the annual conference of the Icelandic Chamber of Commerce was held under the slogan 'Iceland, best in the world?' (Ísland, best í heimi?, 2007). In the University of Iceland's Business Department, an exceptionally well funded research project named *INTICE – Outvasion of Icelandic Companies* was launched the following year, analysing the superiority of the Icelandic *outvasion* model (Ólafsson, 2008). Its success was mostly attributed to informal channels of communication, boldness and quick decision making. The project, which was financed by many of the main *outvasion* companies, instantly ran out of funding after The Crash.

This thinking was also noticeable in the more benign cultural *outvasion*, as illustrated by Georg Holm, bassist of the band Sigur Ros, in March 2008 when explaining that Icelanders were 'intensely proud of our mighty homeland' – adding that it was 'in our Viking blood to want to conquer nations and peoples' (quoted in Hooper, 2008).

Out of this nationalistic discourse emerges a theory of a unique nation which had over the centuries developed special characteristics, but had until recently been limited by its smallness and isolation. The theory explains how this uniquely talented nation would now through increased globalization almost inevitably lead Icelanders to great success on the world stage. This discourse of the uniqueness of the Icelandic nation heard in the boom years draws on the national myth, which has remained central to Icelandic societal paradigms from its creation during the independence struggle in the 19th century. The President directly linked the contemporary Viking Capitalists with the original Viking settlers of the 9th century, claiming that they displayed the same qualities and indeed the same spirit. This is what Anthony D. Smith (1993) refers to as 'the myth of a common ancestry'. This discourse is also evidence of the Viking image being used to refer to a time of political autonomy, as, for example, Nielsen Germaud (2010) explains.

Conclusion

Iceland's economy has been characterized by continuous cycles of boom and bust. In the first decade of the new millennium, Icelanders were, however, taken on a greater economic roller-coaster ride than perhaps any other people in this crisis. After the country had entered the Single European Market, the newly privatized banks flocked abroad en masse in what became known as Iceland's *outvasion*. Inexperienced as they surely were, access to cheap foreign funding allowed the Icelandic Viking Capitalists to embark on one of the world's greatest shopping sprees, snatching up foreign companies in neighbouring capitals through leveraged acquisitions.

Procyclical economic policies did nothing to contain the boom. On the contrary: in conjunction with widespread neoliberal domestic deregulation, massive new industrial construction, increasing public housing loans and far-reaching tax cuts were pumping hot air into an already overinflating bubble. The Central Bank's only response – hiking interest rates rather than tightening its control with broader means – was counterproductive, as it led to hot money pouring even faster into the country over the carry trade. The aspiration to meet inflation targets is thus risky when high interest rates attract capital inflow.

For a while, the new breed of Viking Capitalists were hailed by the international media as business geniuses. Their nouveau-riche lifestyles were, however, ripping apart the fabric of this tiny, egalitarian society. With the consumer price index shooting through the roof and housing prices skyrocketing, the general public was left behind, resulting in massive household borrowing. In order to keep up appearances, ordinary people turned themselves into venture capitalists.

Many economists warned that these policies, which would lead to a prolonged period of major trade deficit, would eventually result in a steep reversal, if not a full-blown depression. However, any words of caution were dismissed, as they countered the age-old desire for modernization and diversification carved out in the independence struggle and developing into the postcolonial national identity. Nothing was to stop Iceland's long-awaited Golden Age.

5
Living on the Edge – Hot Air Flaring Up the Economy

Iceland's booming economy entered troubled waters in early 2006 with flood of negative reports landing on its shores. The response was one of defiance, fuelled by nationalist rhetoric. Instead of contemplating the criticism, our government responded by launching PR campaigns abroad. Any criticism of the new Icelandic financial system was viewed as threat to the entire Icelandic project, to the positioning of modern Iceland as an equal partner within the ranks of prosperous Western states. When liquidity dried up on foreign markets, the oversized and ever thirsty Icelandic banks responded by opening internet-based banks abroad, offering high interest on deposits. Foreign cash floated in through the web and for a while helped to lubricate the failing engine of the monstrosity our Viking Capitalists had created. After a near-death experience, the mini-crisis was believed to be over by late 2006.

With a renewed certificate of good health the Viking Capitalists ripped loose of all chains and blew even more hot air into the economy. After clear signs of overheating in the preceding years, Iceland's finance-driven economy was allowed to grow even faster in 2006 and 2007. Having grown from roughly the size of its GDP at the beginning of the decade to five times that in 2005, the banks doubled in size again in the coming couple of years, still without attracting much criticism.

Negative reporting on Iceland, however, appeared again in early 2008. We later learned that by then the economy was no longer sustainable. With increasingly limited access to funding, Iceland was being pushed out of international financial markets. The downfall leading up to the devastating crash in October 2008 started in January and finally reached the point of no return when, in an extraordinary move, Glitnir was nationalized in late September. This chapter discusses the dramatic events after the mini-crisis of early 2006, leading up to the banking collapse of October 2008. In this period, Icelanders were in economic terms living on the edge – before finally falling off the financial cliff.

The 2006 Geyser crisis

The clouds gathering on the horizon first became visible to ordinary eyes in early 2006 with a row of international reports portraying a negative outlook for the until then booming economy. Its incredible growth and the far-reaching 'outvasion' of Icelandic businessmen had attracted attention around the world. The perceived wealth of ordinary households had grown three times in as many years. Few, however, questioned how this tiny nation could generate so many high-flying international businessmen in such a short period. Initially, the new Vikings had mostly been glorified in the international media but by 2005 more critical voices started to filter through all the praise. The Danish media turned particularly hostile, telling, for example, mostly unfounded tales of Russian mafia money running through Iceland's lava and spreading from the rocky island out to the continent. The tone in many comments – and the way in which the case was framed – pointed to disbelief amongst many in the old colonial master country that poor old Iceland could emerge as a serious player in the global economy.

Analysts and many hedge fund managers were at the same time increasingly noticing signs of a bubble building after extensive overheating. With growth of 20 per cent over three years, virtually no unemployment and a central bank policy rate at 14 per cent, there seemed little room for further growth. The annual current account deficit reaching 20 per cent did not seem very convincing, either. In a report on Kaupthing in November 2005 the Royal Bank of Scotland (2005) voiced investors' concern about the health of Icelandic banks. With a balance sheet two-and-a-half times larger than the country's GDP, Kaupthing alone was growing beyond the capacity of the Central Bank to back it up in time of crisis. The same was becoming true of both Glitnir and Landsbanki. Furthermore, the clearly overvalued Icelandic króna (ISK) was shining like an easy target. It might be easy to take down and pocket the spoils.

Like wolves, hedge funds hunt in packs. In late 2005, a cluster of them had started shorting the króna. Taking out credit default swaps (CDSs) on stocks of the Icelandic banks, they were betting not only on a sharp devaluation of the króna but also on financial firms collapsing as a result. CDSs are credit derivatives contracts in which the buyer insures a financial asset. Shorting banks with CDSs can be very lucrative if the price of the asset falls before payments are due. Branded a 'financial weapon of mass destruction' by investor Warren Buffet (2003), CDSs can be lethal. They are perhaps comparable to others taking out insurance on your house. The increasing spread of such insurance by strangers increases the likelihood of your house being burned to the ground. Similarly, an increased CDS spread on banks raises a red flag on the market.

The source of the CDS spread on the Icelandic banks has been traced to a single fund manager at the Norwegian Petrol Fund, which is reported to have been the first to buy such protection (Jónsson, 2009). Others followed suit. The force of numbers increases pressure and thus the likelihood of a successful takedown. Reportedly, a widespread attack on Iceland was plotted in an informal club of hedge funds named Drobny Global Advisors. In early February 2006, a message was circulated among this group of around fifty hedge funds suggesting that they should go short on the Icelandic króna and other high-yielding currencies (ibid.).

On 21 February, Fitch Ratings (2006) changed its outlook on Icelandic banks from 'stable' to 'negative', mostly because of massive foreign private sector borrowing and slack domestic fiscal policy. The report came as a shock to most Icelanders, who until then had remained oblivious to any economic difficulty. Nervously, the carry traders started constantly monitoring their charts, ready to leave at a moment's notice. As a result, the króna fell by 7.5 per cent, the banks' liability in foreign currency rose and the stock market took a significant hit in this initial shock. Increased business defaults followed.

Two weeks later, Merrill Lynch raised concerns over the Icelandic banks' interconnectedness (and the consequent risk of systemic collapse), their private equity profiles and their reliance on wholesale borrowing abroad (Thomas, 2006). Iceland was being hit right, left and centre. The major blows seemed to come at two-week intervals. The next one was served by the Danish commercial bank, Den Danske Bank, in its very first report on Iceland, called Geyser Crisis, dated 21 March 2006 (Valgreen & Christensen, 2006). The bank claimed that the Icelandic financial system was about to implode and concluded that Iceland had already been frozen out of international capital markets. This time, it was not only the research division that was reporting on the issue but also the operational part of the Danske Bank that was taking action. Before publishing the report, the bank had ceased all trading in króna and closed lines to the Icelandic banks, even to our Central Bank.

Subsequently, some of the Danish media even began warning Danes against working for Icelandic-held companies in their country. By the end of March 2006, the cracks in the Icelandic financial system were becoming plainly evident. A group of investors on a trip to Reykjavik, organized by Barclays Bank, launched into a shouting match with their hosts at Kaupthing's headquarters. Many of the participants had already shorted the króna and taken out CDSs on the banks. During the bank's defensive presentation one guest is reported to have intervened and shouted: 'This is not a bank, but a hedge fund' (Jónsson, 2009).

Icelandic bankers and politicians alike felt the walls closing in. Disaster stories of the country's predicted downfall spread through the international media, with headlines like: 'Iceland melting', 'Icelandic eruption', 'Deep freeze' and 'Geyser crisis'. Concerned investors and analysts were flocking to the country to investigate the health of the economy. Consequently, the CDS spread widened even further and the Icelandic banks found themselves being pushed out of international wholesale financial markets. In only two months, February and March, the ISK fell by 20 per cent. Globally, the pressure had been building on high-yielding currencies such as the New Zealand dollar, the South African rand and the Turkish lira. When critical reports on Iceland's economy emerged in the international media, these other high-yielding currencies fell with the króna.

The 2006 Geyser Crisis took most Icelanders by surprise. We had all been living in a financial fairytale, told through thick nationalistic discourse. The domestic response to criticism of the sustainability of the Icelandic 'economic miracle' was one of defiance, perhaps due to a galvanized spirit of Viking Capitalism. The Icelandic government and most other actors in the society dismissed the warnings as ill-intentioned carping by envious foreigners. Nevertheless, the Icelandic government launched a series of defensive PR campaigns in London, New York and Copenhagen. The Minister of Commerce, Valgerður Sverrisdóttir (PP), said that envy was the root of the criticism by Fitch Ratings and dismissed the concerns of the Danish commercial bank by suggesting that Denmark's self-image had been damaged by Iceland's success (Sverrisdóttir, 2006). Similarly, the Minister of Education, Þorgerður Katrín Gunnarsdóttir (IP), suggested to the Merrill Lynch researchers that they should re-educate themselves, as they clearly did not understand the particular nature of the Icelandic economy (Gunnarsdóttir, 2008).

Volatility was to characterize our economy in the coming months, with repeated rescue missions to save the króna from free fall. The most serious attack came on 21 April, when in a single day trading on the króna amounted to more than 7 per cent the country's GDP. In the whole of the month of April, trading on the króna amounted to more than half of GDP. Finally, the attackers were beaten back with heavy losses. This, however, almost exhausted the Central Bank's capacity to defend the króna. The IMF voiced its concerns over a systemic collapse in a staff report dated August 2006 (International Monetary Fund, 2006).

Domestic actors immediately organized a multi-faced defence. One aspect was to commission world-renowned scholars like Frederic Mishkin (Mishkin & Herbertsson, 2006) of Colombia and Richard Portes (Portes & Baldursson, 2007) of the London Business School to write reports, together with Icelandic academics, which were used to provide Iceland's economy with a renewed certificate of good health. On the basis of a firm regulatory framework and strong institutional back-up, both reports concluded that no real worries were warranted regarding Iceland's financial system.

With a credit reserve of only €1 billion to fend off the attacks there was hardly a euro left in the Central Bank's vaults when it finally ended. Its narrow escape from this near-death experience, however, only re-boosted the self-confidence of the Icelandic bankers, who responded by blowing even more hot air into the already over-inflated bubble, resulting in greater growth in 2007 than ever before. The mini-crisis had not reduced Icelanders' appetite for growth. By mid-2006, Iceland had been able to rebuff the attacks. Illustrative of that was Landsbanki's $2.25 million bond issue in August 2006, brokered between the Bank of America, Citi Group and Deutsche Bank, which perhaps marked the formal end of the mini-crisis. Some have since claimed that the way Icelanders were able to rebuff the crisis created a sort of miracle complex amongst them, a deeply rooted conviction of not being able to fail (Jóhannesson, 2009: 202).

New funding model

Barely surviving the 2006 Geyser Crisis, the banks were, however, not yet out of the wood. Their business model relied on being able to raise funds in the short-term financial market. With restricted access to wholesale funding on international markets, the banks were in desperate need of finding alternative funding to pay their asset purchases. To levitate their exposure to wholesale funding, both Landsbanki and Kaupthing initiated novel, high-interest internet-based retail deposit schemes – which would later be the source of Iceland's greatest international legal dispute to date. As a participant in the EU Single Market, Iceland was inside the European passport system so the banks were able to operate almost like domestic entities throughout the continent.

Landsbanki bypassed its Heritable subsidiary in London and instead, in October 2006, opened a UK branch named Icesave. No one seemed to even contemplate the risk involved. Without any objections from either Icelandic or UK authorities, the bank quoted the EU/EEA directive on Depositors Guarantee Schemes, they claimed to be in place in Iceland, which, they said, would protect all deposits up to €20,887. This was however always very ambiguous.

The difference between a branch and a subsidiary is here significant because branches were under surveillance in the home country of the parent bank, while subsidiaries were subject to such monitoring in the host country. An even more significant difference was that the branch system allows the bank to move deposits across borders. Kaupthing opened a similar high-yielding internet deposits scheme, named Kaupthing Edge. However, unlike Landsbanki with Icesave, Kaupthing used its subsidiary, Kaupthing Singer & Friedlander, to host the deposits. Edge deposits therefore had to be kept in the UK and were under British banking regime surveillance. At the time, few noticed the difference, which after The Crash left those involved in the two cases a world apart.

Playing on an Icelandic symbol, Icesave was marketed to tap into the trust associated with Nordic economies. Soon attracting the favourable attention of the financial media, the scheme became an instant success. The *Sunday Times*, for example, wrote enthusiastically about the scheme under the headline: 'Icesave looks like a hot deal' (Hussain, 2006). Before the end, Icesave had attracted almost as many savers as there were inhabitants in Iceland. In addition many charities, public institutions and municipalities were rushing their money through the wires as the internet-based bank was offering higher interest rates than its competitors. Among them were Cambridge and Oxford Universities, the Metropolitan Police and even the UK Audit Commission. Through the scheme, Landsbanki collected more money than Iceland's entire GDP.

In early 2006, Landsbanki had barely escaped collapsing. By the end of the year, however, it was being inundated with money. The staff monitoring the site could barely believe their eyes when watching the foreign currency accumulating on their computer screens. When foreign deposits seemingly had saved Landsbanki from default in 2006, its CEO, Mr Árnason, declared the high-interest deposit scheme 'pure genius'[1] (Árnason, 2007). In spring 2008, just months before The Crash,

Landsbanki opened a similar Icesave branch in the Netherlands and was planning many such sites in 11 other countries, mainly EU Member States. Later, the celebrated scheme turned into a long-drawn-out nightmare for all involved. The Icesave dispute was not only about to turn friendly nations into Iceland's enemies but was also to rip apart our close-knit society in fierce infighting for years to come.

Love letters and self-inflation

In addition to attracting foreign deposits over the internet, the banks took many measures to broaden their funding base – many of which, in hindsight, were highly dubious. To boost stock prices and keep them afloat, the banks, for example, adopted the practice of accepting their own shares as collateral against loans to employees and related actors for investing in the bank. The government facilitated this measure when increasing its authorization to lend money to buy own shares. This inflated share prices but also created weak accounted equity. Surprisingly, the Icelandic Financial Supervisory Authority FME did not act to prevent this capital manipulation. Right up until the end, the banks employees were ever more heavily pressured to participate in this equity self-inflating exercise.

The so-called 'love letter' triangle similarly served to inflate equity. In order to access more liquidity, the big banks sold securities to smaller banks, which used the bonds as collateral against Central Bank borrowing. The money from the Central Bank was then furthered back as payment to the initial bank. After fine-tuning the scheme domestically, the big three played a similar trick on both the Central Bank of Luxembourg and the European Central Bank via their subsidiaries in Luxembourg. By the end, Iceland had extracted €4.5 billion from the euro system, a third of it collateral in bonds in the Icelandic banks.

This played on a practice also used to boost the equity price of some of the Icelandic holding companies to make room for more borrowing. Company A would sell an asset to company B, which would return it well above the asset value. This created room for more borrowing against fake collateral. The Sterling airline in Denmark, for example, was sold many times between the different Icelandic companies with an ever-higher price tag, which would then be leveraged to the top. Companies would also swap assets well above their value, to the same end. It worked like this: I sell you my goat for a million euros and you sell me your sheep for the same price. We both leverage our newly acquired assets to the top in accordance with the new asset price. Now we are no longer farmers, but a hedge fund. For some reason the FME never tried to prevent this capital manipulation, which led to very weak equity. By the end, 25 per cent of the banks' total capital was without other assets to back it up. The report of Parliament's Special Investigation Commission (SIC) states that weak capital amounted to up to half of the banks' core capital. The banks also practised cross-financing, where one would fund an investor to buy shares in another and vice versa. If cross-financing is factored in, weak capital amounted to 70 per cent of the total (Hreinsson et al., 2010).

However dubious these measures might seem with the benefit of hindsight, they worked beautifully at the time. Even after the steep growth between 2003 and 2005, the economy grew a further 10 per cent in the two years following the early 2006 mini-crisis. With help from foreign workers who flocked to the country at a rate of a thousand a month, a hard landing was avoided in 2006 and 2007. Interestingly, even though Iceland was criticized after the Geyser Crisis for having allowed the financial system to grow from roughly the size of its GDP to five times that in 2005, the banks doubled in size again in the coming couple of years, still without attracting much criticism.

By 2007, the three Icelandic banks had all reached the list of the 300 largest banks in the world. This was the most rapid expansion of a banking system the world had ever seen. Qualifying them as too important to the Icelandic economy to be allowed to fail, Moody's upgraded them all to triple-A ratings in early 2007 (Moody's, 2007). This implicit state guarantee led to a massive miscalculation of risk.

We now know that the banks had grown far too big to rescue. Still, at the time nothing seemed to slake their ever greater thirst for growth. In August 2007, when the Credit Crunch was already biting, Kaupthing announced a planned acquisition of Dutch bank NIBC for €3 billion, which would double its already overblown balance sheet. Kaupthing was considered to be in quite good shape. Only a month earlier, it had won Euromoney's Award for Excellence, which was reckoned to be the most prestigious award in the global banking industry, and Kaupthing was declared the best bank in the Nordic region (Kaupthing Best Bank, 2007).

Already by late 2006, demand for Icelandic bonds had risen again internationally and the Central Bank was gradually able to build currency reserves. By 2008, available foreign cash had doubled since the mini-crisis. Still, despite successfully fending off the 2006 Geyser Crisis and even after accumulating this massive growth, the Icelandic banks were never fully able to shake off the CDS spread, which stubbornly remained between 30 and 40 per cent higher than the CDS premiums on financial firms with similar ratings elsewhere. This, however, only caused minor irritation on the market.

Though the international press was increasingly referring to Icelandic businessmen as Viking raiders, they were being celebrated at home, as if they were the nation's true representatives – rather like a national football team that had succeeded against all the odds to win the World Cup. The domestic reporting might have been influenced by the fact that, like most other sectors of the economy, the media was also dominated by the three banking groups, each of which controlled a major publishing house. The country's only broadsheet newspaper, *Morgunblaðið*, and the largest web-based news portal, mbl.is, were owned by Landsbanki's Björgólfur Guðmundsson. Glitnir's Jón Ásgeir Jóhannesson controlled the largest private media company, 365, which printed the country's largest daily, *Fréttablaðið*, distributed free to all households, and controlled the main private TV channel, Stöð 2, which was the only one that could compete with the state broadcaster. The much smaller *Viðskiptablaðið*, Iceland's equivalent to the *Financial Times*, was held by people of the Kaupthing clan.

The public at large seemed quite content with the state of the economy, as the entire nation was believed to be benefitting from the boom. Iceland was reported as having become one of the richest countries in the world. Our income was ranked the fifth highest, 60 per cent higher than that of the US. By 2008, Iceland had reached the top of the United Nations Development index (United Nations, 2008). In line with the tags given to the booming economies in Asia in the 1990s and to Ireland around the millennium, Iceland was being branded the Nordic Tiger. Most of us, however, never fully understood the basis of our newfound wealth. In fact, we were gradually becoming oblivious to the risk of debt. Iceland was a prime example of a prosperous society blithely living well beyond its means.

Optimism was at its peak when the poles of Icelandic politics, the Independence Party (IP) and the Social Democratic Alliance (SDA), buried their hatchets and entered into a new broad-based coalition in the spring of 2007. Perhaps it tells a larger story that the Ministry for Commerce, which was responsible for banking, was as a result of the coalition treated as a junior ministry and handed to the most inexperienced minister, Björgvin Sigurðsson, who held a BA in Philosophy and had never in his career shown much interest in either business or banking.

Trouble started even during the honeymoon period of the new government. In autumn 2007, the sub-prime housing bubble burst in the US, causing concern throughout the international economy. Even though our banks had not invested much in financial assets holding US housing bonds, Iceland was still extremely vulnerable to any international downturn. Other crisis-ridden states – Greece, Ireland, Portugal, Spain and the Baltic countries – had all experienced capital inflow in the boom years with credit-inflated growth. All enjoyed high investment, increased construction and high asset prices. The scale of all these, however, was greater in Iceland. In fact, our business model relied on constant boom.

Gathering clouds (early 2008)

In early 2008, the massive capital inflow of 2003 to 2007 reversed, as it did in other high-yield countries like the Baltics, Greece, Portugal and Spain. The carry trade, which had helped to keep the lid on inflation by hiking the value of the króna, was now leaving our economy exposed to nervous reversal. Amounting to 40 per cent of GDP, steep reversal was threatening a sharp devaluation, falling output and rapidly rising unemployment. The banks were finding it ever more difficult to access funds. The tide was already turning on New Year's Day.

Economists William Buiter and Ann Sibert (2008) delivered a commissioned report for Landsbanki in which they claimed that it was 'absolutely obvious' that the 'banking model was not viable'. The total liability of the banking system was approaching 750 per cent of the country's GDP. Foreign liabilities were five times GDP. Because of the sensitivity of its content, the report was kept confidential until after The Crash. Morgan Stanley, however, publicly reported similar concerns: that Iceland's financial system was unsustainable (Ineke & Borgstrom, 2008). More and more reports were mentioning the lack of credible lenders of last resort. Already by the end of 2007, short-term loans amounted to 15 times the Central Bank's foreign reserve. Around this time, the first investment company, Gnúpur, fell, causing attention beyond Iceland's border. The negative reporting upset Kaupthing's plan to acquire NIBC and the unfinished deal was finally abandoned in early autumn 2008, leaving Kaupthing even more vulnerable than before and seriously calling its credibility into question.

By the end of January, a select few amongst the Icelandic banking community learned that an attack was under way. They had been invited to the bar at the trendy downtown Reykjavik 101 Hotel to meet a group of hedge fund managers visiting Iceland on a trip which they believed had been organized by Bear Stern and Merrill Lynch. When the cold, dark winter night set in and the champagne bottles multiplied on the shiny black granite table in front of them, they learned that their visitors were shorting both the króna and the banks in the CDS market. In a drunken haze, some of the visitors couldn't refrain from bragging of their plot to take down Iceland. In the hedge fund world, taking down an entire country is much more gratifying than merely killing off a private company. During the small hours of 1 February, the bankers nervously sneaked out of the party and rushed back to their headquarters to report on what they had learned. It soon became evident that the attack had been in planning for months. Many of Iceland's old acquaintances from the 2006 mini-crisis were back; silently, they had again been building up a massive short position. Apparently, many domestic shareholders had been willing to lend the foreign hedge funds their shares for up to a 30 per cent premium.

Soon after the pack of hard-partying hedge fund managers had departed, a flood of critical reports landed on our shores. Before February was out, Bear Stern (2008) analysts, for example, compared Iceland's economy with that of Kazakhstan, with a recommendation to go short. A series of such negative reports ran through the international media, often using similar phrasing or wording, which raised suspicion of unified action in feeding these stories to the press.

Our limited foreign reserves of 15 per cent of GDP would not go far to back up liabilities in foreign currency that amounted to five times the country's GDP. Iceland's financial situation was unsustainable. Moody's was questioning Iceland's triple A-ratings and consequently downgraded Landsbanki and Glitnir (Cailleteau, 2008). The CDS spread on all Icelandic banks was rapidly growing again, while Iceland was getting short of liquidity. Pressure was building fast. Despite the Central Bank's efforts – for example, in keeping a 10 per cent interest differential – the króna fell sharply in early March when Bear Stern fell and the stock market took a significant hit as the banks' stocks dropped. This also created problems for the main holding companies, which by then owned most businesses in the country. If one firm were to fall, there was a real danger of a domino effect wiping out the entire corporate sector.

During the 2006 Geyser Crisis, a CDS premium of hundred points above Libor caused grave concern. In late March 2008, the CDS was ten times higher than that. Interestingly for what was to occur later, the spread on Landsbanki was significantly lower than on the other two because of the perceived success of the Icesave deposit accounts, applauded by the rating agencies.

One reason for the króna falling at what seemed to be regular intervals was that the banks were hedging their foreign assets against it – against their own currency. The linkage between the banks' liquidity position and the rate of the króna was evident. Most of their assets and liabilities were in foreign currency. For a while, they had thus been lobbying for being allowed to operate their accounts in euros in order to smooth out currency fluctuations, which were distorting their books. The government, however, always stood against that, as it was seen as strengthening the argument of those campaigning for joining the EU and entering the Eurozone.

The Icelandic banks were obviously in serious trouble. Although they had clearly far outgrown the state, the government's policy was still to keep the banks domiciled in Iceland. After all, they were the backbone to Iceland's new economy, allowing us not only to underpin our economic independence but also to further strengthen the collective Icelandic Project. This can help to explain the government's vituperative response to foreign critics. Cabinet ministers were now getting involved, accusing foreign hedge funds of a speculative attack and threatening direct government intervention in the currency market and the stock market. Iceland might not possess large currency reserves, but the state was virtually debt free and could, with the help of its neighbours, beat back these rogue attackers, who would as a result suffer significant losses. In a sort of roadshow on behalf of the Icelandic banks, Prime Minister Geir Haarde headed for New York while Foreign Minister Ingibjörg Gísladóttir promoted the banks in Copenhagen. The chairman of the governors' board of the Central Bank, Mr Davíð Oddsson, also asserted that the banking system was essentially sound (Central Bank of Iceland, 2008).

Ironically, however, the hard-partying visitors from Merrill Lynch and Bear Stern, who in January had boasted of their plot of taking down Iceland in the trendy Reykjavik 101 Hotel bar, were by then gone from the scene. Both firms had already fallen victim to the Credit Crunch and been taken over by others. Independent researchers were by now, however, also reporting predictions of Iceland's downfall. In April, for example, Daniel Gros, from the Centre for European Policy Studies in Brussels, wondered if Iceland was already on the brink (Gros, 2008). Around the same time, Standard & Poor's indicated that Iceland, Estonia and Latvia were the 'most vulnerable European countries to a global slowdown' (Anderson, 2008). By now Iceland was in international media no longer grouped with the other Nordics but rather with newly independent Eastern European and former Soviet states.

The lesson learned from the 2006 mini-crisis was to keep calm and weather the storm. At first it seem to work. In spring 2008, the CDS premium finally fell to between 200 and 300 points above Libor. This is perhaps why, despite ever-increasing margin calls, for increased collateral, the bankers were reluctant to sell off assets at a discount price to alleviate the liquidity pressure. Viewed from the experience of the mini-crisis, the worst seemed to be over and bankers and officials alike were uttering sighs of relief. We now know, however, that this was only the calm before the storm.

This time the situation was different. The banks were much more vulnerable than before. Landsbanki had for a while enjoyed better ratings than the other two because it was able to tap into the Icesave deposits to keep liquidity flowing. This was, however, a mixed blessing, as reliance on deposits leaves a bank much more vulnerable to bad news than if it is funded in the wholesale market. Even a minor issue can result in a run if it is portrayed in the wrong light. The next alarm came in June, when Professor Robert Aliber (2008) of Chicago University gave a talk in Reykjavik on Iceland's economic turbulence, describing an unsustainable credit and asset bubble. When answering a question from the audience, Aliber is reported to have predicted the collapse of the banks before the end of the year. Around the same time, all three banks were passing the FME's stress tests with flying colours. In theory, the banks were still doing well. Amongst those buying this story was the *Financial Times*, which as late as August 2008 wrote that 'fears of a systemic financial crisis in Iceland have dissipated after the country's three main banks announced second-quarter results showing that they are suffering amid the downturn – but not too badly' (Ibson, 2008).

The system was, however, evidently becoming ever weaker. One example lies in how the banks met creditors' demands for increased collateral as share prices fell. One of Kaupthing's largest owners, for example, had financed his stakes with funding from Citi Bank, which was demanding increased collateral as Kaupthing's stock was falling. To protect its owner, Kaupthing simply lent him the money to pay Citi. One of its largest owners was thus funding almost his entire stake from his own bank. Landsbanki turned a similar favour to a company run by one of its owners to pay a margin call from Deutsche Bank. Another interesting example of market manipulation leading up to The Crash was the so-called Al-Thani case. In September 2008, Kaupthing announced that Sheikh Mohammed bin Khalifa Al-Thani of Qatar had bought a 5 per cent stake in the bank for $285 million. The investment was claimed to indicate strength and the bank's promising outlook (Davíðsdóttir,

2012). Only much later did it become known that bank lent him the full amount, most of which with no other collateral than the shares themselves. The Sheikh wasn't risking much his own money.

The Central Bank stretched itself to the limit to keep the banks liquidated in domestic króna, for example accepting their own bonds as collateral – the so-called love letters. However, to back up the overinflated banking system in such dire straits it needed a sizable sum in foreign currency. The Central Bank thus went knocking on doors in the neighbouring capitals asking to open swap lines that could be drawn on in time of need. This was meant to boost confidence in Iceland's capacity to back up the financial system. To the surprise of the government, however, it met closed doors in most places. Not only had our banks been pushed out of the international capital market, but our government had as well. Iceland first approached the Bank of England in March 2008. Initially, the request was positively received, but with a suggestion that the IMF would analyse the need. A month later, the climate had changed. It had become clear that the central banks of Europe, the US and the UK had collectively decided not to assist Iceland. We later learned that the governor of the Bank of England, Mervin King, offered instead to co-ordinate a multinational effort to help scale down our financial system. His offer was instantly turned down by the leading governor of the Icelandic Central Bank, Mr Davíð Oddsson, thus only adding to Iceland's subsequent isolation.

For the international financial system tiny Iceland was as a state not thought to be too big to fail. We thus found ourselves quite alone in world, desperately trotting the globe looking for money. In May, Norway, Sweden and Denmark finally agreed on a borrowing line, for €500 million each. This, however, was only on offer at an unprecedented cost: the neighbouring states would dictate a strict fiscal reform, which our government was to implement at home, including changing the Housing Financing Fund, more responsible budgeting and changes in union contracts (Hreinsson et al., 2010). Though the proposed reform was never implemented, this was the most drastic foreign interference in our domestic affairs since independence in 1944 and was indeed a serious threat to our cherished sovereignty.

A loan of €2 billion was also being negotiated with JP Morgan but this was abandoned in June as the interest rate, at 185 points above Libor, was thought too high. By July, all funding possibilities seemed to have been exhausted and the CDS premium on the banks rose again as the rate of critical reporting increased exponentially.

Falling off the waterfall

While Landsbanki and Kaupthing were in late summer 2008 still battling through this extremely troubled water, for example by extracting liquidity from their foreign deposit schemes over the internet, Glitnir was having more serious difficulties in keeping its head above the surface. Glitnir came late to the game of tapping into high-yielding internet savings and was not fully up and running with its scheme when the bank ran into trouble. Its so-called Save&Save deposit accounts had been tried out in Norway but were not properly implemented in time to liquidate the bank when wholesale borrowing was fast drying up, and they were available only for a very short time against sky-high interest. With €600 million loan maturing on 15 October, totalling €1.5 billion in late 2008 and in early 2009, the management was worried it might not be able to jump all the hurdles in time. Its funding model had failed. Selling assets at discount prices now seemed unavoidable. Fortunately, they thought, the bank had some solid assets in Norway to sell or borrow against.

This already grim outlook blackened fast when American investment bank giant Lehman Brothers collapsed on 15 September. Although the Icelandic banks had only small exposure in Lehman, around €150 million, the shockwave that ran through the entire global financial system with its collapse instantly dried up the little liquidity that was left to the Icelandic banks. What was worse, markets for financial assets froze. Subsequently, the króna took one of its repeated nosedives and CDSs on the Icelandic banks shot through the roof, rising by almost half, to reach 1,000 points above Libor. Still, after securing an extension on a €150 million loan from the German Bayerische Landesbank in the wake of Lehman's demise, Glitnir's management was confident of being able to survive long enough past the mid-October deadline for short-term borrowing on international markets to become available to them again. Weak owners were, however, not helping. These were the most highly exposed investment companies, who relied on Glitnir for funding when suffering heavy losses in the equity market and facing an increased flow of margin calls.

After an eventful week weathering this unprecedented storm, Glitnir finally had the wind taken out of its sails when it learned that the Central Bank had quietly taken out €300 million from the same German bank, thereby thus filling its quota for Iceland. When, in panic, Glitnir's representative called Munich to confirm its previous negotiated agreement, the Bayerische Landesbank referred him straight to the Icelandic Central Bank. Emergency money was no longer available to them in Bavaria.

Finally, it dawned on the bank's management that its own Central Bank had in effect stolen its only lifeline. With €600 million maturing in three weeks' time, the bank was about to fall off the waterfall. Clearly, it would survive neither the fall nor the swirling waters below. There were no good options. With the deadline impending, the chairman of the board, Þorsteinn Már Baldursson, decided that the bank must go to the Central Bank to ask for help – after all, the Central Bank had stolen its loan from Bayerische. Perhaps they could have part of it? This was a dramatic decision, which would have grave consequences not only for Glitnir but also for the entire banking system.

To understand some of the peculiarities of Icelandic politics one has to examine personal relationships. When resigning his post as Prime Minister in 2004, Davíð Oddsson, the instrumental force behind the neoliberal regime created in the 1990s and early 2000s, in effect appointed himself the governor of the Central Bank, taking up the position in 2005. By then, he was already at odds with many of the Viking Capitalists who controlled the banks. In an extraordinary move, he had in 2003, when still the PM, publicly withdrawn his deposits from Kaupthing in protest over management excesses, thus hinting a run on the bank. His rivalry with Jón Ásgeir Jóhannesson, however, ran much deeper, starting when Jóhannesson, together with few colleagues in the Orca group, acquired the FBA investment bank in 1998, as described in the previous chapter. At the height of their quarrel, Oddsson had in a TV interview called Jóhannesson, by then Iceland's most powerful businessman, a 'street hooligan' (quoted in Jóhannesson, 2002). In an interview in 2003, Oddsson claimed that Jóhannesson, had through a mutual colleague, offered him 300 million króna to keep off his back (quoted in Friðriksson, 2003). Incredibly, this accusation was never properly examined, leaving it still unclear whether Iceland's most powerful businessman had tried to bribe the PM or whether our PM was fabricating this serious accusation in order to ruin Jóhannesson's credibility.

Vital to the story of Glitnir's takedown in autumn 2008 is that one of Jóhannesson's fellow Orca group investors in the 1998 FBA takeover was Þorsteinn Már Baldursson, by now chairman of Glitnir. Baldvinsson headed Iceland's largest fishing vessel corporation, in the north of Iceland, and had until the FBA takeover been close to the IP establishment. Established knowledge has it that Oddsson never forgets an enemy. It is reported that when Baldvinsson suggested going to the Central Bank for help in September 2008, Jóhannesson, who led the pack of the bank's largest owners, was, to say the least, uneasy with the decision, fearing that his long-standing enemy, now in the governor's chair, would seize the opportunity and snatch the bank from under them – perhaps just as Jóhannesson had done himself in the FBA deal. By the end of the month, when everything was gone, Jóhannesson (2008) spoke of his fears in a TV interview. Baldvinsson, however, still believed that his old, cosy relationship with the IP leadership would prevent such an act of pure revenge. On the evening of Wednesday 24 September, the chairman called for a meeting with Oddsson the following morning. Other board members of Glitnir nervously waited at the headquarters of the Stoðir holding company, from which through Jóhannesson and his colleagues in effect controlled Glitnir.

In the lead-up to all this, the media got wind of something going wrong. An increased volume of reports discussed the until then unthinkable possibility that one of the banks would collapse or be taken over by one of the others. All sorts of scenarios were being discussed. Since early 2008, many plans had been discussed for the others to acquire Glitnir and split its assets. In order to prevent the unthinkable, the government reaffirmed its commitment to the banks. Prime Minister Geir Haarde had for a long time been Oddsson's number two before occupying his seat as chairman of the IP in 2004 and becoming Prime Minister in 2007. He repeatedly announced that the state would indeed back up the banks if they were ever in trouble. On Saturday 20 September the leader of the SDA, Foreign Minister Ingibjörg Gísladóttir (2008a) asserted that the financial system was sound and the government would surely back it up if necessary. In a TV interview on Sunday 21 September, the CEO of Glitnir, Lárus Welding (2008), confidently stated that the bank's position was strong. Most of the banks were indeed arguing that, having learned from the 2006 mini-crisis and since taken precautionary measures, they were now well equipped to weather the storm that would soon hit them.

Despite these bold statements to the press, Glitnir's immediate trouble was worrying all the banks. The writing on the wall was becoming evident. Through cross-lending and cross-ownership they had all become interdependent. The owners of the banks were also their largest borrowers, as was later mapped out in the SIC report (Hreinsson et al., 2010: ch. 9.6). Jóhannesson's family's holding company, Baugur, for example, owed all of them far more than any of them would survive losing. In Glitnir alone, Baugur's credit amounted to half of the bank's regulatory capital (Nielsson & Torfason, 2012). Caught in this incestuous relationship, the Icelandic banks were increasingly being viewed abroad as almost one entity. The demise of

Glitnir would thus almost certainly bring the other two down as well. The threat of a domino effect was imminent.

The Glitnir takedown

In the morning of Thursday 25 September, Glitnir's chairman, Mr Baldvinsson, headed to the Central Bank headquarters in central Reykjavik to meet its governor. The meeting had to be secretive so as not to trigger any reporting, which could result in a run on the bank in this extremely sensitive situation. Glitnir was now at the mercy of the Central Bank – Jóhannesson's business survival was thus in the hands of his old enemy, Oddsson. When sneaking through the bank's corridors, Baldvinsson was still relatively optimistic that the Central Bank would help. Glitnir was, he thought, offering good assets as collateral against an emergency loan of €600 million. By Icelandic standards, however, this amount was astronomical: one-third of the bank's entire foreign reserve as it stood the month before.

At this time, the Central Bank was busy on many fronts. Two days earlier, the news had broken that central banks in the other Nordics had negotiated swap lines with the US Federal Reserve. Our Central Bank was having grave difficulties explaining why Iceland had been left out of the deal – the one of the Nordic five that clearly needed it the most. Flatly refused such access, Iceland was now the only state in Western Europe without a swap line to the Fed. Trading in króna had in effect frozen, as there was no demand for it. This same Thursday, while the Central Bank was still contemplating Glitnir's request, the US investment bank Washington Mutual was taken into administration. As the bank defaulted, its deposits were saved when ushered to JP Morgan. This is significant, as it later served as the template for the Icelandic situation.

Throughout Thursday and by closing time on Friday 26 September, Glitnir owners could not get through to the Central Bank to learn about the fate of the request for an emergency loan. It is revealing that during these few days the Prime Minister and Foreign Minister were with many key government officials in New York promoting Iceland's bid for a seat on the UN Security Council. The government's leaders seemed oblivious to the seriousness of the domestic troubles ahead. While PM Geir Haarde was in ceremony ringing the closing bell on Nasdaq in New York, Glitnir's board was holding an emergency meeting with his Central Bank in Reykjavik. Only on Friday evening did Oddsson finally call Haarde to fill him in on the sensitive situation. Cutting his trip short,

Haarde rushed home the same evening, telling his coalition partner and Foreign Minister, Mrs Gísladóttir, nothing. She thus remained in New York, along with the other SDA ministers, oblivious to anything being wrong back home. Not only was the leader of the other coalition party left out of the information loop amid fear of the country's financial system tanking, but even more dramatically for her personally, a tumour was found in her brain after she fainted while in New York. Just days before Iceland's most dramatic events, on a global scale, the Foreign Minister and leader of one of the two coalition parties was rushed to the operating table in New York.

Meanwhile, the króna kept on sinking and the markets were becoming ever more volatile. Reporters were getting wind of something being seriously wrong and were sniffing around the banks and the government, without, however, finding much to chew on. On Saturday afternoon, the Central Bank's governor was briefing the PM and his aides on his plans. Reportedly, the PM sat quietly in the Central Bank's meeting room, listening without voicing objections. The reader should keep in mind that this was not simply the Central Bank's governor debriefing his PM and awaiting the assessment of the country's leader, but rather a political lion giving his old protégé the heads up. By now, Oddsson was in the driving seat.

Ironically, Sunday proved to be a great PR success for Glitnir, which sponsored the Oslo marathon. Red flags with Glitnir's logo were flying high above the streets of Norway's capital this eventful Sunday. Norway's princess, Mette Marit, was one of five thousand runners wearing Glitnir's red running shirts, which would shine brightly in Norway's media. Back in Reykjavik, however, Oddsson was by now completing his plan. SDA ministers were still not yet involved. Mutual animosity between Oddsson and the SDA Minister for Commerce, Mr Björgvin Sigurðsson, was such that they could not occupy the same room – the governor of the Central Bank and the minister responsible for banking were not on speaking terms. The word was, however, getting out that Glitnir was in serious trouble. Worried that Glitnir's downfall would bring the others with it, Landsbanki was desperately proposing an instant merger of all the banks with government backing. Kaupthing's management was proposing a similar scenario. Distrust amongst the bankers and between them, the government and the Central Bank, however, prevented them from reaching an agreement in time. Finally, in the late afternoon, SDA ministers were informed and in the late evening the opposition heard the news.

Throughout the weekend, Glitnir's board and managers were increasingly impatiently waiting for the Central Bank's reply. After being rebuffed for days, they were finally called to the bank on late Sunday evening. When meeting reporters in the lobby they could before the meeting started tell the answer to their request for emergency loan. Inside the Central Bank's top-floor meeting room, Oddsson had laid out the only deal on offer. The Central Bank would indeed provide the money needed – not as loan, however, but as equity, for a 75 per cent controlling stake in the bank. Glitnir was to be de facto nationalized, leaving only 25 per cent for its owners, who would lose 88 per cent worth of their shears in the takeover. Oddsson dictated that Glitnir's owners were to give their answer before the opening of the markets in the morning. He had already planned a press meeting for that time to announce the deal. Stunned by the offer, Glitnir's owners rushed in panic back to the bank's headquarters, where more reporters awaited them. The game was up. There was no time to find alternative solutions. A run on the bank would surely start when the doors opened in the morning. Chased by the media throughout the night, the bank's board duly threw in the towel at break of dawn on Monday morning. Jóhannesson has said that this was the world's greatest bank robbery (Jóhannesson, 2008). His worst fears of what Oddsson might be cooking up in the days after Glitnir came knocking on the Central Bank's door had come true.

Oddsson's plan was based on his belief that the perceived strength of the state would provide a nationalized Glitnir with enough credibility to be able to weather the storm and eventually make for a fantastic return to the state's coffers. Initially, it seemed to work. American Nobel Prize-winning economist Paul Krugman for example announced his approval (Krugman, 2008). Soon, however, the contrary became apparent. The perceived weakness of Glitnir instead created increased vulnerability for the state, which had taken over the bank's responsibilities. The Icelandic state was subsequently downgraded by international rating agencies, together with the other banks. Another flaw in the plan was becoming ever more visible. The loss of 75 per cent of its shares in Glitnir and 88 per cent of their worth according to the new price tag instantly bank-rupted holding company Stoðir, which had by now become one of the major assets of Jóhannesson's Baugur group. It is reported that the Central Bank's economists were in panic and disbelief, shouting their heads off when, in their separate offices, they read about the deal via domestic internet news outlets. Neither they nor other specialists had been involved in drafting the plan, and they had therefore not had the opportunity to voice their concerns of a domino effect running through the economy, which easily could ruin the country's financial sector. The downfall of Baugur alone would devastate all the banks, which were facing severe losses on their loans. When the news sank in, a silent run started on the banks and the króna went into free fall while the tsunami wave rose all around Iceland's shores.

Conclusion

By end of September 2008, Iceland's banks were on the brink of collapse. The total liability of the banking system had reached almost ten times the country's GDP. Trouble started with the mini-crisis of 2006, which Iceland was barely able to shake off. Instead of downscaling the system and tightening controls, the banks were on the contrary allowed to more than double in size. We now know that by January 2008, the system was unsustainable. Its inherent systemic weakness lay in the operation of large international banks in a small currency regime. A series of mistakes were also made in the lead-up to The Crash, some of the most serious ones mostly because of personal animosity and grievances – perhaps most significantly because of lack of trust.

All roads in this saga seem to have led towards the edge of the cliff: the government's privatization, deregulation and procyclcal economic policies; the ever increasing interconnectedness of the banks and ever more condensed groups of corporations; the risk-seeking behaviour of private corporations with diminished cushions against risk; and the global rating agencies' upgrades of our banks to triple-A ratings. No significant measure was taken to cool the economy and no ventilation built into the machine. The Central Bank lost control of the supply of money when the banks started borrowing wholesale abroad. Furthermore, there was a systemic fault built into the system, as it is extremely difficult for public authorities to control the money supply and asset price inflation and to curb demand when operating a free-floating independent currency. When small states operate a free-flow monetary policy, they need to be able to control the inflow and avoid the risk of a rapid reversal. One measure would be to tax inflow and outflow.

No such preventive measures were taken. On the contrary, practices used to fend off the troubles in the 2006 mini-crisis created weak equity in the banks, leaving them in even more trouble when liquidity dried up. Collectively, this can only be attributed to proactive public policies and the seriously low quality of banking supervision in the country. In fact, the national identity celebrated risk-taking behaviour, as rapid growth served the collective task of broadening the base of the economy to underpin the Icelandic Project. We now see that the very nature of the system, with three large international and interconnected banks, in what can be described as an incestuous relationship, was far too risky, as the failure of one bank would automatically take down the others. This concern was, however, never raised – not by the FME, nor by the Central Bank, nor by the Ministry of Commerce. Neither was it, until March 2008, seriously discussed in the host countries where the Icelandic banks were operating under home-backed protection. The danger of an oversized banking system relative to the state was mostly ignored.

When the crisis was tightening its grip, our cherished sovereignty was also being threatened. Strict conditions for very limited swap lines with the Nordics in spring 2008 meant that Iceland was no longer sovereign when it came to economic governance. This was traumatic for Iceland's postcolonial national identity. Leading up to the collapse, Iceland found itself being further isolated. In September 2008, for example, the government was unable to negotiate swap lines with the US Federal Reserve along with the other Nordics. Iceland was instead, in what seemed a co-ordinated action by its neighbours, pushed towards the IMF. The dream of being a fully functioning and successful modern state, recognized as an equal partner with other states in the West, was turning into a nightmare.

When Glitnir ran into trouble in September 2008, there was no effective plan in place to deal with such a crisis, leaving it to chance what the response would be. In the next chapter I examine the events of the October 2008 Crash.

6
The Crash – Collapse of the Cross-border Banks

In the late afternoon of Monday 6 October 2008, Prime Minister Geir Haarde addressed the nation on TV: the state would not be able to bail out the banks. Over the following three days, the entire financial system collapsed – Landsbanki on Tuesday, Glitnir on Wednesday and finally Kaupthing on Thursday. The Central Bank's decision to acquire a controlling stake in Glitnir, as described in the previous chapter, finally tipped the scales in this extremely volatile situation and caused a domino effect, which wiped out the country's banking system.

When the overinflated bubble finally burst in early October, Iceland not only was financially ruined but also found itself alone in the world. This rapidly growing international banking hub was now reduced to being an isolated rock in the North Atlantic – once again. The UK government invoked Anti-Terrorist legislation to freeze all Icelandic assets in Britain and the entire international society forced the Icelandic state to accept responsibility for foreign branches of the fallen banks before allowing the IMF to open doors to emergency loans. The hostile response of foreign actors, mainly the UK government, induced an increase in bunker mentality within Iceland, where this proud island people felt victimized in the whole horrifying saga.

Domino effect

When news broke on Monday 29 September of de facto nationalization of Glitnir, a slow run started on all Icelandic banks. By lunchtime, the holding company Stoðir, one of the Jóhannesson's Baugur Group's largest assets, asked for a moratorium. Its equity was in ruins when shares in Glitnir instantly fell by 88 per cent. The other two banks, which by now were already in serious trouble, also took a blow, as many of their borrowers held shares in Glitnir and would as a result not be able to meet their repayments. The same was true of the country's pension funds, which had invested heavily in the banks. Many ordinary people who had in the past kept a large part of their savings in bank shares would also be devastated.

In the neighbouring states, governments were frantically bailing out their banks, though by different means. The Irish government, for example, issued a blanket guarantee for all its banks for two years; in the UK, Bradford & Bingley was split, with deposits whisked over to Abbey National; and the Benelux three bailed out Fortis in a joint action. Meanwhile, many measures were taken in the US, where collapsing banks were rescued by rushing them under the wings of others. At the same time, however, it was gradually becoming painfully evident that Iceland did not have the means to do the same.

Liquidity had finally dried up when Lehman fell in September 2008. By then, the total liability of the Icelandic banking system had almost reached ten times the country's GDP, most of it in foreign currency (Halldórsson & Zoega, 2010). Deposits in foreign branches alone were close to the country's GDP and seven times higher than the entire currency reserve. Unlike most other countries, Iceland thus did not have a credible lender of last resort. Illustrative of Iceland's trouble was the fact that apart from the Zimbabwe dollar, our króna had in the preceding year fallen more than any other currency in the word. With inflation on the rampage, many would not be able to meet the increased payments on their inflation-indexed housing loans or foreign exchange-indexed car loans, which had become common in most vehicle purchases.

Already by opening of business on the Monday morning, when news of Glitnir's nationalization broke, depositors were flocking to their nearest branch and withdrawing their savings. When the news travelled abroad, many of the 300,000 Icesave depositors rushed online to withdraw their money. Worries over internet banks were worldwide, but the Icelandic internet banking schemes were now viewed as toxic, as many considered the Icelandic banks almost a single entity. Quite a few Kaupthing Edge depositors were thus also withdrawing their cash, even though Edge accounts fell under the UK's Depositors Guarantee Scheme. At home, our politicians were having trouble convincing depositors that their money was safe. Announcements that the government would in the event of default step in and protect ordinary savings were initially too vaguely worded.

On Tuesday morning, crowds reappeared in front of banks all around the island. The banks' investment advisors had for several months been proactively calling their depositors, advising them to move their savings to money market funds for higher interest, claiming that these were as safe as deposits. We later learned that these funds were used more like petty cash. The banks simply grabbed what they needed and left only bonds in own shares against what they took. By Tuesday 30 September, access to these money market accounts was denied and the crowds were growing more frustrated by the hour. All the banks were now severely bleeding. Despite our PM emphasizing that deposits were safe in accordance with the EU directive that guaranteed protection up to €20,887, elderly women and other locals were seen on Reykjavik streets carrying home sacks filled with cash when emptying their deposit accounts. People were stocking up on necessities in their houses; canned food, foreign cash, etc. In desperation some were investing in luxury goods and real estate to protect the value of their money.

The government finally felt forced to issue a blanket guarantee on all domestic deposits. That, however, was not enough to calm the situation, as it did not cover the money market funds. Though chaos continued on Wednesday, some were already adapting and exploiting the sense of crisis. Many, for example, considered it offensive when Jóhannesson's budget store Bónus advertised that people should 'Stock up at Bónus and choose Icelandic'[1] to prepare for the coming crisis. After all, his Glitnir Bank and his outvasion endeavours had helped to create the crisis. In accordance with Bretton Wood's rule of thumb, Iceland had reserves to last for four months. Still, the CEOs of leading petrol companies were worried they would be sucked dry if people kept hoarding.

Throughout all this, the banks were also kept busy fighting off the increased flow of margin calls. Thursday saw our currency and stock market in free fall while the CDS spread on the Icelandic state rose to 817 points. Reaching the top of the world list, Glitnir and Kaupthing faced a CDS spread of 2,500 points and Landsbanki shot to 3,000 above Libor.

The Glitnir nationalization, which had been meant to save us from economic ruin, was now proving disastrous. Its refinancing needs could exhaust the Central Bank's foreign reserves within a year. Sarcastically, the *Economist* asked: 'What is the Icelandic for "domino"?' (*Economist*, 2008). At home, the government apparatus was finally kicked into gear with a high-level task force appointed to prevent a systemic collapse. The crisis unit, nicknamed the Situation Room, worked around the clock to try to contain the situation.

Throughout the continent, central banks and governments were harmonizing their response to the crisis in Iceland. The ECB and the Bank of England, for example, were providing massive liquidity to European banks, but despite a wide-ranging emergency plea, Iceland would not be allowed access to these funds. The same was true in Washington. Our representatives were flatly refused as neighbouring governments collectively opposed a bail-out, referring our government instead to the IMF. Being the first Western country in four decades to surrender to the IMF was seen as a humiliation and a defeat for the Icelandic postcolonial project – as if we had failed in our eternal quest of securing an independent modern Iceland. During these dark days, representatives of the IMF came to Reykjavik in an informal capacity. Instead of throwing in the towel and surrendering to the IMF, however, our representatives were heading for Moscow.

In the UK, worries over the poor state of the Icelandic banks had been growing for some time. Since May, unsuccessful negotiations had been under way to move the Icesave deposits to Landsbanki's Heritable Bank and thus under the cover of the UK banking scheme. On Friday afternoon, British Finance Minister Alistair Darling called Iceland's PM, Mr Geir Haarde, voicing concerns that money was flowing out of Kaupthing's London subsidiary, Singer & Friedlander. If the flow continued, the bank would be instantly closed. In the evening, the British Financial Supervisory Authority called demanding £400 million from Iceland to cover the Icesave accounts. The European Central Bank also placed a margin call on Landsbanki in Luxembourg, threatening to seize many of its assets. Thus, while Iceland was desperately trotting the globe shopping for money, the UK authorities and the ECB were not only refusing any funding but indeed pressing us for cash. The firm stand of the Bank of England, the ECB and the US Federal Reserve against Iceland also made our Scandinavian neighbours hesitant to help further. The illusion of a shelter amongst the family of Nordic states was thus also shattered during Iceland's crash, which was therefore not only economic but also political and indeed psychological. To stem the bleeding of the Edge and Icesave accounts, both Kaupthing and Landsbanki were frantically selling off assets at rock bottom prices.

The fatal weekend

Many were relieved when end of business finally arrived on Friday afternoon, 3 October. The weekend was surely a welcome break but to halt the run a solution would have to be in place before reopening on

Monday morning. The banks barely coped with the withdrawals. Some branches thus had to limit customer withdrawals. Less than one-fourth of banknotes and coins previously available were left in the Central Bank when the week was finally over. Emergency supplies of fresh bank notes were being printed abroad, as many branches were out of the largest bills. They would, however, take some time to arrive in the island.

Each of the three banks needed at least €500 million in emergency funding to survive only the short-term headwind. Throwing in panic one-and-a-half billion euros, literally the rest of the currency reserve, after troubled banks was never really an option. How would we then meet the next loan payday's? Or indeed pay for vital imports? Many versions of a bank merger were discussed. In all cases, the government and even our powerful pension funds would have to back up the new entity. One of the main hurdles, however, was the deeply rooted lack of trust between the politicians and the bankers. Especially bad was the relationship between the chairman of the board of governors of the Central Bank, Mr Davíð Oddsson, and some of the leading Viking Capitalists. There was also a lack of trust between the rival groups of bankers and indeed between Oddsson and the SDA side of the government. The Minister of Commerce, who was responsible for banking, was, for example, never on speaking terms with Oddsson and his team in the Central Bank – in fact, they despised each other so deeply that they made sure never to be present in the same room. Reportedly, meetings were conducted like poker games.

However, in hectic discussions between the government, the Central Bank and surveillance authorities, the bankers' a plan was gradually emerging. To weather the storm, the Central Bank would need to secure a large buffer, up to €10 billion in total, it was estimated. This was to come from the sale of the foreign assets of Iceland's powerful pension funds abroad and, most vitally, government borrowing on foreign emergency loans. If these solutions came up short, Iceland would be forced to split at least two of the three banks into 'good' and 'bad' banks. In that case, the main idea was to take the banks into administration but immediately establish new domestic banks for each of them where to local loans and deposits would be moved. During this weekend before the storm, the government still hoped that at least one of the banks could be saved by a €500 million loan from the Central Bank. But who would win the lottery was still being deliberated.

By the weekend, the world's attention was turning to Iceland's misfortune, many of the leading international media were flocking over to report on this economic disaster area. Iceland was reported as being on the brink of an economic Armageddon or the equivalent of the last days of Rome. Under a headline stating that the party was now over for an island that had tried to buy the world, Tracy McVeigh (2008) of the UK *Observer* wrote: 'The bars and restaurants of Iceland's capital are packed, the Range Rovers and BMWs are parked nose to tail all along the streets of the central 101 district, and music is pumping from a black stretch Hummer limousine cruising by'. Others described Reykjavik's atmosphere this weekend as like the day before an atomic winter.

With the rapidly increasing flow of negative reporting abroad, the run on Icesave in the UK grew stronger. On Saturday, depositors could no longer access their accounts online. On the website an explanatory note read that this was because of technical problems. Really, however, it was because the bank was already exhausted by the run; it could no longer honour the withdrawals. Out of the £4.7 billion the 300,000 or so depositors held, more than £300 million ran off the accounts on that day alone. Foreign reporters and government authorities responded by asking our government if it would provide the same protection to foreign depositors as it had already announced for domestic ones. Pressure rose when the government struggled to find a diplomatic answer.

The PM's residence by the central Reykjavik pond, in a peaceful wooden building wrapped in traditional corrugated iron, was by now Iceland's crisis centre. Under the watchful eye of foreign reporters and almost all the country's news teams, government ministers, bankers, Central Bank staff and all sorts of advisors were seen rushing about in an ever-increasing haze of panic. Though jumping for everyone in the proximity, the media could not find anyone who was able to provide the public with any coherent overview of the situation. Anticipation was building as news spread that the announcement of a far-reaching rescue package was due in the afternoon.

In the early evening, PM Geir Haarde spoke in secrecy with his British counterpart, Gordon Brown. They were old acquaintances, since both had served for years as finance ministers, meeting on several occasions. The message was, however, still the same as before: no bail-out money would be available internationally for Iceland except through an IMF programme. Brown repeated Alistair Darling's concerns from before, that Kaupthing would unlawfully bring over to Reykjavik one-and-a-half billion pounds from the UK, which would not be tolerated. The UK was in this regard already burned by Lehman, which prior to its default had sneaked back to the US eight billion dollars from the City of London, and would not allow the same thing to happen again. The call ended without a solution, with Brown all but begging Haarde to call in the IMF rescue team.

Outside the PM's residence a pounding rainstorm was punishing all spectators. Tension grew again when the hours passed without any clues as to what the rescue package, which reportedly was being negotiated behind the closed doors, would entail. The people were thus still impatiently waiting for news on the fate of their country. What we did not know was that all attempts to shift the Icesave accounts into British banking space had already failed. Negotiations with the British Financial Supervisory Authority (FSA) to allow Landsbanki to move the deposits to its London Heritable Bank and thus under the UK banking regime were stuck. The British were asking for more money alongside it than either Landsbanki or indeed the Icelandic state could possibly raise.

Finally, just before midnight on Sunday, our PM, Geir Haarde, stepped out of the door the news cameras had all been focused on. To the astonishment of most of those who were nervously waiting at home in front of their TV sets and computer screens, he told reporters that the result of the work over this dramatic weekend was that there was in fact no need for a special rescue package. He then quietly excused himself, mentioning in passing he had hardly had any breakfast yet – he was only stepping out to get a bite to eat after a long working day. At home, the population was left in complete dismay. The following day, Haarde's statement proved to be a blatant lie, which many have never been able to forgive him for. But what could he say? What indeed would have happened if the PM had honestly explained that our financial system was already collapsing and about to fall on our heads? His words have since been considered the last decade's anti-climax.

Implementing the master plan

In the small hours of Monday 6 October, the last desperate attempt to move Icesave to the UK ended with a flat refusal in Westminister and Plan B, which had been in preparation for a few days, was kicked into action. One of the banks would get Central Bank backing but the others would be split between 'bad' international banks taken into receivership and 'good' new domestic banks. Specialists from JP Morgan who had worked out the WaMu acquisition were already in the PM's residence polishing the plan. A defensive wall was to be raised around Icelandic homes. Unlike in most other countries, in these trying times the taxpayer was not to be asked to foot the bill for reckless bankers abroad. According to international rules, bondholders and depositors over the

€20,887 threshold would have equal claims. The emergency laws that had been in the making in the Ministry of Commerce would have to be rushed through Parliament, most importantly moving deposits to the front of the rank of priority and push bondholders and other creditors towards the back of the queue. In the morning, when some of the staff finalizing the emergency plan were heading home just before opening hours, they are reported to have stopped at cash machines to withdraw as much as they could.

When the markets opened, the FME had stopped trading the banks' stocks and the banks themselves froze all fund transactions. To counter the almost inevitable avalanche of withdrawals, the government issued a blanket protection for all deposits *within* the country. The UK and Netherlands were issuing top-off guarantees for deposits above the €20,887 stipulated in the EU directive: up to €40,000 in Holland and, by Wednesday, up to £50,000 in the UK. Many European states were also issuing complete guarantees, including Ireland, Germany, Denmark and Austria. Iceland was, however, only guaranteeing *domestic* deposits but could not explicitly state what would happen in foreign branches, apart from a vague general pledge to the effect that the banks' Depositors and Investors Guarantee Fund would be 'supported'. This would, however, always be difficult, as deposits in foreign branches of Icelandic banks, most of which were on Icesave accounts, amounted to around £8.5 billion, about 80 per cent of the country's GDP, whereas the fund held only about 1 per cent of that total amount, which was comparable to other countries. The ambiguity of the statements coming out of Reykjavik was thus worrying our neighbours, especially government officials in Whitehall.

Around noon on Monday, Alistair Darling called again to discuss these and other grave matters with Finance Minister Árni Mathiesen. When he could not get a clear state guarantee out of his Icelandic counterpart, an assurance that UK depositors would be protected, at least up to €20,887 according to the EU directive, he stated that this would be 'extremely damaging to Iceland in the future' and then ended the call saying, 'the reputation of your country is going to be terrible' (Samtal Árna og Darlings, 2008). Mathiesen could not but agree, but he understood from their conversation that he would still have some time to work things out.

Kaupthing won the lottery of which bank to save. It was the biggest of the three, with the strongest assets abroad. It would have the best chance of surviving. The Central Bank thus provided a €500 million short-term loan against all shares in Kaupthing's Danish FIH Bank subsidiary as collateral. This came as a bitter blow to Glitnir, as the loan to Kaupthing was identical to the one Glitnir had been denied just a week before. The government decided to go even further and revoked the planned nationalization of Glitnir for €600 million. It would not be saved. The Central Bank also denied Landsbanki's request for a similar emergency loan. Landsbanki and Glitnir were now on their own, while Kaupthing still had the Central Bank's backing. By noon on Monday it was clear that Landsbanki would be already defaulting the following day. The owners were furious at the government's decision. This was a stark reversal of the bank's situation of just a few months before, when it seemed to be well funded with a comfortable €800 million liquidity and strong inflow of foreign deposits. Furthermore, redemption of loans was low until late 2009. And even though it was exhausted of foreign cash by the run in the UK, the bank still had enough money in Icelandic króna to survive this storm; the problem was that the króna was no longer tradable for foreign currency.

By afternoon the króna was once again in free fall, being traded at different rates by different actors, so that no one knew its real value. Icelanders abroad were having trouble withdrawing cash. For example, students abroad, funded by the state Student Loan Funding scheme, could not access their money to pay rent or for other necessities. Even those abroad who could get money with their cards or from online accounts did not know the exchange rate they would get. This was thus a double crisis – a banking crisis and a currency crisis – which had already started in March.

God bless Iceland

At four in the afternoon on Monday 6 October, Geir Haarde was ready to address the nation on TV. This was an extraordinary event, as apart from the traditional New Year's Eve address, it is something our PM never does. We were all gathered in our workplaces: around radios, TV sets and computer screens. The entire nation was listening to his grave concerns: the banks were in serious trouble, he said. The state would not have the means to bail them out. If it tried, we ran a risk of being sucked with them into an economic abyss. This was a shock to most, as just hours earlier he had told reporters that all was well, that no action needed to be taken. Many were thus in disbelief when he now, in this strange address, tried to reassure Icelanders that their deposits were safe; all normal domestic banking would still be operational. He stated that if they united in these trying times, Icelanders would withstand the storm and then ended his unprecedented address by asking God to bless Iceland (Haarde, 2008). This is when we knew we were in serious trouble. In a secular country this was as unusual as any of the other new experiences we were going through in these days of rapid, dramatic events.

From the TV studio the PM rushed to Parliament, where he introduced the government's emergency legislation, which allowed the banks to be split and altered the order of payments out of the fallen banks by moving depositors to the front. This was a *force majeure* situation. The action was part of the defensive wall being raised around ordinary households. Foreign creditors would simply have to accept losing most of what they had loaned to the Icelandic banks. Before midnight, the emergency legislation had been rushed through all formalities and parliamentary procedures. At 1:30 in the morning, government officials were sneaking past doctors and nurses to find the President of the Republic, who had been committed to Iceland's national hospital for heart treatment. Only when his signature had been secured could the banks be taken into administration. The President was the second of the nation's leaders to be taken ill, but not the last. SDA leader Ingibjörg Gísladóttir was still in a New York hospital recovering from severe brain surgery and later, Prime Minister Haarde would also fall ill, as I will discuss in the next chapter. These illnesses weakened the leadership of the country during these days of crisis.

Before opening of business on Tuesday morning, a new board for Landsbanki had been appointed. The members of the new board were mostly lawyers, who had almost randomly been called in the middle of the night. Miraculously, the bank remained operational. If it had not been for the media frenzy its customers might hardly have noticed that they were now banking with a new, state-owned financial institution. At the same time, in the UK, the FSA issued a moratorium on Landsbanki's London subsidiary, the Heritable Bank. The world's media were now covering the Icelandic collapse night and day from the ever-growing media camp in downtown Reykjavik.

With all funding opportunities closed, the situation was growing bleaker by the hour. European rescue money was still out of reach and the US refused our Finance Minister, Mr Árni Mathiesen, once again when he came begging. An informal delegation of the IMF had trav-elled to Reykjavik but the government was not yet ready to enter into a formal IMF programme. Then out of the blue, as it seemed, the Central Bank's leading governor, Davíð Oddsson, announced to the press that the Russians were lending us €4 billion. So, unexpectedly, Moscow of all places was jumping to our rescue. This broke all previous alliances, as Iceland had been heavily invested in Western interests, a founding member of NATO and host to an American army base until just two years before. Senior SDA minister Össur Skarphéðinsson said the US's denial of help was pretty harsh given that Icelanders had for decades believed that they were in a specially friendly relationship with the US – which now in times of trouble was not amounting to much (Skarphéðinsson, 2008).

The jubilation quickly calmed, however, when we learned that Oddsson had somewhat misunderstood the Russian ambassador – Moscow was not committing any money, only saying it was willing to consider such a plea. The money never materialized. Perhaps Moscow was only dangling its feet to the possibility of upsetting NATO's consolidation.

If the Icelandic authorities still enjoyed any credibility abroad after the misreporting of the availability of Russian roubles, it was finally exhausted this same day when the Central Bank announced that it was setting a unilateral exchange rate for the króna, well above its current trading rate. Once again, the main governor of the Central Bank took a vital economic decision without consulting the bank's experts (Jóhannesson, 2009: 160). As a result, the bank had to use a significant portion of its foreign reserves to keep an impossible peg, which therefore held for only two days. Wade and Sigurgeirsdóttir (2012) claim that those in the know were able to exploit the situation and pocket the spoils. Finally, some hope was again held out when Norwegian PM Jens Stoltenberg called offering help – hopefully the united front of foreign leaders was cracking. This was, however, both too little and, seemingly, too late.

In the evening, the Central Bank's governor Davíð Oddsson appeared on the country's main TV news talk show to discuss the crisis and defended the Central Bank's decisions. In simple terms he explained the Washington Mutual (WaMu) method of splitting the banks in a good domestic banks surviving and bad foreign ones collapsing. Ordinary Icelanders would not be asked to pay the foreign liabilities of reckless bankers. Foreign creditors would simply have to accept getting only 5 to 15 per cent of their claims. As a result, however, Iceland would be cleansed of the unsustainable foreign debt of private banks and very soon ready to start growing again (Oddsson, 2008). This sounded too good to be true – later we learned that it was. For now, however, Oddsson, once again, sounded like the country's real leader. The following day, he was proposing a new emergency government of all parties. He also proposed the formation of an ad hoc crisis committee comprising representatives of the Central Bank, the FME and the ministries of finance and commerce, which in effect would control most economic affairs in the country. Though hesitant about a new emergency government unit, PM Haarde proposed that Oddsson, his old boss, should head the crisis committee. This was more than SDA ministers could take; many of them went berserk, claiming that Oddsson was exploiting the crisis in an attempt to steal back control over the state.

By the end of Tuesday, Glitnir was exhausted. The planned nationalization had been cancelled and it was clear that the bank would not receive the promised €600 million for 75 per cent of its shares. By Wednesday morning, Glitnir was thus also taken into administration. Its operations in Norway and Luxembourg followed soon afterwards. Public discussion mirrored the general sense of decay. Paralysed and in panic, the public was worried about their savings in stocks, bonds and money market funds, much of which was gone by now. The largest loss was that of Landsbanki's owners. Its main owner, Björgólfur Guðmundsson, suffered one of the greatest individual bankruptcies in world history. His son, Björgólfur Thor Björgólfsson, who had enjoyed a place amongst the richest people in the world when his name was on the Forbes 500 list, was also all but wiped out in one go. His trouble had started a bit earlier, when British travel group XL Leisure collapsed on 15 September, leaving many holidaymakers stranded. For Samson this was a potential exposure of more than €200 million. All hope was, however, not yet gone for Iceland, as Kaupthing, our largest bank, was still standing.

The UK attack

With the Icesave website down, a run was also blazing in the UK on Kaupthing's Edge accounts at Singer & Friedlander. Though protected by the UK's Depositors Guarantee Scheme, the bank was still having trouble convincing customers that their deposits were safe. During these difficult days, Kaupthing was being challenged on many fronts. The Finnish Financial Supervisory authority, for example, was freezing movement of its assets until the situation in Iceland had cleared.

Seen from the UK and the Netherlands, the situation was simply that Icesave depositors were left without access to their accounts. The website was unaccessable and no trace of the bank was left in the UK or Holland. No one answered the phone and there was not even an address to go to. Depositors were in an intolerable position – the bank had disappeared without a trace from the face of the earth. This caused a seriously strained relationship Reykjavik had with London and The Hague. The British and the Dutch governments decided to compensate their depositors, even beyond the €20,887 mark guaranteed by the EU directive. For this they demanded payback with interest from the Icelandic government. The Icesave dispute became our greatest international dispute since the Cod Wars – once again with the British. During these repeated conflicts between the two islands a characteristic, postcolonial-like love–hate relationship developed.

In Whitehall, preparations had been under way for dealing with the Icelandic crisis. Icelanders would not get away with simply cutting off its foreign debt, shutting the doors and leaving British citizens out in the cold. It did not help when UK officials learned of Oddsson's message on TV, in which he almost triumphantly stated that foreigners would be left out in the cold. The plan was to be kicked into action. The British claimed that giving preference to depositors in domestic banks over those in foreign branches was a breach of European regulations, which Iceland subscribed to through the EEA.

In the early morning of 8 October 2008, Alistair Darling appeared on two of the UK's most popular morning TV programmes, on ITV and BBC, and claimed that the Icelandic government was reneging on its responsibility to UK depositors, and that this would not be tolerated. On the BBC he said, when referring to his conversation with Iceland's finance minister Mathiesen: 'The Icelandic government, believe it or not, told me yesterday they have no intention of honouring their obligations here' (Darling, 2008). In a joint press conference at 9:15 Darling and Gordon Brown announced a massive bail-out of UK-based banks, to the tune of £500 billion. As a result of pumping the money into the banks, the British state acquired a majority stake in the Royal Bank of Scotland and steered the merger of HBOS and Lloyds TSB, in which the state had acquired third of the shares. There was, however, not a penny for Icelandic-owned banks in the UK. On the contrary, Brown claimed that Iceland's authorities must assume responsibility for the failed banks and announced that the UK government had taken 'legal action against the Icelandic authorities to recover the money lost to people who deposited in UK branches of its banks' (quoted in Balakrishnan, 2008).

Earlier in the morning, the UK FSA had called Kaupthing demanding £300 million instantly be moved from Reykjavik to Singer & Friedlander to meet the run on Edge accounts and then a further £2 billion over ten days. This was of course an impossible demand for Kaupthing to meet, and it instead called the Deutsche Bank, asking it to sell off Kaupthing's operations in the UK. Deutsche's brokers thought that could be done within 24 hours.

The legal actions Brown had mentioned in his press brief, however, went much further. At 10:10 in the morning, deposits in Landsbanki's

Heritable Bank were moved to the Dutch internet bank ING Direct when the 'Landsbanki Freezing Order 2008' took effect (The Landsbanki Freezing Order, 2008). The action was based on the Anti-Terrorism, Crime and Security Act, which had been put in place after the terrorist attacks in the US on 11 September 2001. Not minding that around a hundred thousand people worked for Icelandic-held companies in Britain, the UK government invoked the Anti-Terrorism Act to freeze the assets of Landsbanki in the UK and for a while also all assets of the Icelandic state. Subsequently, Landsbanki and for a while also Iceland's Central Bank and our Ministry of Finance was listed on the Treasuries home page alongside other sanctioned terrorist regimes, including Al-Qaeda, the Taliban, Burma, Zimbabwe and North Korea. This was in stark contrast with the response elsewhere. Authorities in the Netherlands, for example, saw no reason to freeze assets and in Stockholm the Swedish Central Bank was still trading with Kaupthing's Swedish branch.

While Kaupthing's CEO, Einarsson, was in his London office in the late morning discussing with Deutsche Bank over the phone the fastest way to liquidate its assets, he read a banner running on the TV screen saying that the FSA had already moved Kaupthing's Edge accounts to ING Direct in the Netherlands. Their phone conversation quickly ended, as there was no longer anything to talk about. In the afternoon, the UK authorities issued a moratorium on Singer & Friedlander, showed its Icelandic CEO, Ármann Þorvaldsson, the door and sealed the offices. This instantly prompted a flow of margin calls and a further run on the mother company. When the dark set in, Kaupthing Bank was itself taken into administration in Reykjavik. Thirty thousand shareholders lost all its worth. As had happened to the holding companies Samson and Stoðir when Landsbanki and Glitnir fell, the Exista holding company was instantly ruined with the collapse of Kaupthing. The Icelandic economic miracle was over. Interestingly, the British FSA later found out that no money had illegally been moved from Singer & Friedlander to Iceland (Júlíusson, 2009), which, however, had been one of the main justifications for the UK's attack on Iceland.

These actions were a co-ordinated attack. Indeed, it was a bomb, which was to blow up the defensive wall that the Icelandic government was trying to build around domestic households. Access to the estimated 7 billion pounds the Icelandic government and banks held in assets in the UK no longer being available, the wall came tumbling down. Invoking Anti-Terrorist legislation against a neighbouring state and fellow NATO and EEA member was virtually an act of war. This was an unprecedented move against a friendly state, which cost Iceland dearly, in both economic and political terms. Moody's instantly downgraded Iceland by three full points, to A1. Money transactions to Iceland were stopped not only in the UK but as a result also widely in Europe, where many banks refused to trade with Iceland after it had been listed in the UK with terrorist actors.

The payment and clearing system for foreign goods collapsed. In only two days, all trading in króna had ceased outside Iceland's borders. When PM Haarde called to complain about this brutal treatment, Brown did not even answer. Later in the day, Brown told Sky News that Iceland, as a state, was bankrupt. We were being completely rebuffed. In fact, in the coming days Brown's rhetoric against Iceland was only to harden, and he said that further measures would be taken to recover money (quoted in Brown Condemns, 2008).

With UK depositors holding a stake of £700 million in Icesave, including many charities' funding, Brown stated that the Icelandic authorities were now responsible for the deposits. Even in the UK, many were stunned by Brown's harsh response to the Icelandic crisis. Many claimed that by attacking Iceland, a foreign actor, Brown was attempting to divert attention from difficulties at home, perhaps much as Margaret Thatcher had done during the Falklands crisis (Murphy, 2008b). Initially it did indeed work. On its front page the *Daily Mail* declared 'Cold War' (2008) on Iceland and the *Daily Telegraph* screamed across its front page: 'Give us our money back' (2008). And these were papers that did not even support Brown or his Labour Party.

Perhaps part of the reason for this harsh response can be found in the fact that Iceland's economic fragility turned the mirror on the UK and its own volatile financial situation. Economist Willem Buiter (2008), who had studied the state of the economy in both countries, saw the similarity and wrote that it was no great exaggeration to also describe the UK as a huge hedge fund.

Financial devastation

By Thursday 9 October 2008, almost the entire Icelandic financial system had collapsed in a dramatic chain of events, which later became known simply as The Crash. Ironically, this was a full week before Glitnir's 15 October deadline – which had started the whole thing. Only weeks before, all the three banks had passed the FME's stress test with flying colours. Landsbanki, Glitnir and Kaupthing were all private firms. Still they fell on the state and indeed on the general public. In the coming days and weeks, many smaller savings and loan companies, investment banks and holding companies fell as well. Most businesses suffered severally, as around 70 per cent of corporate loans were foreign exchange-indexed. The vast majority of investment companies suffocated as a result and indeed most businesses in the country were technically bankrupt when the currency tanked.

Though panic was perhaps not visible on the streets, many were worried for their economic survival in the short term, let alone what their financial state would be on the other side of the immediate crisis. Many were thus stocking up on necessities and shortages were felt in stores, though nothing close to what the most pessimistic had been predicting or what could be read in some of the international media. Many long-lasting trading relationships were strained. Icelandic shops, for example, were often refused imports unless they paid up front, which they were not accustomed to doing. Iceland was being isolated on many fronts simultaneously. As the external payment system broke down, many transactions were stuck abroad and some amounting to significant sums were even lost. On international markets, all things Icelandic had become toxic. Icelanders abroad who were relying on the collapsed króna instantly lost more than half their income and many were having serious trouble meeting their obligations regarding rent, loans and bills.

Before The Crash, the banks had held assets worth €150 billion, almost double the value of WorldCom before its collapse in 2002 and around three times that of Enron before its failure (Benediktsdóttir et al., 2011). On Moody's list of the largest bankruptcies, the collapse of each of the Icelandic banks was ranked 11th in world history; collectively, their demise was ranked third, after Lehman and Washington Mutual. The total loss by creditors was thought to be around €47 billion – outstanding loans by German banks alone amounted to €15 billion. A higher recovery rate out of the fallen banks than was initially expected has, however, since significantly diminished the loss.

Initially, this seemed to be the mother of all financial crises. With the collapse of the banks more than three-quarters of the stock exchange was wiped out. At its lowest level the stock market was only 5 per cent of its July 2007 high. The currency market froze and the external payment system seized. In free fall domestically, the króna became virtually worthless abroad. By the end of 2008, it had fallen by 80 per cent and property prices by 25 per cent. Investment instantly fell as well as imports and lending. Real wages fell and unemployment rose. Out of all the OECD countries Iceland suffered the third-biggest fall in output during this financial crisis and the fourth-biggest fall in employment (Wade & Sigurgeirsdottir, 2012).

While many of the banks' assets proved dubious at best, their liabilities were very real. The Icesave liabilities alone amounted to €8.5 billion. The number of depositors in the UK was almost equal to Iceland's population. The UK authorities were thus in effect asking every man, woman and child in Iceland to foot the cost of an Icesave account of their own. Not only had the banks left them a gigantic bill to pay, but their demise had also blown a hole in the state's coffers, as their tax revenues, which had amounted to quarter of the state's budget, had disappeared overnight. People also felt the economic turmoil privately. The widespread financialization of society had turned many ordinary people into risk investors. Many had grown fantastically rich through 'amateur' investments. Now, all of a sudden, this counted equity was wiped out as well.

Only after the collapse did Icelanders learn of the many dubious dealings the banks had engaged in. Their owners seemed to have had almost unrestricted access to borrowing in their respective banks. Right up until the end, they had been borrowing massive amounts from the banks' money market funds, which staff had vigorously been pushing onto customers in order to keep their owners afloat. The banks' holding companies would simply leave securities in their own shares and take the cash. While it became clear that these funds would lose up to a third of their value, many were angry when learning of this money market manipulation.

The owners of the banks had also freely been exploiting the limited liability of companies when establishing new businesses, which would borrow from their bank and use the money to fund something entirely different. These new, heavily indebted companies were then left without any assets, which quite often, we learned after the Crash, had been moved to Luxemburg or to tax havens in the Caribbean, mainly to the British Virgin Islands – where Tortola for some reason became a popular destination for cash out of Iceland, hosting 130 Icelandic companies. This is just one example of how the banks and holding companies were looted from within. Many ruses were used to suck money out of the banks, for example through excessive salaries and bonus payments and ridiculous expenses.

We were all stunned when learning of the scale of the debt left behind. Jón Ásgeir Jóhannesson and his companies alone owed more than a thousand billion ISK, between 70 and 80 per cent of the country's GDP. He had started his career as a small grocery store owner, undercutting the slow moving established conglomerate and offering better prices by stripping off fat and bringing down overhead costs. Leading up to The Crash he had, however, himself become the conglomerate, on steroids, with little control over his empire.

Our authorities were also at fault. The groups of Viking Capitalists were allowed to merge investment banking with commercial banking and exploit the implicit government guarantee for both operations. Through the domestic trade of love letters alone the banks were able to generate liquidity amounting to 13 per cent of GDP. As a result, the Central Bank was technically bankrupted by The Crash, when it lost what amounted to quarter of the country's GDP. The state had to step in and bail out its own Central Bank with an injection of 270 billion króna.

Evidently, in the days and weeks before The Crash, the banks had loaned massive amounts, literally their last liquidity, to their owners. When this came to light, we learned that in the days leading up to The Crash Kaupthing's management had in a London meeting decided to free key staff from being responsible for personal loans they took out in the bank to buy Kaupthing shears. On realizing all this, the people in Iceland became angry. The Viking Capitalists were no longer their heroes but had rapidly become the villains in this horrific saga. Many of them could be seen fleeing on their private jets from Reykjavik airport 'like the last helicopter out of Saigon', as one foreign reporter put it (Jackson, 2008).

Immediately after The Crash, Reykjavik was almost invaded by foreign vultures manoeuvring among the ruins to acquire assets on the cheap. Amongst them was UK shopping mogul Philip Green, Jóhannesson's old business partner, who was attempting to snatch up Baugur's assets for only 5 per cent of its debt. Though Green was not successful, lots of valuable assets were squandered in this way. When forced to sell, Glitnir's branch in Norway was practically stolen for only a fraction of its worth. This happened when the Norwegian Depositors Guarantee Fund issued a margin call on Glitnir without any warning. Only few years earlier, the bank had been bought for 3.1 billion Norwegian krona. Now it was taken for only 300 million. Later we learned that the chairman of the Norwegian Depositors Fund, Finn Haugan, was also leading the banks heading the takeover. Soon the asset was almost up to its previous worth, turning a massive profit for those who had plotted the hostile acquisition. Another group of travellers visiting us in these days were lawyers representing creditors. In the week right before The Crash, most Reykjavik hotels were filled with lawyers and other crisis travellers.

Ruined reputation

When Foreign Minister Ingibjörg Gísladóttir, leader of the SDA, finally arrived home after successful brain surgery in New York, where she had gone before the crisis hit to promote Iceland's bid to be part of the UN Security Council, she found her country in a state of financial devastation. Its reputation had also been destroyed. The rhetoric in the world's media was aggressive. *The Australian*, for example, suggested that alongside the US Iceland was the most 'immoral country in the world' (Devine, 2008). Making no distinction between the actions of the different actors, the media lumped Icelandic bankers, politicians and the public together in a claim that *Iceland* as a whole had failed (for more, see Chartier, 2011). *Le Monde*, for example, reported that Iceland in its entirety was bankrupt (Mamou, 2008). The fear was that others would soon follow, most pressingly the Baltics, which were tilting towards a financial cliff of their own.

Appetites for disaster stories out of Iceland seemed insatiable. Ironically, in the evening of the day Landsbanki fell, the CEO of advertising agency Indentica in the UK, Franco Bonadia, accepted an award for 'best marketing campaign' for the Icesave deposits advertisements. Bonadia later described how strange it felt that his successful campaign had become a running gag at the London gala award ceremony (Montgomery, 2008). In Copenhagen, a journalist from the Danish tabloid *Ekstrabladet* started a collection for poor Iceland outside Magasin du Nord, one of the main landmarks of the Icelandic Viking Capitalists in Copenhagen. On the eBay website, Iceland was listed for auction with a starting price of 99 cents and the mock listing was reported by news media around the world. Iceland's fall from grace was emphasized in the UN Security Council election, in which we lost to Austria and Turkey by a much greater margin than expected.

During these dramatic days, many reports told stories of Icelanders being verbally abused by strangers on the street in some of our neighbouring capitals, of people being laid off or having their rent cancelled just for being Icelandic. In Copenhagen, a young Icelandic mother was refused service in a central H&M store, and a customs official at Stansted airport in London reportedly asked Icelanders passing through if they worked in a bank; if they said 'yes', they were not allowed to transit (for more, see Jóhannesson, 2009).

Via foreign TV, Iceland's reputation was being flushed down the toilet. Foreign media were flocking to the country and with an almost anthropological interest reporting on this extraordinary, finance-driven society in ruins. In the boom years, Reykjavik had undergone a transformation, with many new high-rise buildings and luxury neighbourhoods built from scratch. The titanic Harpa concert hall under construction by the old harbour, which was to cost almost 1.5 per cent of the country's GDP, was viewed as symbolic of the megalomaniac boom years. One of the new villa neighbourhoods on Reykjavik's eastern outskirts had newly laid, illuminated roads but no finished houses. These unfinished constructions became the icons of a crisis-ridden Iceland when foreign news people delivered their reports standing in front of what looked like ruins.

In *Vanity Fair* Michael Lewis reported on the 'single greatest act of madness in financial history' (Lewis, 2009), claiming that the state owed a thousand billion dollars in banking losses, each individual, man, woman and child thus being owed roughly $330,000. He wrote that in a 'stunning collective madness' Iceland had re-invented itself around 2003 from a tiny fishing island to a global financial power. On a more upbeat note, he wrote that after the collapse, the women had given up on the men, who had ruined Iceland, and taken control of the country.

In the more serious press, our leaders were ranked amongst those blamed for the larger international financial crisis. The *Guardian* listed Geir Haarde among the 25 world leaders responsible for the crisis (Finch, 2009), *Time Magazine* did likewise, naming Davíð Oddsson as one of the main villains (25 People to Blame for the Financial Crisis, 2009) and the *Huffington Post* listed Finance Minister Árni Mathiesen as one of the world's worst bankers (Graham, 2008).

Conclusion

Iceland's Viking finance-dominated economy was the first casualty of the international financial crisis when its three big banks, Glitnir, Landsbanki and Kaupthing, came crashing down in October 2008. On the back of emergency legislation they were in quick succession split up and partly nationalized. The króna went into free fall and inflation sky-rocketed, rendering both consumer price indexation-based mortgages and foreign currency loans unsustainable, 40 per cent of households soon went into significant arrears on their mortgage repayments. The collapse of the currency was a test of strength in which it was impossible for the Viking historic bloc to pass.

Though differently orchestrated, Cyprus played a similar trick in 2013 when its overinflated banking system came to a grinding halt. After cancelling a proposal to tax deposits to bail out the oversized banks, the government took its second largest bank, Laike Bank, into administration. The Mediterranean island's banks were filled with foreign deposits, mostly Russian. Deposits of up to €100,000 were moved to the Bank of Cyprus, with the rest partly nationalized. Shareholders and creditors lost almost all their worth, as did rich foreign depositors, who lost everything above the €100,000 mark. This was the first sign of Europe adopting an Icelandic method of dealing with troubled oversized banks.

One of the main mistakes of the Icelandic banks was accepting equity as collateral, as this created weak capital. To boost equity, key staff of the banks were pressured to invest in its stock, which the bank would loan against. Before the fall, employees of Kaupthing, for example, owned 9 per cent of its stock. Perhaps this helps to explain the loyalty of key staff and the lengths they were willing to go to in order to save the banks from defaulting.

When the dust had settled, we saw that the Central Bank really did all it could to bail out the banks; its vaults were emptied of almost the entire reserve and the Central Bank was in the end technically bankrupt. It simply did not have the means to prevent the collapse. With a reserve-to-external debt ratio of only 8 per cent the Central Bank never had a chance to back up the system.

The collapse of the Icelandic banks clearly revealed a serious weakness in the European banking passport system, a macroeconomic imbalance within the Single European Market. It was a weakness that some of the more established banking nations had warned against when the system was being constructed (for more, see Benediktsdóttir et al., 2011). The main flaw lay in the fragmented nature of supervision on an otherwise common market – European-wide regulation but only local supervision. This had caused a mismatch between access to market and adequate supervision.

In Iceland, there was a further local problem to add to this European weakness. Unlike the supervision authorities in many European countries, who understood their function as to holistically monitor the financial system in both practical and legal terms, the Icelandic FME followed an ultra-legalistic approach, claiming that it had no authority to intervene to prevent the collapse and that its only function was to make sure the banks followed the letter of the law. It is evident, for example, that the British FSA was much more active than our small FME both leading up to and during The Crash.

Despite these unfavourable external factors, we can still conclude that the Icelandic growth model collapsed under its own weight. The hard-driven procyclical economic policies explained in Chapter 4 proved to be a recipe for disaster when crisis hit: young, inexperienced but over-ambitious managers drove the rapid expansion of an interconnected banking system based on high gearing to equity, which was dependent on foreign funding. When explaining what went wrong, Kaupthing's CEO, Sigurður Einarsson, noted that the capitalist system had been contaminated by elements that contradicted its principles, meaning that public guarantees and state banking had compromised the morals of the banks' management and owners (Einarsson, 2008). Be that as it may, the incredibly rapid expansion of an unsustainable financial system surely does help to explain the world's most spectacular financial collapse.

Still, the Icelandic banks were in principle perhaps not all that different from banks elsewhere during this time of international boom. What separated them from others was clearly the limited capacity of the small Central Bank to back them up. Iceland's far too exposed banks no longer had a credible lender of last resort. The banks' oversized liabilities were in foreign currency and outside the reach of the state. For some reason the bankers, the government, the surveillance authorities and the public at large ignored this systemic risk. The reason for this collective ignorance can be found in Iceland's national identity, as explained in Chapter 1.

Being in the Single European Market but outside the fence of EU institutions left us without shelter when the crisis hit. The Crash not only was economically very detrimental but also dealt a blow to our national identity. The Icelandic *outvasion* was no longer a heroic conquest but an international joke.

Even as the contradictions of Icelandic Viking finance-dominated capitalism became undeniably visible, nationalistic rhetoric retained its foothold. The dispute with the UK and Dutch governments over the Icesave deposits fell into familiar trenches. Though ambiguity remained as to who was legally liable for the loss, the UK government was using all means available to pressure Iceland to accept responsibility. Internally, Iceland was represented as a victim of vicious and conspiratorial foreigners. Even the Nordic states were viewed as 'traitors', especially the Swedish government, which soon became the main villain of the piece in the minds of many Icelandic parliamentarians. Surely there were some merits in this feeling as later evidence discussed in the following chapter point to an joint international action, lead by the UK, of not assisting Iceland. During this horrible week in October 2008, Iceland not only was frozen out of international markets but also suffered a co-ordinated attack from abroad. As Jónsson (2009: 187) claims, the actions of the UK government are perhaps best described as a sort of corporate ethnic cleansing. When Iceland was vindicated of any wrongdoing in the Icesave affair by the EFTA court in 2013, many saw the feeling of victimization as justified, as is further discussed in the following chapter.

Within Iceland, many were also angry at the seeming incompetence of our government to meet the crisis. The passivity of the authorities leading up to The Crash is indeed noteworthy. The seeming inaction of Prime Minister Geir Haarde became notorious, resulting in a common term named after him: 'To do a Haarde'[2] – meaning to do nothing. In his defence, Haarde maintains that the banks lied to him, for example claiming to have access to enough liquidity to keep going until the end of 2009. In the next chapter I turn to the response of the ordinary public, which in the aftermath ousted the government in a series of protests that became known as the Pots and Pans Revolution.

Part III
Revolution and Recovery

7
The Pots and Pans Revolution – and Defiance Abroad

By mid October 2008, Iceland's banking system had collapsed and the country was in financial ruin. Mixing a libertarian ideology of privatization and market liberalization with weak public institutions and cronyist processes had proven to be a recipe for disaster. The public was in state of shock, uncertain of its economic future. This was not only a financial crisis but also a crisis of politics and a fundamental blow to our national identity, which was in tatters. Instantly, the public took to the streets, protesting against the government's seeming incompetence in dealing with the crisis. Already in March, however, truck drivers had started a smaller and more segmented protest against rising petrol prices accompanying the sharp devaluation of the króna, which was devastating their highly leveraged business – many could no longer meet rising loan repayments. Now, in the wake of The Crash, the general public was taking to the streets, banging on pots and pans and other kitchen utensils. The government's apparent weakness in responding to the UK attack, described in the previous chapter, added to the public's frustration, especially when it had become clear that no money had illegally been moved out of the UK.

In order to prevent the economy from grinding to a halt, with devastating effects, Iceland was in desperate need of foreign funding. After being pushed out of international financial markets in the lead-up to The Crash, it found doors still closed in most places. Though ambiguity remained over many legal aspects of this highly complex situation, the UK and Dutch governments were pressuring Iceland to accept full responsibility for the Icesave accounts. While also pressuring Iceland to turn to the IMF, these governments were, with the help of the EU apparatus, lobbying neighbouring capitals to refuse us any loans except through an IMF programme. Our government, however, was still afraid of the stigma of being the first Western state in four decades to surrender to the IMF. In late October, Iceland finally caved in to the collective pressure and sought help from the fund. To our surprise, the IMF board refused help unless, we were made to understand, we first cleared up the Icesave dispute with the British and the Dutch. Holding out for less than a month longer, the government threw in the towel and under impossible pressure accepted to guarantee deposits up to the minimum €20,887 stipulated by EU law.

The forced Icesave agreement angered the public, which took to the streets in ever greater numbers. Caving in to foreign pressure and accepting a forced agreement was seen as violating the Icelandic Project, the eternal and sacred quest of protecting Iceland's sovereignty. After a series of protests, which later became known as the Pots and Pans Revolution (*búsáhaldabyltinging*), the grand coalition of the Independence Party and the Social Democratic Alliance was ousted from power in late January 2009, paving the way for a new left-wing government – the first purely left-wing coalition in the history of the republic. This chapter discusses the unprecedented events leading up to the Pots and Pans Revolution and further analyses the nationalistic rhetoric politicians used in the blame game that immediately emerged in the wake of the Crash and rose to a new high in the Icesave-dispute with the UK and the Netherlands.

Taking to the streets

On the basis of emergency laws rushed through Parliament the previous day, Landsbanki was taken into administration in the early morning of Tuesday 7 October 2008. Glitnir fell on Wednesday and Kaupthing before dawn on Thursday. Capital controls were introduced and the economy seemed paralysed. The severity of the currency crisis which followed the banking collapse can for example be seen in the fact that Iceland was the only country that had to revert such extreme measures as implementing capital controls. On Friday 10 October, the first of many popular protests started. After only a few hours' promotion via Facebook, around 300 protesters gathered in front the Central Bank in Reykjavik demanding that its leading governor, Mr Davíð Oddsson – our long-standing previous Prime Minister and leader of the IP – step down. Though he was not in the government any longer, the protesters saw Oddsson as the main architect of the failed neoliberal model.

The Crash of October 2008 was nothing if not sudden. However, Iceland's economy had, though, for months been on a downward spiral. As early as March, a bunch of truck drivers had initiated a public protest against rising petrol prizes when the currency sharply devalued by a quarter. It is telling of the extreme financialization of the society and general lack of fiscal caution even amongst the ordinary public that many truck drivers had leveraged their assets to the top, leaving very little margin to maneuverer when payments suddenly rose. Many had taken out foreign currency loans to finance their trucks and other equipment for their businesses. When the currency fell and prices started rising, many suddenly found themselves on the wrong side of their balance sheet as monthly payments exceeded income.

Artists played a prominent role in structuring the protests in the wake of The Crash. A couple of classical musicians, for example, initiated the first protest in front of the Central Bank. A well known folk song singer and stage actor – a veteran campaigner for gay rights – followed suit and started a series of regular protests in front of Parliament on Saturday afternoons. Social media became the main instrument for promoting these events. Initially, this was a diffuse bunch of protesters with a variety of demands gathering in small groups around the country, in front of banks and government buildings. The protesters often used rhythm to create an underlying beat for their messages. Soon, however, the regular Saturday protests became the focal point for protesters. On the grass in front of Parliament a stage was built for writers, academics and other intellectuals to deliver dramatic speeches to the protesting public.

Though the protesters held different and often contradictory views, three collective demands soon emerged: first, for the government to resign and hold an election; second, for the heads of the Central Bank and the financial supervisory authority to be sacked; and third – a more long-term goal – to resurrect Iceland on a reformed platform, for example, by writing a new constitution (for more, see Jóhannesson, 2009; and Sveinsson, 2013).

Adding insult to injury: the Icesave dispute and the IMF

The dispute with the British and Dutch governments over the Icesave accounts added to public frustration. While the crisis was tightening its grip leading up to The Crash, our neighbours had refused help unless it was through an IMF programme. Though a fact-finding team from the fund arrived in Reykjavik during the week of The Crash the coalition government remained split on the issue. While SDA ministers were advocating applying to the IMF, the IP leadership still believed that the fund was only for bankrupt and in effect failed states, which Iceland was not. Most significantly, entering into an IMF programme was viewed as surrendering our sovereignty, which is never an option in Icelandic politics in view of the previously described postcolonial national identity.

However, after the collapse of the banks, the IMF gradually emerged as the only solution to our immediate problems, as Iceland was still being isolated internationally. The British and Dutch governments had been successfully lobbying both the ECB and other European states not to aid Iceland independently, while at the same time pressuring our government to accept responsibility for the Icesave deposits. Our government, on the contrary, insisted that according to the relevant EU directive it was only obligated to ensure that a Depositors Guarantee Fund was in place and not explicitly responsible for foreign branch deposits (Blöndal & Stefánsson, 2008). The problem was that, as in most EU countries, the fund held only around 1 per cent of the liabilities of the banking system. Referring to a report written for the French Central Bank in 2000, Iceland argued that the directive did not explicitly dictate that the state had to pick up the balance in the event of a systemic collapse (Banque de France, 2000).

This was, however, a difficult argument to get through in the crisis-ridden climate at the time. In order to prevent a further run on their own banks and to regain enough credibility to keep them afloat, the British, during these same days, led a coalition of G20 and EU states promoting collective international action emphasizing almost blanket depositors protection (see, for example, Pilkington, 2008). Allowing Iceland to leave depositors in foreign branches without such protection was seen as countering these efforts and indeed undermining the entire global financial system. In Whitehall, many feared that the Icelandic crisis was spreading to the UK, which also had approached the brink of widespread banking collapse. As a result, Iceland was being turned into an international villain. We felt trapped. Only our closest neighbour, the tiny Faroe Islands, was willing to swim against the current and sent over €45 million without any conditions. This was a lone friendly voice in a time when the international community was collectively condemning us. Even today, Icelanders are extremely grateful for the friendly gesture of our tiny neighbour. It thus called for a celebration when we were able to pay the loan back in early 2013.

Though Iceland was still stubbornly hesitating, a joint economic programme was informally being negotiated that would include

$2.1 billion from the IMF and a further $3 billion from the Central Banks of Denmark, Finland, Norway and Sweden in addition to a separate loan from Poland. Our resilience was diminishing by the day. The pressure to accept responsibility for the Icesave deposits grew. According to some reports, Iceland was even threatened with being expelled from the European Economic Area (EEA), our economic lifeline to the outside world (Hálfdanardóttir, 2008). With dwindling foreign reserves and at risk of a serious shortage of, for example, medicine, food and other necessities from abroad, Iceland finally threw in the towel and applied to enter the IMF emergency programme on 25 October.

Based on informal query our government expected that the IMF board would accept our application on 3 November (Sveinsson, 2013: 46). In the meantime, however, the British and Dutch governments, which previously had been pressuring us to go to the IMF, were now lobbying behind the scenes *against* us being allowed into the programme unless we first accepted responsibility for the Icesave accounts (Duncan, 2008). The *NRC Handelsblad* in the Netherlands reported that the blockage was being orchestrated by Dutch Finance Minister Wouter Bos and his British colleague Alistair Darling (Banning & Gerritsen, 2008). Later, the chief IMF representative in Iceland admitted to a block by not only the British and Dutch governments but also the Nordic states (Rozwadowski, 2013). When Iceland would not concede, the IMF board postponed its decision on our application. We were made to clearly understand that our plea would be blocked until our acceptance of liability for Icesave. During this time, a senior advisor in the IMF's external relations department publicly acknowledged that the delay was directly due to unresolved disputes with Holland and the UK (Transcript of Press Briefing by David Hawley, 2008). As Iceland was not a member of the EU and thus not subject to the European Court of Justice, and as the EFTA Court had no jurisdiction in the UK and the Netherlands, there seemed at the time to be no available legal body to rule on the dispute.

Iceland was thus caught in a tight spot. We needed money to prevent further deterioration of our already devastated economy but that meant agreeing to liabilities we did not want to accept. Though Norway finally broke away from the unified bloc within the IMF and agreed to send over €500 million, as later did Poland, which unilaterally pledged $200 million, companies and households in Iceland were feeling the effects of the prolonged lack of access to currency. Holding out for only a couple of weeks longer, we finally surrendered on 16 November. According to the revoked 11 October agreement, which Finance Minister Mathiesen had been forced to sign, Iceland was to repay the Icesave dept over ten years, starting three years after signing, with 6.7 per cent interest on the loan. With the new guidelines agreed between the disputing parties, brokered by the French EU Presidency the government of Iceland agreed to cover the deposits of depositors in the Icesave accounts in accordance with EEA law. These so-called 'Brussels Guidelines' also entailed that the EU would continue to participate in finding arrangements that would allow Iceland to restore its financial system and economy. A stabilization package of financial assistance from the IMF was an explicit part of the agreement, which was to be discussed at the IMF Executive Board meeting on Wednesday 19 November (Agreed Guidelines, 2008).

Three days after surrendering, Iceland was thus the first developed economy to enter an IMF emergency programme since the UK in 1976 – many other states were, however, soon to follow. Though this first agreement on the Icesave deposits was meant to end the quarrel, the dispute was only just starting. Amibutiy still remained. To keep up the pressure, and even to increase it, the Dutch Foreign Minister, Maxime Werhagen, threatened to veto Iceland's EU bid in July 2009 (The Hague Threatens Iceland, 2009). In the end, two additional agreements were proposed, both rejected by the public in extraordinary referendums initiated by the President when he refused to sign them into law, as discussed later in this chapter. In January 2013, the EFTA Court finally vindicated Iceland of any wrongdoing, thus refusing the EU's and the UK and the Dutch governments claim of a state guarantee, such as Iceland had been forced to accept in the earlier Icesave agreements (Judgment of the Court, 2013).

'God Damn, Fucking Fuck'

The seemingly imposed agreement had angered the public, and within Parliament there were MPs who insisted they would not consider themselves bound by what they viewed as an 'unlawful, coerced agreement' (Blöndal, 2008). The government justified the signing by claiming that it had had no choice. Either we bit the bullet and accepted responsibility or we would remain frozen out, thus without access to vital imports such as medicine and food. The government explained that no one supported us; not even our Nordic neighbours were willing to listen to our legal arguments in the case. Without the agreement, Iceland would no longer have been considered a modern state, internationally recognized as equal to others, but would rather have been relegated to being an isolated outpost surviving on local agriculture and fisheries alone. The signing was, however, a serious blow to our political identity, as our postcolonial national identity insisted on our not giving in to foreign pressure. It thus caused great strain domestically. Referring to the distinctive title of the Danish colonial governor stationed in Iceland in the old days, *landstjóri*, one critic of the IMF, a well known intellectual of the IP, said that we now had just such a governor from Washington, a new *landstjóri*, who, much like our former Danish colonizers, would control the country's economy (Magnússon, 2008).

Frustrated by the government's apparently weak response to the UK attack when Iceland was listed with terrorist regimes like the Taliban and Al-Qaida, a group of Icelanders with ties to the UK formed a citizens' movement called InDefence. Under a campaign titled 'Icelanders are NOT Terrorists' the group collected more than 83,000 signatures, by far largest signature collection in our history, which was handed to the UK Parliament in protest against the UK government's use of anti-terrorism legislation against Iceland. The group then organized a PR offensive in the UK, publishing articles and giving countless interviews in the British media. Later, the InDefence group led the domestic campaign against the Icesave agreements (InDefence, n.d.).

After Iceland's concession to the British and the Dutch over Icesave, the general public took to the streets in even greater numbers than before, now not only protesting against our government's mismanagement of the economy but also against apparent foreign oppression. We were being flooded with bad news. According to estimations, the cost of fully protecting domestic deposits and establishing new banks out of the ruins of the failed ones would bring public debt from 29 per cent of GDP up to 109 per cent by end of 2009; before 2010 was out, we would need a further $24 billion from abroad (Jóhannesson, 2009: 258). Many compared the agreement to the Treaty of Versailles when, after the First World War, the Germans were forced to accept impossible liabilities – as Foreign Minister Gísladóttir had argued in the *New York Times* before the agreement was signed (quoted in Lyall, 2008).

Frustration grew as businesses closed and more and more people were laid off while inflation rose to 20 per cent. The protest was now spreading around the country. The foreign media was also becoming increasingly interested in the events as the crowds grew larger. Initially, only a couple of hundred protesters showed up for the weekly Saturday protests in front of the Parliament building. By November, the crowds had grown to several thousands. In January, the numbers would reach five figures.

The country was in a state of shock and the cracks in the government coalition were becoming increasingly apparent. A vicious blame game was being played throughout society, with no one accepting any responsibility. The Central Bank blamed the bankers, the bankers in turn blamed the government, and the SDA part of the government blamed the Central Bank and financial supervisory authority while the IP leadership attributed all the blame to the 'international financial crisis'. Professor Gissurarson, a promoter of the failed neoliberal model, for example refused any responsibility. Furthermore, he said that capitalism as such was not to blame for the events either, but rather reckless individual capitalists. 'We must differentiate between capitalism and capitalists,' he said (quoted in Jóhannesson, 2009).

All the while, the public was growing increasingly tired of everyone's refusal to accept responsibility. The signs protesters waved portrayed the frustration quite well. Amongst the hand-painted slogans were: 'Government go away', 'Stop paying', 'Stop the corruption', 'Out with Oddsson.' The one that was, however, believed to best capture the protesters' frustration simply read: 'God Damn, Fucking Fuck'.[1]

To lighten the mood during these grave times, sarcastic humour also played a prominent role. During the boom, the new class of Viking Capitalists had been keen on showing off their wealth by, for example, driving around Reykjavik in luxury cars like Hummers, Land Cruisers and Range Rovers, which were imported to Iceland in large numbers. Now, these previously prestigious vehicles were being referred to as 'Bummers', 'Grand Losers' and 'Game Overs'.

The apparent public frustration in addition to the Icesave agreement and the involvement of the IMF, was challenging the unity of the government. The SDA was by now aggressively pressuring the IP to apply for EU membership, providing a fast track into the Eurozone, as a way to protect the currency from falling even further – 'First IMF then EU', wrote SDA party leader Gísladóttir (2008b). While the IP was still hesitating, its leaders agreed to hold an extraordinary party convention in early 2013, at which the party's anti-EU policy would be re-examined (Sveinsson, 2013: 224).

During this period of widespread upheaval the country was flooded with all sorts of miracle workers selling simple, quick-fix solutions to complex problems; on the currency issue, for example, we were advised to create a new one and leave behind all debts in the old króna or to unilaterally adopt several foreign currencies and thus surrender monetary policy to Central Banks we were not even connected. One of these miracle workers offered massive loans from Hugo Chavez in Venezuela; another advocated deep-pocketed capital injection from a Hong Kong based investor.

The government was generally criticized for infighting, inaction and being incapable of providing guidance to get the country out of the mess. Though stalemate persisted on many pressing issues, Parliament did agree to establish a Special Investigation Commission, kind of a truth committee, which was to examine the cause of The Crash and would eventually point to the legal responsibility of ministers and high-level government officials. The government also decided to appoint a Special Prosecutor, who was to investigate possible illegal actions of the banks leading up to The Crash. However, if this was meant to soothe the angry public, it did not work, as the protests were only gaining momentum.

'In-com-pe-tent go-vern-ment': an all-Iceland revolution

2008 ended with a bang when protesters forced themselves into the traditional live TV show on New Year's Eve where the country's political leaders were in a celebratory setting discussing the events of the year. Protesters claimed they were in the right to invade what they believed was an ivory tower where leaders out of touch with the ordinary public were hiding. This set a more violent tone for the coming January protest – when the government was finally ousted from power.

Within the government and amongst the established elite many initially tried to dismiss the protesters, claiming that they were mostly old acquaintances: radical lefties and young anarchists skipping school for something more exciting. This attitude, however, underestimated the weight of the undercurrent. Alongside the young anarchist one could find his grandmother banging her wooden spoon on saucepans and other kitchen utensils. The Pots and Pans Revolution was gaining momentum.

Through theatrical, musical and rhetorical means the protest developed characteristics of its own identifying aesthetics. To convey its message a collective mantra gradually emerged whereby, over a ritualistic drumming beat created by banging on anything that could deliver a sound, protesters shouted the same words over and over again: *Van-hæf-ríkis-stjórn* – meaning 'in-com-pe-tent go-vern-ment'. This repeated mantra grew into what can be viewed as a distinctive mass musical event. The protest has for this reason been defined as a specific cultural organization with structural elements (Sigurjónsson, 2011).

Anticipation grew and many expected that Parliament would face a greater number of protesters than ever when resuming on 20 January. Two weeks earlier, the government had officially decided not to take the UK government to a British court for freezing Icelandic assets by the so-called Landsbanki Freezing Act, which was based on the UK Anti-Terrorism legislation. This angered many even further. The action of the UK government was seemingly in violation of several international laws, including the European Economic Area agreement. It could therefore be argued that the British Labour government had by default also taken over the bank's obligation in the UK – including payments from the Icesave accounts. Why the Icelandic government did not used this obvious argument to transfer the responsibility onto Brown's own shoulders was a mystery to most people in Iceland.

Growing friction within the government was also becoming evident. SDA minsters wanted Oddsson out of the Central Bank and were still pressuring the IP to agree to apply for EU membership. Many smaller SDA associations around the country were now calling on the party leadership to end the coalition and hold an early election.

Though most were protesting in peace, violent outbursts and incidents grew more common in the New Year: the flags of the banks were burned; fireworks were shot at government buildings; Parliament's historic brick and stone building in central Reykjavik was pounded with eggs, yogurt and tomatoes, which had to be cleaned every morning; the homes and luxury cars of the Viking Capitalists were vandalized – in the early morning, it was not uncommon for some of the most recognized Viking Capitalists to find their houses covered in red paint.

Then, on 20 January, while Barack Obama was being sworn into office on Capitol Hill in Washington, the people of Iceland started the first revolution in the history of the republic. The weather was unseasonably mild when Parliament resumed in Reykjavik that Tuesday after the traditional Christmas and New Year break. Many thought that it was illustrative of how out of touch Parliament was with the ordinary public that the first item on its agenda was a bill proposing minor changes to the country's alcohol laws. By noon, the crowds had already grown larger than before. The police were now having trouble protecting the Parliament building, which had been surrounded by protesters. Parliamentarians were locked behind the stone and brick walls, though some were able to sneak out through a secret tunnel leading to a neighbouring house. The ritualistic mantra had now grown into a continuous cacophony of drumming masses. In the evening, protesters kept warm by lighting bonfires and burning torches in front of the building. This added a dramatic visualization to the distinctive musical aesthetics of this unprecedented event in Iceland's history.

A noteworthy aspect of the nature of the Pots and Pans Revolution can be found in what happened when the protest seemed to be getting out of hand, for example when the police found itself late one evening being stoned with cobbles from the pavements. When pepper spray and tear gas failed to keep the rioters away, a group of more peaceful protesters broke ranks and shielded the police from the stone-throwing hooligans. This event started what became known as the Orange Group – a citizens' movement promoting protest while also condemning any sort of violence. This changed the nature of the protests; violence mostly ended when it was noticed that most protesters were wearing orange in support of peaceful protest.

Though the tide had surely turned, the excessive and out-of-touch high-society culture of the boom years had not yet completely disappeared. A surreal encounter occurred when a group of artists were heading with their hand-painted posters to the Parliament lawn. On their way they heard a familiar voice call in English from a balcony above: 'Darlings, come up and have some champagne!' The voice belonged to wealthy Baroness Francesca von Habsburg, a patron of the arts and friend of the President's wife. Some of the now protesting artists had once enjoyed her hospitality and graciousness, so they stopped for a glass of champagne, which they drank from crystal glasses while rubbing shoulders with diamond-wearing members of international high society before heading out to join the other protesters banging on their pots and pans (Ásmundsson, 2009).

While the IP leadership mostly still remained defiant in the face of the protesters' demands, many SDA members were growing increasingly uneasy. It added to the complexity of the situation that the SDA's leader, Mrs Ingibjörg Gísladóttir, was still fighting brain cancer and was during these dramatic days again away, this time in a Swedish hospital. Many party members thought it would to be too rebellious to end the coalition without her. Further adding to the strained atmosphere, the leader of IP, Prime Minister Haarde, was also diagnosed with cancer and would as well need to seek treatment abroad. This unavoidably weakened the country's political leadership. The very fabric of society seemed to be coming apart at the seams. Many protesters felt guilty about revolting against sick leaders. On Gísladóttir's return, on Friday 23 January, the relevant party apparatuses of the SDA, however, passed resolutions calling for an end to the coalition. The Minister for Commerce, Björgvin Sigurðsson, resigned on Saturday while also dissolving the board of the financial supervisory authority. On Monday, Gísladóttir formally told PM Haarde that the SDA no longer supported his government and offered her resignation.

This is how it happened that the Icelandic government was the first to collapse in the global financial crisis, ousted from power in what became known as the Pots and Pans Revolution. The word 'revolution' might sound a bit of an overstatement, but given the calm temperament that usually prevails in Icelandic politics, the unfolding events represent, at the very least, a revolution in political activism. No one died, few were injured and just 12 protesters faced prosecution for violence. According to research conducted at the University of Iceland, a quarter of Reykjavik's inhabitants participated at least once in the January protests (Bernburg et al., 2010). Opinion polls indicated that two-thirds of the population generally supported the protests (Tveir þriðju, 2009).

Left-leaning landslide

Before the government's downfall, a new leadership within the Progressive Party had offered to support a minority caretaker government of the Social Democratic Alliance and the Left Green Movement (LGM) until early elections were held in the spring. This was a time of political turmoil. Having been accused of co-sponsoring the failed neoliberal model, the PP had been in ruins after leaving a longstanding coalition with the IP in 2007. By early 2009, the party had a completely new leadership, headed by novice Sigmundur Gunnlaugsson, who had been at the forefront of the InDefence group and one of the most defiant voices against the foreign pressure Iceland had faced over the Icesave accounts.

Jóhanna Sigurðardóttir, Minister of Social Affairs in the ousted government, who had belonged to the more critical left wing of the SDA, led the new minority left-wing government, which took office on 1 February. She not only became Iceland's first female PM but also the world's first openly gay head of government. Usually, the leader of the larger coalition party would head the government. SDA leader Gísladóttir had, however, already exhausted her political capital in the co-operation with the IP and was also still recovering from brain cancer. Sigurðardóttir, often accused of being a stubborn and eccentric idealist, seemed at the time to be the only politician in the country who still had credibility. A long-standing campaigner for social reform and a vigilant fighter against corruption, she was the only person whom both the LGM and the SDA – and in fact the protesting public – would accept at the time. Approaching retirement age, she had in the boom years rather been sidelined within the party. Now, however, her time had come.[2]

The situation was grave when the minority government took office. The public debt level had grown well above a year's GDP, the CDS spread on the state stubbornly remained at a staggering 820 points above Libor, and our currency had more than halved in value despite being locked behind capital controls. With massive losses in tax revenues, it would take years to bridge the vast state budget deficit. In addition, it was estimated that close to half of households were in negative equity, while the housing market remained frozen. The building industry was wiped out, car dealerships were closing and shops were empty of customers. Businesses were filing for bankruptcy in record numbers while mass lay-offs were still increasing. Many responded by moving abroad, mostly to Norway, which seemed to have well paid jobs for anyone willing to emigrate.

Though the task ahead was herculean, the left-wing parties felt quite comfortable when seeing their support surge. In the late April 2009 election, the SDA and LGM earned a healthy majority in a landslide to the left and emerged as the country's first purely left-wing majority government, headed by Sigurðardóttir, who had by now become the leader of the SDA. The IP suffered its greatest loss in history but the PP was able to prevent being wiped out by throwing out the old guard and parachuting in a completely new leadership. The Icelandic party system allows room for a variable, fifth party and sometimes also a sixth, alongside the four main parties. A new such party called the Citizens Movement, established by a group of protesters, was able to pass the 5 per cent threshold and slot into 4 of the 63 seats.

The Icesave dispute heightens

The new left-wing government contested some of the premises of the Brussels Guidelines in the amended first Icesave deal, which they claimed was unlawfully imposed by foreign forces. Under the leadership of Finance Minister Sigfússon, chairman of the LGM, the new government abandoned the multinational approach of the Brussels Guidelines and instead sent their representatives to London and The Hague to renegotiate terms. The new agreement reached with the two countries' finance ministries stipulated that Iceland would get a seven-year grace period without payments in return for agreeing to foot the part of the bill that the fallen Landsbanki's assets would not cover. The payments were to be made between 2016 and 2023. Interest was brought down to 5.5 per cent. The British and the Dutch governments had already paid out to depositors. This result, which in effect was merely a loan agreement with the foreign ministers of the Netherlands and the UK, where Iceland accepted to cover up to €4.5 billion, instantly became one of the most unpopular agreements in the history of the country. Only after its signing, however, was Iceland's name removed from the list of terrorist regimes on the UK Chancellor's website.

Parliament reluctantly accepted the agreement, but only after adding to it new preconditions, referring to Iceland's ability to pay. These the UK and the Dutch refused. A new negotiation committee was thus formed, which was able to lower the interest rate a little further. After a fierce debate, the amended agreement was accepted in Parliament on the last day of December 2009. Our new government was now also accused of caving in to foreign pressure and surrendering Icelandic interests to external forces. The government also saw a rebellion within its own ranks, with five of its MPs abstaining and the Health Minister resigning in protest.

The saga took a dramatic turn on 5 January 2010, when the President of Iceland, Ólafur Ragnar Grímsson, denied signing the law necessary to ratify the new agreement after receiving a petition of 60,000 Icelanders asking him to reject the deal. This was an exceptional move. Our elected President has traditionally been a symbolic figure rather than one with any real power. Usually, it is a mere formality for the President to sign parliamentary bills; only once before had the President rejected one. The constitution says that when the President refuses a bill, the matter shall be put to a national referendum. In the previous incident, however, the legislation was simply withdrawn by the government. The second Icesave bill thus became the first such parliamentary issue to be put to the public.

Refusing the bill was an extraordinary but a highly popular move on the part of President Grímsson, who was able to claw his way out of the doghouse that he had found himself stuck in after The Crash, when he had been accused of having been the main cheerleader of the Viking Capitalists: travelling in their private jets, extolling them in the international media and providing them with the credibility of his office. A sarcastic and humiliating depiction of the President was, for example, the running gag in the vastly popular annual New Year's Eve TV comedy programme, which almost the entire population always watches.

In early 2010, Icelanders once again found themselves in unknown waters. A quarter of the electorate had signed a petition to be put to the President asking him to veto the bill, which subsequently was refused by 90 per cent of voters. The country was in a mood of defiance. Many felt betrayed by the UK government when it had invoked the Anti-Terrorist Act – an action that ultimately drove our last bank into the ground. Icelanders therefore found the idea that they should foot the whole bill alone difficult to swallow. There was also a legal twist. The EU directive upon which the British and Dutch had based their claim was rather unclear. It stipulated only that states are obliged to set up special deposit guarantee schemes. It did not speak of a state guarantee. Many Icelanders were thus frustrated by the fact that the British and the Dutch had refused our request for an impartial court to rule on the issue.

The general perception in Iceland was thus that our government had been bullied by an overwhelming foreign power into signing an unjust agreement. It is generally accepted that our government and Parliament only accepted the initial deal to achieve other ends, rather than because they felt under obligation to pay. It was simply a necessary evil to gain access to the IMF. And then there was the cost. €4.5 billon might have seemed a small figure by UK standards but this was almost half our GDP. Divided by Iceland's small population, the bill amounted to more than €12,000 per head, or just under €50,000 per household. If Landsbanki's assets deteriorated any further, this would place a devastating burden on an already debt-ridden population.

The rhetoric some UK leaders were using in the dispute was a further source of frustration. During Prime Minister's questions in the House of Commons on 6 May 2009, PM Gordon Brown said that the Icelandic authorities were responsible for the loss of the cancer charity Christie's in Manchester and claimed to be in discussion with the IMF on how Iceland would repay the losses it was responsible for. Brown went on to wash his hands of the matter and repeatedly said that the UK was not the regulatory authority. This was, however, not true. Christie's business was with Kaupthing's Singer & Friedlander, a UK-based bank that was regulated by the British FSA and therefore covered by the UK depositor protection scheme. This was clearly stated in the House of Commons Treasury Committee report (2009) published in April 2009. Not only was Brown's statement false but in fact the opposite could be argued. By killing off Kaupthing, the Labour government was itself partly to blame for the troubles Christie's was facing. Many felt that in attributing blame to Iceland Brown was once again trying to save his own political skin: now, with regard to the troubles of the cancer charity in Manchester, which he himself was partly responsible for. Leading up to the referendum this sort of rhetoric in the UK only fuelled the No camp in Iceland.

In addition to the wide-ranging general feeling of frustration, the appearance of leniency towards the British and Dutch spurred a new wave of protest in mid-2010, which heightened when Parliament resumed in the early autumn, to find thousands of protesters surrounding the building, once again. Flags symbolizing Iceland's independence could now be seen flying high in front of the Parliament building. Amongst them were blue EU flags on which a red no-entry sign had been painted right across the yellow stars.

After twice going back on signed agreements, the government found it difficult to go knocking on doors in London and The Hague asking to renegotiate the deal once again. Headed by a hired American negotiator, our new team was nevertheless in the end able to bring the interest rate down to 3 per cent. This time, a large majority emerged in Parliament when the IP joined ranks with the government in backing the new deal. Only the Progressive Party still opposed any agreement. Yet, to the surprise of most, President Grímsson also refused the third bill.[3] In a second referendum, on 9 April 2011, the new agreement was refused by a two-thirds majority, illustrating a clear division between Parliament and the public. Now, there was no longer anything to negotiate. The case was sent to the EFTA Court, where the EU was backing the claim of the UK and the Netherlands against Iceland. Finally, on 28 January 2013, the court ruled in favour of Iceland, which was vindicated of any wrongdoing in its handling of the Icesave deposits (Judgment of the Court, 2013).

Post-crisis discourse

To understand the sentiments that arose when Icelanders felt themselves under siege by foreign forces, it is helpful to analyse the discourse used. At once, the dispute with the British and Dutch governments fell into familiar trenches of nationalistic rhetoric. Tapping into this rhetoric, prominent figures claimed that Iceland was a victim of vicious foreigners who had conspired to bring Iceland to its knees. Commentators explained how we had come under siege by the 'central banks of the US, UK, Holland, Europe, Luxembourg and the Nordic states, which joined hands to lock us in while the British FME launched an attack on Landsbanki' (Gunnarsson, 2009). Iceland was seen as the victim of this international conspiracy led by the EU and some of its Member

States to force the country into the hands of the IMF – where the British and Dutch were waiting to force Iceland to agree to an unjust deal on the Icesave accounts. Many parliamentarians echoed this notion of a European-led conspiracy and some said they would not accept anyone from the Nordic states as a mediator between Iceland and the British and Dutch governments, as they had aligned with the EU against Iceland (Hreyfingin, 2010). When the amended agreement was drafted in June 2009, the government was instantly accused of high treason by the opposition and pundits.[4] PP leader Mr Sigmundur Gunnlaugsson, who was to replace Mrs Jóhanna Sigurðardóttir as PM in spring 2013, accused her of 'humiliating the nation' by 'forcing her nation to pay the Icesave debt burden'[5]. Instead of protecting the nation, he claimed, the government was working on behalf of the British and the Dutch to attack Iceland. When he became Prime Minister himself, Gunnlaugsson used the PM's traditional celebratory address on Iceland's national day, 17 June, to remind us that the EU had participated in the dispute in an illegal attempt to coerce Icelanders to accept enormous burdens (Gunnlaugsson, 2013).

When the result of the first referendum became clear, the President was quick to exploit Iceland's wish to be recognized as an equal in the modern international system. He explained how the referendum on Icesave would have an impact on a global scale. Referring – like historian Jónsson Aðils at the turn of the century – to ancient Athens and the US constitutional convention in Philadelphia, he insisted not only that the vote mattered for Icelanders but that it 'had changed people's views around the world on the way that it was possible to develop democracy and bring direct power to the people in this new century.' He said that all around the world people were asking why they had not got the rights Icelanders enjoyed (Grímsson, 2010).

The Icesave dispute was directly linked with the debate on EU membership. After explaining how the EU had forced Iceland to agree to an unjust deal, one parliamentarian (IP) said it was strange that any Icelander would like 'to join this club that is beating on us'[6] Another (LGM) was offended by the fact that Iceland was applying for membership at the same time as the big countries in the EU were 'shamelessly forcing a nation like ours to surrender to their interests'[7]. Associated with the country's historical enemies, the European Union was repeatedly referred to as a club of former colonizers – contrary to Iceland, which had been colonized by one of its members, Denmark. An MP for the Citizens' Movement explained: 'Iceland is an old colony and we are negotiating with historical colonizers who have not protected their colonies in the past. Are we going to surrender to becoming their colony?'[8].

Similarly, the new IP leader, Bjarni Benediktsson, referred to the most historically important quote of Iceland's independence struggle: 'We all protest.' The main leader of the independence struggle, Jón Sigurðsson, had voiced those words when protesting against the Danish authority after it had unilaterally ended Iceland's Constitutional Assembly in 1851. Benediktsson said that Iceland should now send the UK the same message[9]. Another example is found on the blog of the anti-EU 'Organization for Research on the European Union, and on its Relations to Iceland', when it emphasized that the most powerful EU members – at least ten of the then EU-27 (amounting to two-thirds of the vote within the Council) – were former colonizers, whom Iceland should stay away from (Tíu aflóga, 2012).

After a long-drawn out dispute, the Icesave agreements appeared to have become the most unpopular since the Old Treaty with Norway in 1262, when according to the national myth Iceland's economy started to deteriorate after it had fallen under foreign rule and entered into a period of humiliation by losing its independence.

The change in the national rhetoric, from the superiority discourse of the boom years discussed in a previous chapter to the idea of being under siege by ill-willed foreigners after The Crash of 2008, was quite rapid. On the surface it might even seem that those two ideas were in contradiction. However, when analysing the harsh nationalistic rhetoric of the Icesave debate, it can be seen that it had the same origin as the rhetoric on the Icelandic economic miracle heard in the first decade of the new millennium: Iceland's postcolonial national identity. The core of both ideas is found in the national myth created during the independent struggle in the 19th century, written down by Jón Jónsson Aðils at the beginning of the 20th century and kept alive and nourished by politicians of all ranks throughout the decades and then put into new perspectives by the likes of President Ólafur Ragnar Grímsson. As Jón Jónsson Aðils did more than a century ago when describing the old settlement society, President Grímsson linked modern Iceland with ancient Greece.

Conclusion

With the country in financial ruin and a bleak outlook for the future, the public took to the streets in protest. This was a time of great economic upheaval and political turmoil. When the British and the Dutch increased the pressure, the International Monetary Fund was called in to stabilize the economy and co-funded a loan package together with the Nordic and Polish governments. The suffocating feeling of surrendering to foreign forces in the Icesave dispute further added to public frustration. The government thus stood accused of not only failing to protect our economic well-being but also of caving in to foreign oppression, which was in direct violation of our postcolonial national identity.

Amid a series of protests, which became known as the Pots and Pans Revolution, the IP/SDA coalition government fell in January 2009 and was replaced by a fragile left-wing caretaker coalition. The protest gradually gained momentum and grew into flood of events, which through theatrical, musical and rhetorical means developed their own identifying aesthetics. A left-leaning landslide in the ensuing election saw the minority government win a healthy majority. Though the government faced astronomical difficulties in restructuring the collapsed economy, it was its handling of the Icesave issue that first undermined its credibility in the eyes of the voters.

An interesting shift in public opinion occurred after the President refused the government's proposed solution. The President had stood accused of having become a cheerleader for the Viking Capitalists in the boom years while most government ministers were thought to have been free of any such corruption. The table turned in the wake of the referendum. The President, who had lost credibility in the eyes of the public and had by end of 2009 all but been laughed out of office, suddenly became the country's principal hero. The leaders of the new left-wing government were then in their turn accused of sacrificing Icelandic interests while surrendering to the will of foreign forces. The public thus not only revolted against the IP/SDA government which collapsed during the Pots and Pans Revolution but also turned in a similar way against the new left-wing government when they believed it was not holding its ground against foreign pressure.

When studying the post-crisis discourse, we see Iceland's postcolonial identity emerging through the domestic language game, with an emphasis on formal sovereignty, which insulated Iceland against submission to foreign authority. This is what characterizes the rhetorical manoeuvring: both insisting on formal sovereignty and striving for external recognition as being an equal partner with its neighbours. Accordingly, the rhetoric which clearly indicates the importance of this postcolonial national identity myth travelled through all political shifts, historical turns and changing environments, taking on different forms in different times, as it can be utilized for different purposes. The President's comment after the Icesave referendum in 2010 is a good example on how the nationalistic discourse of the boom years had survived The Crash of 2008.

In the two final chapters I will examine Iceland's economic recovery and political reform.

8
Rising from the Ruins – A Fragile Economic Recovery

Iceland suffered a more brutal blow to its economy in the international financial crisis than perhaps any other nation. The small island was severely hit in autumn 2008, when 90 per cent of its financial system, including its three main banks, collapsed. The tiny currency lost more than half its pre-crisis value, inflation escalated and unemployment rose rapidly, with an avalanche of bankruptcies in its wake. While government expenditure surged, the state's revenues were evaporating. The economy contracted by almost 13 per cent from its peak in late 2007 while both public and private debt grew way beyond sustainable levels. The country was financially devastated.

The severity of the crisis called for extraordinary measures. While neighbouring states were frantically bailing out banks by pumping capital into the system and issuing public guarantees to private banks, Iceland was not able to follow suit. In late September 2008, Ireland, for example, provided a blanket guarantee for all liabilities of banks domiciled in Eire. This was only deemed credible because of backing from the ECB – and thus also from Germany. Without access to enough foreign currency to prevent its big banks, by then worth nine times GDP, from collapsing, the Icelandic state had no other option than to take them into administration. This approach contrasts with responses elsewhere and is thus a unique case in this crisis.

When new domestic banks were established out of the ruins of the fallen ones, most of the old banks' liabilities fell on the shoulders of foreign creditors. Though this was indeed contrary to responses in most neighbouring states, where the state emptied its coffers and sent a huge bill to future taxpayers, the public cost of the Icelandic banking collapse was also severe. To make this grave economic situation worse, foreign investors holding glacier bonds amounting to 40 per cent of GDP, denominated in króna, were looking to escape the country, which would devastate the króna even further. Introducing capital controls was thus deemed necessary, as well as locking in the foreign creditors when the fallen banks were being wound up and pressure on the króna further increased.

When the fierce dispute with the Dutch and the British over the Icesave deposit accounts was temporarily calmed in November 2008, the IMF arrived in Reykjavik with a handsome rescue package. In order to stabilize the currency further, the interest rate was hiked to 18 per cent. In a highly unorthodox move in relation to its previous positions elsewhere, the fund supported extensive capital controls and allowed the left-wing government to implement its policy of mixed measures to deal with the crisis rather than forcing through strict austerity, which for example was the case in the PIIGS – Portugal, Ireland, Italy, Greece and Spain.

The sharp concentration of the economy finally stopped in late 2010, with modest growth in 2012 and 2013. The fisheries still generated healthy foreign income. In June 2011, Iceland re-entered capital markets with the successfully auction of $1 billion worth of bonds at a premium below that offered by many crisis-ridden states. Subsequently, rating agencies lifted Iceland again from junk bond status to investment level. Many workers who had lost their jobs in the crisis, left the country, most of them heading to Norway. In early 2013, the flow reversed as more people came back than left. A further vital contribution to the recovery was that, despite the financial sector's devastation, many of our international production companies, which had also grown rapidly during the boom years, were able to survive the turmoil and generate significant foreign currency income.

In this chapter I will analyse Iceland's fragile economic recovery. The next chapter deals with strives for accompanying political reform.

The IMF emergency programme

Many measures had been taken during and immediately after The Crash to insulate the state from excessive amounts of bad debt when the banks fell and to minimize socialization of private sector losses. However, without the IMF rescue package the state was almost sure to default on its obligations, which might have locked us out of international markets for years (Guðmundsson, 2013). To the surprise of many Icelanders, the Dutch and the British still enjoyed the full backing in the Icesave debacle of our neighbours in the European community. Iceland had been frozen out in terms of diplomatic relations. Suffering the deepest crisis in its postwar history, the country was already sucked dry of foreign cash when the IMF finally opened its doors in November 2008, after we had, under coercion, finally agreed to guarantee the Icesave deposits. The emergency programme provided financing amounting to $5.1 billion in total. $2.1 billion came from the IMF's coffers. The rest was from the Nordic states and Poland.

The seriousness of the situation was such that the IMF Mission Chief to Iceland, Paul Thomsen, described it as unprecedented. Three years later, when Iceland had successfully completed the programme, he explained how during The Crash Iceland had suffered a 'near-death experience' (Thomsen, 2011).

Renewed access to foreign currency allowed us to build credible foreign currency reserves. The flipside, however, was that taking on foreign loans also makes it difficult to re-enter international capital markets. The pressure on the króna was such that comprehensive capital controls were viewed as a key element of the programme. Had the carry traders and creditors of the fallen banks been allowed to leave, the currency would surely have tanked. This solution of implementing capital controls was a vital break from the IMF's traditional practice. Usually, the fund insisted on the free flow of capital and was adamant in pushing through strict austerity measures. Iceland thus saw a softer side of the IMF than others had previously faced. For the most part, rather than forcing through its traditional neoliberal one-size-fits-all design, the fund agreed to our government's own economic programme. Indeed, the IMF agreed to use a greater variety of economic tools than was usually found in its toolkit. It can be argued that we were at this time in a favourable position, as the IMF was eagerly shopping for a success story after years of harsh criticism. Three main goals were set: stabilization of the exchange rate, fiscal sustainability and reconstruction of the financial sector (Guðmundsson, 2013).

Bank restructuring

During the crisis, countries on both sides of the Atlantic saw banks fail, but most were bailed out in one way or another by their respective governments – though some were allowed to default. What set Iceland worlds apart from the others was that the country's entire oversized financial system collapsed virtually in one go: the three big banks in October 2008 and most of the large investment companies in the following months.

Small domestic banks were raised on the ruins of the fallen cross-border ones. Arion Bank was created out of Kaupthing, Glitnir's domestic operations were renamed Íslandsbanki and the old Landsbanki simply became the new Landsbanki. Local deposits were moved to the new entities, as were domestic loans, which were transferred at a discount price – the write-off on average was around 50 per cent. This, though, only accounted for about a tenth of the old banks' bloated balance sheets. In line with the 6 October emergency law, the rest, mainly international operations, was put into administration. It was then the task of court-appointed returning committees to wind up the assets of the fallen banks, most of which lay outside Iceland. The old banks were thus in effect turned into asset management firms with the primary aim of returning to creditors as much value as possible from their foreign assets. The new banks were right from the beginning quite well funded. With also cash instalments from the government they were started off with equity amounting to around 13 per cent of GDP. Their combined balance sheet was roughly twice GDP, down from nine times before The Crash (Alþingi, 2011).

It should be stressed that even though Iceland was able to cut off most of the banks' liabilities abroad, it still had to foot a large bill. According to an OECD calculation, Iceland suffered the second-greatest direct fiscal cost of all OECD states in this crisis, amounting to 20 per cent of GDP. Only Ireland had to shoulder more per-capita cost. Ireland in fact separated completely from the pack, with a spectacular direct cost of almost half its GDP. In comparison, the cost to the UK was well below 10 per cent (OECD, 2011). In the end, the cost of the crisis was such that public debt in Iceland rose from below 30 per cent of GDP in 2007 to over 100 per cent of GDP in 2010. One of the largest one-off bills stemmed from the bankruptcy of the Central Bank, amounting to 13 per cent of GDP – which is amongst the many special Icelandic features of this crisis (Byrne & Þorsteinsson, 2012).

Controlling stakes in two of the three new banks, Arion Bank and Íslandsbanki, were handed over to creditors, but Landsbanki was kept in public ownership – partly because of the trouble over the Icesave deposits. The new owners of Arion and Íslandsbanki were mostly foreign hedge funds, which had acquired the bonds at rock bottom prices in the secondary market after The Crash. Most of them were looking to quickly get out for as wide a margin as possible.

Iceland's relations with its neighbours for the most part normalized when the IMF arrived in Reykjavik. There were, however, still examples of foreign authorities exploiting the volatile situation to squeeze out assets. One such case is found in events around the Danish FIH Bank.

Our Central Bank had come into possession of the Danish investment bank when Kaupthing collapsed. In early 2011, the Danish financial supervisory authority suddenly called for more cash to insure its operation, thus tightened the thumbscrews and in effect forced the sale of the bank, threatening otherwise to take it into receivership – rendering its shares worthless. Iceland's Central Bank had in October 2008 taken the bank as collateral against a €500 million emergency loan to Kaupthing just a day before its collapse. In the sale pressed by the Danish FSA only €255 million was paid out, with up to twice that amount due in 2015, depending on the performance of the bank up to that point. Poor performance of the bank in that period would mean that the CB had lost most of its worth (Lán Seðlabankans, 2012).

Welfare-orientated recovery

The crisis blew a black hole into the state's coffers. A quarter of the state's revenues evaporated with the collapse of the banks, while public expenditure shot up, along with costs. The government thus had to bridge an impossible gap. Its focus was on protecting the Nordic welfare model, thus shielding the lowest income group while shuffling costs onto the upper classes. Against its previous practices, the IMF agreed to our left-wing government's proposal to tackle the budget deficit over time and through mixed measures instead of implementing strict austerity. The $5.1 billion currency loan provided a necessary buffer. Public services were, however, still cut significantly three years in a row while taxes were gradually raised to just below 36 per cent of GDP in almost a hundred different changes to the tax code.

While taxes on higher-income groups were significantly increased, the tax burden on the lower strata was brought down even further. Several additional measures were introduced mainly to cushion the lowest income groups. Those on lower salaries, for example, were shielded from nominal wage cuts. Redistribution mechanisms such as benefits and interest subsidies were also strengthened and welfare measures further geared towards the lowest level. From 2008 to 2010, the average disposable income of households fell by 27 per cent. In the lowest income group, however, the fall was only 9 per cent, at the middle level it was 14 per cent, while the highest income group suffered a full 38 per cent drop (for more, see Ólafsson & Kristjánsson, 2012). This was significantly different from the strict austerity measures in many other countries. In Ireland, for example, the lower income level was shouldering even more of the burden than the upper level.

Ranking 14th out of the 34 OECD countries, Iceland still had a generally lower tax level than the other Nordic states (Þorláksson, 2013). Significant new fees on fishing quotas were also introduced (though later abolished again by the right-of-centre government that took power in mid-2013). The budget deficit, which had risen to 13.5 per cent of GDP in 2009, was reduced to 2.5 per cent by 2011, when the IMF programme ended, finally reaching small primary budget surplus in 2012. For 2014, six years after The Crash, the budget was more or less balanced.

Production base intact

Our tiny currency, the króna, also factored significantly into both the build-up to the crisis and then also the apparent recovery in the aftermath. An independent currency exaggerates economic cycles at both ends: it increases the risk of collapse but also helps in turning the economy around after a collapse. The smallest currency in the world on free float, the ISK lost half its value in 2008, the crisis year. With most loans linked either to inflation or to foreign currency, the sharp devaluation led to spiked debt and rocketing prices, resulting in a much higher cost of living.

On the other side of that equation, however, the devalued currency also provided sudden stimulus to the export industry. The prolonged double-digit current account deficit rapidly reversed and grew into a surplus, in the region of 3 to 4 per cent a year. This is especially important, as the root of Iceland's relatively rapid recovery is to be found in the fact that the production base remained intact.

With the financial sector gone, we were able to fall back on fishing, which still generated significant income in foreign currency, amounting to a yearly export value of more than €5,000 per inhabitant (see Íslandsbanki, 2012). Furthermore, many of our main international production companies, which had also grown rapidly during the boom years, survived the storm and were in the wake of the crisis able to bring foreign income into cash-thirsty Iceland. Among them were food processing company Marel and prepared food producer Bakkavör, as well as the many fish production companies. Adding to the pool we can also count world-leading orthopaedics producer Össur and pharmaceutical manufacturer Actavis.

The robust production power found in Iceland's fishing grounds and the strength of these production companies is really what kept Iceland afloat. There is, though, a limit to further growth, as fishing and aluminium production, which collectively account for 80 per cent of

Iceland's merchandize exports, both face natural capacity constraints. These limitations are, however, not on the IT industry or tourism, which also have flourished.

Debt restructuring

Several measures were taken to deal with the unsustainable debt burden many households faced after the collapse of the currency. Parliament passed numerous laws increasing the rights of debtors, for example, making it more difficult to evict people from their homes and repossesses of assets. A new institution, the Debtors' Ombudsman, was established to protect the interests of borrowers against their creditors, with powers to force through debt reduction. Real house prices had dropped by 30 per cent. Loans exceeding the value of the property were brought down to 110 per cent of market value. The tax system was also used to repay some of the interest on housing loans. Many measures were taken to alleviate pressure on households, including allowing early pension withdrawals.

Foreign currency loans, which had shot up with the collapse of the króna, were suffocating many households. The pressure was somewhat alleviated in mid-2009 when the Supreme Court ruled many of them unlawful. As it turned out, linking housing and consumer loans to a foreign exchange index, in the way that the banks had formulated many of them, was in violation of Icelandic laws on the structure of loan agreements. This cut much of the short-term car loan debt from many debt-ridden households. Furthermore, a large fraction of the foreign currency exposure was in holding companies that had already defaulted and was cut off (Halldórsson & Zoega, 2010).

Collectively, these examples of debt restructuring and write-offs brought the country's debt level down significantly. They were mostly provided to businesses that had grown debts far beyond sustainable levels. Ordinary households, however, also significantly benefitted from the measures. Household debt dropped from 132 per cent of GDP in 2009 to around 100 per cent in early 2013. One criticism prevailed, however: that the Viking Capitalists and reckless borrowers were being rewarded with most of these write-offs, thus undermining the legitimacy of the efforts. The ordinary public gradually grew frustrated at always being asked to foot the bill for other people's recklessness.

The turn-around of the economy started in late 2010 and continued in 2011. In June of that year, for example, Iceland was able to re-access international markets by selling $1 billion worth of five-year bonds at

3.2 per cent above Libor, which was well below the premium many other crisis-ridden states had to pay. In May 2012, another $1 billion was raised on ten-year bonds. Part of the proceeds was used to repay more than half the IMF loan provided by the Nordics and Poland well before its maturity. Predictions that Iceland would for decades be locked out of international markets because of not bailing out its banks and for not agreeing to guarantee Icesave were thus proven wrong.

To help alleviate currency trade pressure, the Central Bank regularly held foreign exchange auctions at which it bought currency for krónas at a favourable rate for investors, to be used for long-term domestic investment. Concurrently with these auctions, foreign investors were invited to sell ISK at a lower price in exchange for foreign currency. In these cross-actions the Central Bank aimed to bring together actors interested in long-term investment in Iceland and investors looking to unwind their króna position, without destabilizing the exchange rate. Within these measures were also bond swaps in which the Central Bank issued long-term liabilities in foreign currency for Icelandic assets (Ministry of Finance and Economic Affairs, 2013).

Rising from the ruins

Only the Baltic three and Ireland suffered greater economic contraction than Iceland. Iceland, however, topped the list of crisis-ridden states in terms of the fall in purchasing power of disposable income (Ólafsson & Kristjánsson, 2012). After three years of sharp contraction, the economy started to grow again in late 2010 and expanded by 2.6 per cent in 2011 and by 2.4 per cent in 2012. The output gap, which had averaged around 3 per cent a year after the crisis, was essentially closed (International Monetary Fund, 2012). The growth, which however was set to slow again in 2013, was mostly driven by domestic demand: private consumption and investment, which after a sharp contraction grew again, in addition to increased exports. Essentially, per-capita GDP and disposable income were set to be similar in 2013 to their 2005 levels (Ministry of Finance and Economic Affairs, 2013).

The prolonged trade deficit in the boom years had also reversed to a surplus after The Crash, averaging in the region of 6 to 7 per cent a year. Fiscal consolidation was well on track. Measured from the deficit peak at roughly 13 per cent in 2010 to the closure of the gap in late 2012, Iceland had outpaced all other developed economies in terms of fiscal consolidation (Fitch Ratings, 2013), including Greece, where the consolidation was roughly 10 per cent. The domestic banking sector had furthermore been quite successfully rebuilt. The new banks were well liquated, fully capitalized and profitable. After extensive write-offs and loan restructuring, non-performing loans had been reduced from 18 per cent high in 2010 to well below 10 per cent.

In August 2011, Iceland completed the IMF programme when the fund approved its final loan. The fund's representative, Nemat Shafik, was pleased with the success of the 33-month rescue mission, concluding that strong policy implementation had ensured that key objectives were met, that public finances were on a sustainable path and the exchange rate had been stabilized and that the financial sector been restructured (quoted in International Monetary Fund, 2011).

Iceland was the first developed country to be downgraded leading up to the crisis, starting in 2006. In the wake of The Crash, the country was relegated to the junk bond category. Rating rehabilitation began in May 2011, and Iceland was back to investment level in early 2012. In February 2013, Fitch Ratings and Moody's upgraded us further while many other countries were still on a downward trajectory – like the UK, which lost its triple-A rating. Fitch concluded that the new rating reflected Iceland's 'impressive progress in its recovery from the financial crisis of 2008–2009' (Fitch Ratings, 2013). Moody's concluded that with the help of the EFTA Court ruling in favour of Iceland over the Icesave dispute, which had freed it from potentially large costs, the Icelandic economy had also clearly emerged from crisis-induced recession and was now expanding at a reasonable pace. The key factor supporting the rating was, however, Moody's view that 'the Icelandic authorities are able and willing to pursue economic policies that allow the country to return to a sustainable economic, fiscal and external position within a reasonable period of time' (Moody's, 2013).

The Fitch report further stated that the economy was growing, that fiscal consolidation remained on track and public debt was falling and, vitally, that the resolution of Icesave had 'removed a material contingent liability for public finances and brought normalization with external creditors' (Fitch Ratings, 2013). In the report, Iceland was viewed less at risk of slipping back into recession than some troubled Eurozone countries.

Both public and private debt had slowly but surely declined since shooting up after the crisis hit. This too was partly because of debt restructuring and write-offs. The net international investment position reversed after the Crash, rising to a negative level of 568 per cent by end of 2011. This position was, however, distorted by the impact of the continuing wind-up proceedings of the fallen cross-border banks. The failed banks amounted to three-quarters of Iceland's external debt, which would evaporate from the books when the wind-up was completed. With the completion of the winding-up process, Iceland's external debt was set to reduce to a sustainable level. Landsbanki was, for example, expected to return all primary debt, including the entire principal of the Icesave accounts. Already in early 2013, more than half of the Icesave claims had been paid to the British and Dutch governments. Despite the EFTA Court ruling, the rest was to follow as the winding-up progressed. This was because of much better return out of the fallen banks than had been expected.

Sovereign debt was also on a downward trajectory. Since peaking way above a year's GDP in 2010, public debt had dropped below the 100 per cent mark. Holding the equivalent of more than 30 per cent of GDP in deposits at the Central Bank, the government was also highly liquid. This was enough to reduce net public debt to around 65 per cent, compared with roughly 80 per cent in Spain and almost 110 per cent in Ireland. This positive outlook was mirrored in a lower CDS spread; in 2013 five-year Treasury bonds carried only 1.7 per cent, the lowest rate since mid-2008 (Central Bank of Iceland, 2013).

Another indication of a gradual rising from the ruins was found in the fact that emigration had stopped. Unemployment had peaked at over 9 per cent in 2010, up from only 1 per cent in the boom years. The government then instigated several measures to create jobs and promote higher work market participation, for example subsidizing salaries for companies hiring from the unemployment registry. By early 2013, unemployment had fallen below 5 per cent, for the first time since The Crash. The labour marked proved quite flexible. It helped to alleviate the pressure caused by many workers leaving the country, mostly to Norway. With a falling unemployment rate, the migration flow reversed in early 2013. By international standards, the activity rate in Iceland was high, above 80 per cent in 2013, averaging 44.1 hours per week.

Inflation, which always seems to strain our economy, remained stubbornly high in the wake of the crisis, finally dropping below 4 per cent in early 2013, much later than expected. Despite prolonged difficulties in bringing inflation down, real wages had risen. Even the stock market, which had been wiped out in The Crash, was already in 2012 starting to recover. The index climbed 11 per cent in 2012, with an even sharper rise in early 2013 before calming again. In line with the increasing purchasing power of disposable income, property prices were also on the rise. For the first time since the crisis hit, building cranes could again be seen in Reykjavik in 2013.

In the wake of the crisis, Iceland also enjoyed a vital windfall in the form of a massive influx of tourists, eventually amounting to almost three times the population. Iceland became a fantastically popular tourist destination after The Crash. The drop in value of the currency certainly made the country cheaper but more vital was the unprecedented media attention during The Crash, which put Iceland on the tourist map. When the Eyjafjallajökull volcano erupted a couple of years later, shutting down European airspace for a full week as it spewed volcanic ash over the entire continent, the attention of the world was back. At first we were afraid that these devastating events would destroy the rest of our already tarnished reputation, but then we saw that they only made more people interested in travelling to Iceland. Their euros, pounds and dollars were very welcome.

By applying mixed measures rather than implementing strict austerity, the government was able to prevent rising inequality, as had occurred in many European countries and in America. In fact, inequality diminished in Iceland over the course of the crisis (Ólafsson & Kristjánsson, 2012). Iceland's relatively rapid recovery compared with, for example Ireland, thus perhaps supported Joseph Stiglitz's claim that surging inequality was stifling recovery in America (Stiglitz, 2013).

Challenges ahead

When taking stock five years into the Credit Crunch, Iceland in many ways showed remarkable progress. Though recovery was taking root, however, we still faced many grave challenges. The capital controls had certainly helped to cushion us from the Eurozone crisis, but they had also seriously distorted the domestic economy, for example promoting a seemingly unstable local asset price bubble. The controls also discouraged much-needed foreign investment, to the point of prolonged difficulties. Over time, the side effects of capital controls can easily become worse than the sickness they were meant to cure. Here, the national postcolonial identity was also at play. Most interest for foreign direct investment was in the field of energy. Our government had, though, in line with the nationwide suspicion of foreign investors, been hesitant in allowing external investment in land and in the energy sector. Examples of such suspicion were the difficulties the Canadian energy company Magma Energy faced when refused investment in a natural heat energy company and when Chinese investor Huang Nubo was refused permission to buy a piece of privately held but mostly deserted land in the north of Iceland where he wanted to build a tourist resort. Criticisms of these planned investments aside, it was interesting in both instance that the main objection in the public discussion revolved around the foreign ownership aspect rather than whether operations like these should be privately owned or not.

Iceland's main economic challenge was tackling the currency issue. An independent króna proved to have procyclical effects. Massive amounts of krónas looking to emigrate put immense pressure on the exchange rate, which had already dropped by more than half. Solving the balance of payments problem, primarily the so-called *overhang*, was pressing. The overhang consisted of the trapped carry trade and foreign-held króna assets of the fallen banks. In all, this amounted to more than €5 billion or around half the annual economy (Áskorun, 2013). Though a third of liquid assets in króna held by non-residents, mainly from the carry trade, had by 2013 been eased out of the system through the Central Bank's auction channels, krónas amounting to 23 per cent of GDP were still trapped (Fitch Ratings, 2013). This was excluding the króna assets of the creditors of the old banks that still were to be liquated in the winding-up procedures. Allowing these krónas to leave could easily lead to another currency crisis. There was thus still a pressing need to control liquid offshore krónas, for example by anchoring them to longer maturity or releasing them at a reduced price.

Iceland was not a fully fledged currency control regime, but rather a capital control regime that limited certain classified capital transactions (Ministry of Finance and Economic Affairs, 2013). These controls still made it difficult for many cross-border companies in Iceland to grow properly. One of the country's largest IT companies, the much celebrated internet gaming developer CCP, was amongst those that were, as a result, contemplating moving their headquarters abroad (Scrutton, 2013).

The government had a strategy of gradually lifting the capital controls, conditioned on the rate of the currency holding. It was in our interest to securely evacuate these assets without devaluing the króna too much. The creditors' main interest, on the other hand, was to gain access to their foreign currency assets linked to the fallen banks abroad. Under Icelandic law these assets could be paid out in krónas and thus held within the controlled currency regime. This is something most creditors wanted to avoid. Negotiation were thus under way to allow the krónas to be exchanged for foreign currency and leave cross the controls over a prolonged period for significantly reduced value in exchange for liquidating the external assets in foreign currency. The more their value was reduced in terms of foreign currency, the faster the controls could be lifted. The Central Bank's governor hinted at around a 75 per cent discount on the króna when leaving (quoted in Ægisson, 2013).

Solving the overhang, however, would not automatically allow the lifting capital controls – when Iceland was locked behind capital controls for 63 years, between 1931 and 1994, there was no overhang problem. In fact, there is a vicious cycle here, as the controls themselves can distort the economy to the extent that it is no longer fit for the free flow of capital.

Furthermore, the general outlook for Iceland's recovery was linked to economic development in Europe, as three-quarters of our exports were to the continent, 60 per cent of which went to the Eurozone.

Conclusion

After experiencing one of the most profound financial crises a developed country has suffered, Iceland soon began to show signs of an impressive recovery. The macro economy had stabilized, which perhaps was best evidenced by the fact that there was no longer much talk of the sovereign defaulting. Marginal growth, which started in the second quarter of 2010, was in 2013 set to continue, but on a lower pace. Fiscal consolidation was on track and public debt had been on a steady downward trajectory since The Crash. Furthermore, the domestic financial system was quite well funded and resolution of the Icesave dispute in early 2013 normalized relations with external creditors and removed potential further contingent liabilities for the state. Very much contrary to predictions when the crisis hit in 2008, it can thus be concluded that Iceland had performed better than for example the Eurozone countries.

The commonly held prediction that Iceland would suffer devastating damage to its reputation by not bailing out its banks and by not covering Icesave with interests was also proved utterly wrong. The contrary can actually be argued, as in the wake of the crisis Iceland was praised in the international media for going against the current and being the only country refusing to dump the private debts of the banking system onto taxpayers' shoulders. Though this picture is not entirely accurate, as has been established here, this positive change in media attitudes to Iceland served the economy well.

Most importantly, however, many structural aspects in the economy remained favourable. The country's strong production base was still intact as well as the countries highly lucrative natural resources. Many of our main international production companies had survived the storm and were able to generate much needed foreign revenues. In addition, Iceland had a robust, young, well educated population and strong industrial infrastructure. We were thus ready and able to take on a greater burden and move faster through the crisis than many less flexible and older populations.

The outlook was thus rather positive, but fragile. There were still significant systemic risks to overcome. The debt burden of households and small businesses was still much too high. The pressure on the exchange rate was such that lifting capital controls was not in sight, which could result in prolonged difficulties, as capital controls gradually distort set the set-up of the domestic economy and, thus, create strong groups with interests in keeping them in place. A comprehensive agreement with creditors to leave over a long enough period and at a low enough exit rate also needed to be completed. And though most economists did agree that the króna was too small and vulnerable to be set on completely free flow again, there was still no consensus domestically on a future monetary policy. This was perhaps the greatest systemic flaw to overcome before a more sustainable recovery could be reached.

In addition to alleviating pressure on the króna and solving the capital control problem, the main challenges were low growth, uncertainty as to the health of the fragile new financial sector, low investment and ongoing inflationary pressure. In addition to these challenges, prolonged difficulties in the Eurozone diminished the room for further growth in Iceland. However, though the recovery remained fragile, the outlook was for continued expansion, declining inflation and a strengthened external position.

9
Reconstituting Iceland – and the New Critical Order

The Crash of 2008 not only was a severe financial crisis but also served a devastating blow to Icelandic politics. Key government institutions stood accused of having sponsored the rise and collapse of the failed neoliberal model. This was a crisis of capitalism, which opened new opportunities for political reform in addition to the economic recovery discussed in previous chapter. In the wake of the crisis and the following Pots and Pans Revolution, many initiatives were embarked upon to not only resurrect the failed model but also to implement more permanent changes to the political system. There was a clear popular call for political reform; a *New Iceland* was to emerge from the ruins. Many non-governmental groupings were founded, and they deliberated and promoted different avenues out of the crisis. Ordinary people not only took to the streets in protest in the wake of The Crash but also engaged much more actively than before in public discussion – in the mainstream media as well on blogs and through social media outlets. Many called for the establishment of Iceland's Second Republic or, in data lingo, the updating of the system to Iceland 2.0.

Many measures were taken in the aftermath of The Crash, which collectively had the aim of widespread political reform. Parliament appointed a Special Investigation Commission – a 'truth committee' – to analyse the events leading up to The Crash and estimate whether government ministers had been at fault. The government established a Special Prosecutor, who was to investigate criminal activity in the financial sector leading up to The Crash. In order to regain access to international markets, the government agreed to cover the Icesave deposits and applied for EU membership, mainly to underpin its monetary policy by adopting the euro. Jointly these moves were aimed at securing Iceland's economic framework for the future. The political party system was also being challenged not only by widespread leadership renewal within the established parties but also by a flood of new parties emerging; for example, the Best Party, led by a well known comedian, took control of the capital city and becoming Mayor of Reykjavik in 2010. Calling for an extraordinary election for a Constitutional Assembly, which was to write a new constitution, was perhaps the most ambitious of these efforts for political reform.

However, as I will explain in this chapter, even as economic recovery was taking root, as discussed in the previous chapter, most of these initiatives for significant political reform were caught in what can be described as a *new critical order*, which took hold in post-crisis Iceland and, in effect, contradicted the many reparative moves.

Political accountability

The report of the Parliament-appointed Special Investigation Commission (SIC), published in 2010, had been awaited with great anticipation. It claimed leaving almost no stone unturned in its analysis of the lead-up to The Crash and ran to 2,700 pages in 9 volumes. The report concluded that three ministers had been criminally negligent: the Prime Minister, the Minister of Finance and the Minister of Commerce. The three governors of the Central Bank and the director of the financial supervisory authority were also found to be at fault. The main conclusion of the SIC's Working Group on Ethics was that 'the most important lessons to draw from these events are about weak social structures, political culture and public institutions' (Árnason, Nordal & Ástgeirsdóttir, 2010).

One of the first tasks of the new left-wing government was to replace the politically appointed leadership of the Central Bank with a more professional management. The Bank's leading governor, former PM Davíð Oddsson, fought tooth and nail against being sacked but was in the end removed by a new law changing the bank's management structure came in to force. The significance of the move towards more professional practices was, however, somewhat diminished by the fact that an economist with close ties to the Social Democratic Alliance, Már Guðmundsson, was appointed the bank's single new governor.

On the back of the findings of the SIC, the new left-leaning Parliament decided to invoke a hitherto dormant clause in the constitution and prosecute former PM Geir Haarde before a special court that could be called to hold ministers accountable for wrongdoing. This special Country Court (*Landsdómur*) had never been convened before. Haarde faced many charges but was in the end sentenced only for neglecting to hold government meetings leading up to The Crash, when he should, according to the Country Court's interpretation of the constitution, have kept his ministers better informed of the critical situation. His punishment was suspended, so in the end, this was only a slap on the wrist (Dómur Landsdóms, 2012). In addition, the fact that his political opponents had singled out only Haarde for prosecution undermined the whole exercise.

Criminal investigation

The office of Special Prosecutor set up to investigate criminal activity in the financial sector leading up to The Crash was seen as a vital instrument for holding those responsible for the devastating events accountable. Both the public at large and many politicians were keen to hold bankers accountable. For that purpose, the famous Norwegian/French financial crime fighter, Eva Joly, was hired to advise the new institution. Over a hundred cases of suspected fraud had been opened, many quite large in scope (Act on the Office of a Special Prosecutor, 2008).

Many of the top management of the old banks were held in custody while under investigation but few sentences were passed. Amongst the most high-profile cases was an accusation of fraud against Glitnir's former CEO, Lárus Welding, who was sentenced to nine months in prison, but six of them were suspended. Another high-profile conviction was the two years prison meted out for insider trading to the Permanent Secretary of the Ministry of Finance, Baldur Guðlaugsson, who had belonged to the Locomotive group discussed in Chapter 4. Kaupthing Bank's top management and key owners were also prosecuted for widespread market manipulation in the previously discussed Al-Thani case.

Though it was hailed as the one of the 'world's most sweeping investigations into the bankers whose action contributed to the global financial crisis' (Higgins, 2013), many in Iceland were still frustrated by the slow pace of the prosecution.

Re-entering international society

As discussed in Chapter 3, where I analysed Iceland's foreign relations, the EU had been becoming more appealing to many Icelanders before The Crash and immediately afterwards. The volatile Icelandic króna had proved a burden to many households when it devalued by more than half before being locked behind capital controls. In order to stabilize the economy, the Social Democratic Alliance (SDA) thus made it a condition of entering into government with the Left Green Movement that application for EU membership be sent to Brussels and a draft accession agreement put to national referendum when completed. The SDA hoped that the adoption of the euro would underpin the crisis-ridden economy and provide a more solid base for recovery than continuing to rely on the constantly devaluating króna.

Support for EU membership, however, rapidly declined as the Iceave dispute heightened. The EU was thought to be supporting its members, the UK and Netherlands, against Iceland. This commonly held belief was reinforced when the European Commission joined in with the EFTA Surveillance Authority in its case against Iceland before the EFTA Court. Soon, support for EU membership reversed, with polls showing fiercer opposition against membership than ever before (Samtök Iðnaðarins, 2013). This led the government to slow down the accession negotiation process leading up to the May 2013 election and promising not to open any new chapters in the negotiation. After the election, the right-of-centre government formally put the accession negotiation on hold and in effect stopped the process.

In order to re-access international financial markets after The Crash, the post crisis left wing government saw it as a necessary evil to accept responsibility for the Icesave deposits. This proposal was, however, firmly rejected by the Icelandic electorate in two referendums initiated by the President of the Republic, as was discussed in Chapter 7.

Challenging the party system

The Icelandic political party system traditionally consisted of four main parties, as discussed in Chapter 2; the Independence Party (IP), Iceland's old right-wing hegemonic power, the Progressive Party (PP) which is based on traditional national sentiments with roots in agriculture, the rather internationalist and left-of-centre Social Democratic Alliance (SDA) and the further-left-leaning, feminist and environmentalist Left Green Movement (LGM). Alongside the four main parties there had always been a fifth and sometimes a sixth ad hoc or shorter-term parties, often formed around specific issues. The longest standing of these was the Women's List, which persisted during the 1980s and the 1990s.

Standing accused of having been corrupted in the boom years, the conventional parties were challenged in the wake of The Crash. The Progressive Party, with a completely renewed leadership, the old guard having been purged after leaving government in 2007, offered to back the left-wing minority government led by Jóhanna Sigurðardóttir, the post-crisis leader of the SDA. The LGM had been in opposition in the boom years and thus was not seen as having been contaminated by the Viking economy. Forces emerging out of the Pots and Pans Revolution were able to fill the fifth party slot when the Citizens' Movement won 4 of the 63 seats in Parliament in the 2009 election. More devastating for traditional politics, however, was the victory of the Best Party, which in 2010 won 35 per cent of the votes in the Reykjavik City election by mocking conventional politics. 'All kinds of everything for losers and fools'[1] was the party's slogan. The party was led by comedian Jón Gnarr, who, together with a number of colleagues mostly from the Reykjavik underground Punk Rock scene, was able to secure control of the city, in a coalition with the Social Democratic Alliance.

Leading up to the 2013 parliamentary election, a record number of parties, 13 in total, stood in the country's six constituencies. The Progressive Party, under its new leadership, emerged as the winner, grabbing a quarter of the vote. This is remarkable because the PP had for decades gradually seen diminished support and was rather expected to leave Icelandic politics, or to survive only as a symbol of times gone by. Then, spectacularly, the party surged in opinion polls immediately after the EFTA Court ruled in favour of Iceland in the Icesave dispute in late January 2013. The ruling gave credibility to the new PP leadership, which was the only of the four main parties that had remained firmly against giving in to the British and Dutch throughout the dispute. The PP gained further popularity by promising to force foreign creditors, which they systematically referred to as 'vulture funds' (*hrægammas-jóðir*), to pay for a 20 per cent debt relief household loans. The money to pay for this one off debt relief was to be retrieved when the creditors would be allowed to leave cross the controlled currency borders. On the back of its firm stance in the Icesave dispute and by promising to squeeze money out of foreign creditors, the PP more than doubled its support.

In the 2013 election, the SDA and LGM were heavily punished, mainly for accepting liability in the Icesave dispute when in government. In fact, the SDA suffered the greatest loss of any party in the history of the republic. Interestingly, however, the previously hegemonic IP won only a few more votes than in the 2009 election, when the party had had its worst result in history. Down from its traditional level of almost 40 per cent, the IP now received only roughly a quarter of the votes. Throughout the first half of the post-crisis parliamentary term, the IP had consistently been polling around its traditional level. The descent had started when its new leadership decided to back the last Icesave agreement in Parliament.

The volatility of Icelandic politics was perhaps best illustrated by the fact that two new parties were in the 2013 election able to pass the 5 per cent threshold necessary to win seats in Parliament. Bright Future, which was created out of people from the Best Party and splinters of the SDA, won six seats and the Icelandic version of the international Pirate Party won four seats. This was the first time a Pirate Party had won seats in any national parliamentary election.

However, even though a record number of the electorate voted for non-traditional parties, the conventional party system withstood the challenges waged against it. With the Citizens' Movement dissolving in the 2013 election, the revolutionary forces from four years before were mostly gone.

It was an illustration of the IP's weakened position in Icelandic politics that after the election it had to settle for serving under the PP leadership in a new coalition, despite still being the countries largest party, with, however, only few more votes than the PP. In his first address on Iceland's National Day, on 17 June 2013, Prime Minister Gunnlaugsson placed himself even more firmly than most of his predecessors within the established postcolonial discourse, mainly emphasizing Iceland's heritage and celebrating the nation's defiance against foreign oppression in the Icesave dispute. Referring to the IMF's concerns over the new government's debt reduction plan for households, he added that international institutions would no longer dictate Iceland's economic policies (Gunnlaugsson, 2013).

In line with the persistence of the traditional political party system was the success of President Ólafur Ragnar Grímsson in fending off challenger Þóra Arnórsdóttir in the 2012 presidential election. President Gímsson had lost credibility in the eyes of most Icelanders when standing accused of being the greatest cheerleader of the Viking Capitalists in the boom years. Post-crisis, however, he had regained popularity when referring the Icesave agreements to referendums. These moves were nevertheless still controversial. His challenger, Þóra Arnórsdóttir, a young mother of five and a non-controversial TV presenter, ran – while pregnant – on a ticket calling for renewed unity and an end to crisis politics. But by referring to Arnórsdóttir's adolescent involvement in pro-EU and social democratic politics, Grímsson was able to discredit his opponent and he gradually emerged as Iceland's main post-crisis hero – mainly because of his firm stance against the British and Dutch in the Icesave dispute.

Constitutional reform

As stated, crisis in capitalism can open up our imagination to alternative 'economic imaginaries' (Jessop, 2004). Similarly, constitutional revisions are usually only embarked upon in the aftermath of severe political or economic crisis (Elster, 1995). This is what can be called a constitutional moment. A constitutional moment emerges when a catastrophe mobilizes societal forces for fundamental change (Teubner, 2011). In the wake of the crisis, Iceland came closer than most countries ever get to a clean slate situation. As I will demonstrate, the constitutional revision process embarked on after The Crash was an integral part of the 'imagined recovery' of Iceland from the most profound crisis to hit the republic since its creation in 1944. As a result, the process became highly politicized, which makes it a interesting case to study the *new critical order*, which emerged through the crisis and was contesting most of the initiatives for reform.

Pressured by the angry public, the new left-wing government decided in 2010 to start a constitutional review process, which would draft a new constitution in three phases. First a *National Forum* of a thousand people selected by stratified sampling were gathered for a one-day meeting to discuss what principles and values the new constitution should be based on. This was based on a civil movements initiative, called the Anthills, which the year before had held a similar event to map ideas for reform. A seven-member political party-appointed *Constitutional Committee* was then created to gather information, analyse core issues discussed by the National Forum and propose ideas for constitutional revision. Finally and most importantly, Parliament called for a national election of an independent, 25-member *Constitutional Assembly*, which should on the basis of the work of the National Forum and the Constitutional Committee review and revise Iceland's constitution or possibly draft a completely new one.

The process was heavily politicized right from the beginning. The IP, recently ousted from government, fought fiercely against it every step of the way, perhaps feeling that the whole exercise was an attack on their political heritage. Leading up to the spring 2009 election, the new leadership of the PP had focused their strategy for regaining trust on this proposal for a nationally elected Constitutional Assembly, which they insisted would serve as a healing process to reconstruct Iceland's 'Social Contract', which had been ripped apart in The Crash. It is indicative on just how polarized Icelandic politics were becoming that when the new left-wing government agreed and did exactly that, however, many PP parliamentarians suddenly started to distance themselves from the process and gradually emerged amongst the most forceful critics of the project. While the new PM, Jóhanna Sigurðardóttir, and many of her colleagues were eager supporters of the project, there was also quite hefty opposition amongst prominent ministers within the government. Many parliamentarians of the coalition parties either remained silent or were suspected of only paying lip service to the project while quietly plotting against it.

Unfinished project

Constitutional reform had been on the agenda of Icelandic politics ever since the republic was established in 1944, when the country finally came out from under Danish rule while Denmark was still under Nazi occupation. The celebrations were held in Parliamentary Fields (Þingvellir), the site of the medieval parliamentary court, which in the hundred-year-long independence struggle had become the holy site of Iceland's national spirit (Hálfdanarson, 2001). In order to show the world that Icelanders were united in announcing their independence, in 1944 Parliament agreed not to make other changes to the constitution of the Icelandic kingdom than those directly stemming from the establishment of the republic – thus, only changing the articles on the role of the Danish king to include references to a nationally elected Icelandic President. As a result, 95 per cent of the electorate agreed to establish the republic on the basis of the temporary constitution that the king of Denmark had handed to us in 1874 on the thousandth anniversary of Iceland's settlement, which had until then been changed only marginally to provide for Home Rule in 1904 and Sovereignty status in 1918 (resulting in the 1920 constitution of the Icelandic kingdom). The Union Act of 1918 contained a sunset clause stipulating that either country could end the relationship after 25 years. The massive support for the 1944 constitution was thus due to the fact that a Yes vote was seen as the national duty of all Icelanders, but it was not necessarily an approval of the content of the constitution itself.

At the foundation of the republic in 1944, the founding fathers (they were all men) had announced that complete constitutional revision would be instigated immediately (Jóhannesson, 2011). However, mostly because of political infighting, our parliamentarians were usually able to agree only on minor changes. When the process was jumpstarted after The Crash, constitutional revision was thus in many regards very much an unfinished project – perhaps even a thorn in the side of the young republic, as our parliamentarians were never able to agree on either the process of reform or the content of a new constitution. It was thus only in the wake of crisis that our politicians were able to find a way out of the trenches of traditional party politics, outsourcing the drafting of a new constitution to a nationally elected external body. The primus motor for that initiative was PM Jóhanna Sigurðardóttir, who had been one of very few long-standing supporters of the call for such an external constitutional assembly.

Problems and participation

In all, 522 candidates stood for election to the Constitutional Assembly, marking unprecedented political involvement. Each had collected signatures from more than 30 supporters, which collectively amounted to almost 10 per cent of the entire population signing for one of the candidates. Only roughly 37 per cent of the electorate, however, participated in this unique election. In accordance with the nature of the assembly and perhaps because of the troubled political climate suspiciousness of party politics, the political parties did not field candidates and interest organizations refrained from intervening but instead supported certain individuals. Days before the election, however, the IP secretariat distributed to its members a list of candidates that were considered 'favourable' to the party.

Twenty-five members from a broad background were elected, including a few of those the IP secretariat had listed in its circular. Among the elected were lawyers, artists, priests, professors, political scientists, media people, erstwhile MPs, doctors, company board member, a farmer, a campaigner for the rights of handicapped people, mathematician, a nurse and a labour union leader. Soon after the results were announced, however, opponents of the process complained that only previously well known individuals had been elected, mostly from the ranks of the left-leaning Reykjavik elite. In fact, though, most were not affiliated with any political party or party political association.

To deal with the complexity of the voting and the fact that voters would have to spend much more time in the ballot booths than in parliamentary elections, the electoral authorities decided to change the set-up, mainly by increasing the number of election booths. This proved to carry grave consequences when the election was announced null and void on technical grounds (Meuwse, 2012). This was an extraordinary decision, which almost delivered a fatal blow to the whole process. The ruling was criticized for 'not only being poorly reasoned but...also materially wrong' (Axelsson, 2011). Professor Gylfason, one of the elected members, has indicated that the leading judge in the case, a 'staunch party man' of the IP, is suspected of having drafted one of the complaints, which he then in his capacity as the judge leading the charge 'used as pretext for invalidating the election' (Gylfason, 2012: 11). This, however, has not been proven.

Faced with this unique decision – the first general national election in modern times to be invalidated, not only in Iceland but in the whole Western world, solely on trivial technical grounds, Parliament decided to simply appoint those individuals elected to the Constitutional Assembly to a Constitutional Council, which would more or less have the same tasks. This, however, severely damaged the legitimacy of the process.

It was thus in a rather awkward situation that the Constitutional Council started its work in April 2011. The country had recently collapsed amid a financial crisis, the previous government had been ousted as a result of widespread popular protest and the Council's own mandate had been called into question by the invalidation of the constitutional election.

The Council, working full time, was nested with a 700-page report from the Constitutional Committee and an extensive value map from the thousand-person National Forum. The message of the National Forum was both vast and far-reaching. Among its main demands were better protection of human rights, the protection of Iceland's sovereignty and language, and guarantees that the nation's resources remain in public ownership. The Forum also agreed that each vote should have equal weight and that representatives should be elected through preferential voting (The Main Conclusions of the National Forum, 2010).

Despite members holding very different positions, the Council was able to unite on three main initial tasks: first, to update the human rights chapter so that it incorporated social and civil rights and to add a chapter on nature protection and collective ownership of common natural resources; second, to divide more clearly the branches of government and third, to develop functional tools for increasing direct democracy, for example with preferential voting in parliamentary elections and clear guidelines on how the people can call for referendums on vital issues.

'Crowdsourced' constitution

Contrary to the advice of many constitutional experts, such as professor Jon Elster, the Council decided to open its work up to the public as much as possible. This interactive engagement with the public was at the expense of the more typical professional distance. The whole process had been heavily politicized in a harsh exchange between politicians. The Council believed that it might help it to regain legitimacy in the eyes of the public to invite all those interested to participate.

Opinion polls indicated that popular trust of Parliament was at a historic low, with only one in ten feeling content with its work. Professor Jón Ólafsson claims that the Council in fact made a point of distancing itself from Parliament and that some of its members 'expressed openly their hostility to the "political elites".' He claims that the members saw themselves as representing the common public rather than the privilege elite, and that as a result of the widespread anti-establishment rhetoric the Council 'alienated itself from the Parliament' (Ólafsson, 2012).

Through social media outlets like Facebook and Twitter, the Council attracted several thousand inputs in addition to 370 proposals via more traditional correspondence. The Council also opened up its meetings and working documents online. Viewing it from a distance, the international media was branding the production as the world's first 'crowdsourced' constitution, drafted by the interested public in clear view of the world. The Council welcomed this focus and even played on it and used it to its advantage in domestic politics. This was, however, never a realistic description of the drafting. Despite the open access and the existence of a robust secretariat staffed with many experts to assist the Council, the Council was not able to systematically plough through all the extensive input, as it only had four months to complete its task.[2] Many in the international media, including the *International Herald Tribune*, nevertheless reported that enthusiasts of open government around the world were insisting that the Icelandic constitutional process should serve as model for ordinary people to wrest power from the political elites that have monopolized political decision making (Morris, 2012).

Professor Jón Ólafsson (2012) claims that the Council in effect worked without a clear methodology as to the approach to the main principles of its work. However, rather than developing the document in a traditional linear fashion, the Council had decided to apply the *agile* method often used in software development, gradually completing a holistic document in several rounds. Each week, the Council posted on its website new provisional articles for perusal by the public. When comments and suggestions had been received from the public as well as from experts, the Council posted revised versions of the articles on its website. In this manner, the document was gradually refined and the final version of the new constitution arrived at. Despite initially wide differences in opinion and on occasion vigorous open disputes, the Council adopted the new constitution unanimously. The emphasis on solidarity and unanimity grew stronger among the members as their work progressed, precisely because it was viewed as being vital in order for the Council to present a unified front against expected political resistance.

Scholars in the Comparative Constitutions Project at Chicago University, who analysed the draft, claimed that this constitution-making process was tremendously innovative and participatory and concluded that it would be at 'the cutting edge of ensuring public participation in on-going governance,' (Elkins, Ginsburg, & Melton, 2012).

New, not only amended

Amongst the Council's main challenges was that the mechanics of the existing constitution, which was based on the Danish 19th-century governmental model, no longer mirrored the democratic governmental system in the country. Since independence in 1944, a comprehensive constitutional debate had mostly been missing, fostering an ever-larger list of constitutional problems.

The 1944 constitution, for example, attributed a range of governmental duties and powers to Iceland's largely ceremonial President – for example to appoint ministers, suspend Parliament, negotiate treaties with other states, and even exempt people from specific laws. After attributing all of these and many other powers to the President of the republic, the constitution whisked them back in two articles, which stated that the Presidents transferred his power to government ministers and was not responsible for governmental decisions. This had left an ambiguity as to the proper role of the President and even as to the nature of our governmental system. Traditionally, the President had operated as a ceremonial head of state but not as head of the government. As in other parliamentary democracies, the Prime Minister was the head of government. Iceland had therefore been classified as a Parliamentary Republic, like Ireland, Italy and Germany. However, in recent years, some scholars had been reinterpreting the constitution as describing a semi-presidential system (e.g. Kristjánsson, 2012). President Ólafur Ragnar Grímsson, first elected into office in 1996, had gradually been merging into that interpretation. In the 2012 presidential election, candidates could not even agree on the role of the President or the nature of the governmental system (Bergmann, 2012). Despite the constitution's claiming that governmental power could not be transferred abroad, because of the ambiguity in the 19th-century text Iceland was able to enter into the European Economic Area agreement, which, as explained in Chapter 3, had brought the country into the EU Single Market in exchange for its implementing all relevant EU laws.

The 1944 constitution was full of misconceptions like these, which had resulted in ambiguous and often contradictory interpretations of the text. The Council understood that the greatest danger of the old constitution was that the blurred lines between branches of government made it possible for strong leaders to gradually gain control of all three branches of government – the executive, the legislative and even the judiciary, through political appointments to the bench. The Council therefore came to the conclusion that it would be impossible to keep the old constitutional model for a Western republic of the 21st century, which would be like basing a new space shuttle design on the architecture of a horse-drawn cart.

The 1944 constitution had allowed the executive to assume power from the legislature and the courts. Through the decades, leaders of coalition governments had gained almost complete control of the Parliament. This had been illustrated when the leaders of the IP and the PP (Prime Minister Davíð Oddsson and Foreign Minister Halldór Ásgrímsson) had decided without consulting Parliament or any of their colleagues to support the US by listing Iceland in the 'coalition of the willing' before the invasion of Iraq in 2003. Another example is found in the appointment of judges to the Supreme Court. The justice ministers of the same parties (IP and PP) had throughout the decades appointed the vast majority of all new judges. Under the proposed constitution, Parliament would be more independent from the government and the misleading articles on the purely formal power of the President removed or moved to appropriate sections.

The proposed constitution furthermore explicitly stipulated that natural resources are in the collective property of the nation. This is key to understand the harsh political debate over the constitutional reform process and the politicization of the whole project. The dispute over the ITQ system, has has been branded 'The battle of Iceland'. Over more than three decades, control of Iceland's fishing quota had amounted to the greatest political dispute in the country. For years, there had been a clear majority in opinion polls for rolling back the fishing quota virtually given away in the 1980s. However, despite massive public support, an article acknowledging the public ownership of the fish stock had not previously been added to the constitution. The IP, which has close links with the Association of Fishing Vessel Owners (LÍU), had always stood against such an amendment. This might partly explain the IP's opposition to the project.

A healing process or a pet project?

By mid 2011Council members had reached a consensus on a draft constitution. This came as a surprise to many, including Parliament, which had no set plan on how to proceed. Professor Ólafsson (2012) claims that the main reason for the cool reception of the draft in Parliament was that the Council had refused to cooperate with Parliament or political parties on the drafting; that the politicians and the political elite therefore felt alienated from the draft.

No sooner had the draft been handed over than the traditional political quarrel started – perhaps not surprisingly, as throughout the process the establishment of the IP had fought tooth and nail against the entire project. Holding an extremely fragile and even fluctuating majority (several MPs crossed lines in both directions during the term), the coalition government spent a full year navigating the draft through parliamentary procedures.

Finally, Parliament settled on holding an 'advisory referendum on 20 October 2012. Around half of the electorate turned out for the referendum, of which two-thirds accepted the draft as the basis of a new constitution, which Parliament was to complete (Niðurstöðum þjóðaratkvæðagreiðslunnar lýst, 2012). The overwhelming support for the proposal came to the surprise of many. The fate of the whole exercise was, however, still in the hands of Parliament. Running out of time leading up to the April 2013 election, the government reached an agreement to delegate the decision on the bill for a new constitution to the next Parliament. Further changes to the bill were required by the new Parliament, which appointed a new parliamentary constitutional committee to navigate through the complexities the process was caught in. The new right-of-centre government however had no intention of ratifying the draft constitution.

Repeatedly, the process was hijacked by party political infighting. From the outset, many criticized the whole exercise for being only a pet project of Prime Minister Sigurðardóttir, even an unwelcome distraction from dealing with serious economic reform, which was of much more vital interest to the public. Caught in the new critical order of Iceland's post-crisis politics, the constitutional process, like many other proposals for political reform, ran into trouble. Still, and perhaps somewhat paradoxically, the public discussion spurred by the project served as a healing process for the society after The Crash. Through it many had been able to contribute to the promise of a resurrected and reformed Iceland. The exercise as such is thus likely to have contributed to the expectation of greater public participation in decision making in the future.

Conclusion

Five years after The Crash fragile economic reform was taking root. Many ambitious proposals and initiatives for widespread political reform had, however, been caught in what can be described as a new critical order taking hold in the Icelandic post-crisis society, which was marked by political infighting. The post-crisis left-wing government thus failed in its quest to create a *New Iceland*, which was to develop from the ruins. Though former PM Haarde was, in a controversial move, sentenced to imprisonment for not holding enough government meetings leading up to The Crash, politicians were not really being held accountable for the devastating events. Admittedly, some of the bankers responsible for the crisis were investigated and some sentences were passed, but for the most part, those involved were still able to embark upon new business adventures. Meanwhile, the government was not able to push the Icesave agreement through referendums and opposition grew against EU membership, ultimately bringing the accession negotiations to a halt. The constitutional process was also caught in the political infighting characterizing the new critical order as most proposals for reform were discredited.

Interestingly, the Icesave dispute was to dictate political development in the post-crisis period, rather than the settling of scores with those responsible for The Crash. After winning a landslide victory in the 2009 election immediately after The Crash, the two left-wing government parties were heavily punished in the 2013 election. Their support started to deteriorate when they pushed the first Icesave agreement with the UK and Holland through Parliament in late 2009. After the IP decided to support the left-wing government's second Icesave agreement in late 2011, its support also started to fall, while the PP, which was the only party always vigorously campaigning against any agreement, surged in the polls when the EFTA Court in early 2013 cleared Iceland of wrongdoing. Only by applying postcolonial analysis can these phenomena be explained, as was discussed in Chapter 1 and will be analysed further in the short conclusion to this book, which I turn to next.

Conclusions and Final Remarks

Iceland was the first casualty of the Credit Crunch. In early 2008, its three oversized cross-border banks, amounting to 85 per cent of the island's financial system, fell in three consecutive days, leaving the country in economic devastation. In the preceding years, the financial system had grow to nine times GDP, to become the crown jewel in what was commonly phrased the Icelandic economic miracle. This was the Nordic Tiger's last roar. The equity market was wiped out, the króna tanked, inflation spiked and unemployment rose to unprecedented levels. Abroad, Iceland's reputation was in ruin. Collectively, these events have simply been branded *The Crash*.

Devastating as this certainly was to our economy, it was also a crisis of politics and political culture. The rise of high-level cross-border financial services and the far-reaching *outvasion* in the new millennium had marked our entrance onto the world stage. The *Icelandic Project* – to be internationally recognized, as an independent state on an equal footing with others in the West – seemed to have been completed. Now it was in tatters. The Crash thus delivered a severe blow to our national identity. It was thus a profound psychological shock as well as an economic debacle.

The severity of the Icelandic Crash makes for an exceptional case to study in this international financial crisis. Initially, the Icelandic banking collapse was collectively estimated to amount to the third-largest bankruptcy in world history. In terms of the country's size, it was perhaps the greatest national crisis of them all. Still, five years later, fragile economic recovery was taking root though a prolonged new critical order had halted much sustained political reform.

The Icelandic crisis stands out in many ways. Instead of bailing out its privately held financial firms, as most governments tried to do – often at great cost – the Icelandic government took its cross-border banks into administration and split them into old 'bad' international banks, which were put into wind-up procedures, and new 'good' domestic banks, which were created out of the fallen ones. This, however, did not free Icelanders from shouldering fiscal cost as sovereign debt shot up from around 30 per cent of GDP to almost 100 per cent of GDP. In fact, Iceland suffered the second-greatest direct cost in this crisis, after only Ireland, which towered far above others on the list.

Icelanders' response to the crisis also set the situation worlds apart from others. The Icelandic Crash was much more sudden than elsewhere. The whole world was watching when the country collapsed on live TV. This was a much greater shock than a gradual disintegration, like those in the PIIGS (Portugal, Italy, Ireland, Greece and Spain), which saw public debt grow much more steadily. As Europe fell into recession, strict austerity measures slowed its economy even further, causing more prolonged public hardship in the PIIGS, where there was, for example, lower labour market participation. After the ousting of the accross-the-centre grand coalition in the so-called Pots and Pans Revolution in January 2009, the post-crisis left-wing government initiated various complementary measures to ease the crisis rather than implementing strict austerity. This prevented inequality from surging as it did in many other countries, cushioning the drop in purchasing power of lower income groups. The evidence from the Icelandic case thus perhaps supports Joseph Stiglitz's (2013) argumentation in his dispute with Paul Krugman (2013) over the effect of inequality on recovery and growth. By preventing the purchasing power of the middle class from dropping too far, domestic consumption became one of the main motors generating growth again. Vital for recovery was, however, that the production base in fishing and other manufacturing industries remained intact, and many production companies still held a strong international marketing position.

The turnaround came in late 2010 with marginal growth after steep contraction. International financial markets were re-accessed in 2011, when the Central Bank was able to auction a $1 billion bond for a decent rate. In late 2012, the rating institutions recognized Iceland's recovery as 'remarkable' and lifted our bonds back to investment level. Fiscal consolidation was finally achieved in 2013, when the EFTA Court ruling in favour of Iceland also normalized relations with neighbours. This 'remarkable' recovery, however, remained fragile. The tiny economy still faced grave challenges. Household debt, for example, was still beyond a sustainable level and pressure on the króna was such that the lifting of capital controls was not yet in sight, with the accompanying danger of serious distortion in the set-up of the economy. In combination with the prolonged economic difficulties in Europe, Iceland's main export market, these challenges would further slow growth.

Iceland was rushed into rapid modernization in the 20th century. Though average annual growth was at 2.6 per cent throughout the century, the economy was characterized by repeated cycles of boom and bust. The saga of the troubled Íslandsbanki in the early 20th century relates in an interesting way to the devastating events suffered in the early 21st century, when our oversized cross-border banks collapsed. When the foreign-owned Íslandsbanki was established in 1904, capital came pouring into a closed off and backward economy, which was thirsty for liquidity from abroad. Icelanders bought engines for their primitive trawlers, creating the beginnings of a fishing-based economy. The fish could be sold abroad and soon Iceland was awash with foreign cash. Holding a central banking licence, with a firm peg to the Danish krona, Íslandsbanki prompted the trans-nationalization of Icelandic capital accumulation and the early, fragile financialization of the society. When it ran into trouble, the cross-border Íslandsbanki was refused help and allowed to default, while the central banking licence was moved to the domestic Landsbanki, which was saved. Capital controls were introduced in 1931, locking Iceland out of international capital markets for 63 years – until it entered the EEA agreement in 1994.

The next wave of foreign cash came in the Second World War, when the British and American armies landed in Reykjavik. Enjoying generous funding from the Marshall Aid plan, Iceland was able to invest in high-tech fishing vessels, and because of its new geostrategic importance in the Cold War, it was able to expand its fishing ground in the so-called Cod Wars and push the British out of its waters. During the decades immediately after independence from Denmark in 1944, Iceland's economy thus continued to be characterized by extensive accumulation based on fishing, which became the engine room of our economy. This created a new historical bloc around fishing exports with close ties to the hegemonic Independence Party. Foreign currency was now pouring into the country, increasing inflation, which rose to unsustainable levels in the troubled 1970s. A generational shift within the IP leading to a neoliberal accumulation strategy occurred in the following decade. The introduction of an ITQ system in fishing, in effect turning uncaught fish and their production into property and based on historical catch figures, then paved the way for the vast capitalization in the coming period of incredible boom.

These repeated cycles of boom and bust spurred an increased effort towards diversification, leading for example to widespread use of natural energy, mostly for aluminium production. This collective move towards diversification in turn led to an emphasis on high-tech industry in the 1990s and financial services in the first decade of the new century, both of which were to suffer devastating blows.

The procyclicality of governmental economic policies was only to grow further, leading to perhaps the greatest national economic collapse in the present financial crisis. Iceland's new finance-driven economy had taken shape around the turn of the century, replacing the old resource-based growth model. This change was also facilitated by the neo-corporatist agreement in 1990. The so-called National Concensus Agreemety linked interest of the labour movement with that of the financial sector through operating accumulative pension funds which invested heavily on capital markets. This removed a potentially significant source of opposition to further financialization.

After a prolonged drought, Iceland was again thirsty for foreign money. By accessing the Single European Market in 1994 and subsequently privatizing the state-owned domestic banks, Iceland was rushed towards a neoliberal, finance-driven economy: Icelandic Viking Capitalism was born. The much celebrated outvasion was considered necessary to break the constraints of smallness that were holding back growth. Further growth was viewed as necessary to broaden the base of the economy in order to ensure its economic independence. It can thus be argued that Iceland was too small for its own national identity.

Thanks to a neoliberal deregulation strategy, Iceland moved in one decade from being amongst the most heavily regulated and backward banking regimes to being one of the most liberal in the world. Three banking conglomerates emerged out of the almost simultaneous privatization, deregulation and internationalization of the economy, each entrenched in its own power networks. Hailed as a new breed of brilliant businessmen, the competing groups flocked en masse onto international markets, embarking on one of the grandest shopping sprees in world history – collectively termed the Icelandic *outvasion*.

The expansion was not entirely self-driven. Rather, it was also a result of procyclycal governmental policies. In addition to the previously mentioned policy changes came increased public housing loans, massive new industrial construction, far-reaching tax cuts and a reduction in banks' reserve requirements. This only blew more hot air into the overinflated bubble, until the economy imploded. The Central Bank's sole response, hiking interest rates to counter the rising inflation, only attracted more hot money, which came pouring in as the carry trade looked to exploit the vast interest rate difference. To add to all this was the risk-seeking behaviour of private corporations, with diminished cushions against risk while operating in increasingly interconnected banks and condensed groups of corporations. The Icelandic political economy had become incestuous.

Several macroeconomic imbalances thus grew in the boom years, leaving the economy ever more vulnerable. Nothing was, however, done to counter the procyclycality. Corporate and household debt built to staggering levels, private consumption surged, house prices rocketed and shares multiplied in value. Ordinary people were turned into venture capitalists in a far-reaching financialization of the society. Banks' balance sheets were over-extended and the current account deficit grew unsustainable. When the crisis hit, these imbalances would take long time to reverse.

When analysing these policies and events, we cannot ignore Iceland's national identity, carved out in the struggle for independence from Denmark in the 19th and early 20th centuries. The national myth indeed laid the foundation on which the Icelandic republic still rests. Importantly, the struggle did not end when full independence was won. The year 1944 rather marks the start of Iceland's new *everlasting* independence struggle. The fragility of Iceland's sovereignty is always present, with constant threats to the very existence of the nation.

The postcolonial national identity, which is based on a commonly held national myth of our history, puts emphasis on *formal* sovereignty and insistence on being recognized as an equal partner in Europe, rather than a microstate that relies on a larger neighbour. This is what can be called the *Icelandic Project*. The duality of the national identity often creates tension between emphasis on *internal* independence and *external* recognition – between *isolationist* and *internationalist* approaches.

The colonial experience is still very present in contemporary politics, in terms of both rhetoric and praxis. In line with the poststructural emphasis in IPE, I thus maintain that Iceland's colonial past and postcolonial relations still decisively impact on Iceland's political economy. To contextualize contemporary Iceland, our historically based national memory has to be taken into account. Indeed, the discursive representation of the past is continually present in Icelandic politics, and contemporary interpretations of the state of the economy stand in a dynamic relationship with a common notion of our past.

It is thus also in this light that these procyclical policies need to be examined. The economic development throughout the 20th century, and especially in the boom years in the new millennium, served to underpin Iceland's *internal* economic independence and *external* recognition as a modern state at least equal to others.

The effect of the postcolonial identity is perhaps most evident in Iceland's foreign relations. Participating fully in the Single European Market through the EEA serves our insistence on being economically on an equal footing with others, while formally staying out of EU institutions supports our notion of formal sovereignty. In fact, Iceland's relationship with the EU only makes sense when taking into account its colonial history and postcolonial national identity, which emphasize formal sovereignty. It has since become the core of the Icelandic political identity to guard formal sovereignty. This neither-in-nor-out situation was, however, costly when the crisis hit and Iceland found itself vulnerable and quite alone in the world.

The desire for modernization and external recognition as an independent equal partner – Iceland's postcolonial national identity – can help to explain the sudden and often uncritical implementation of procyclical economic policies, especially in the boom years leading up to The Crash. Iceland was in a hurry to modernize and grow. These sentiments can also help to explain some of the seemingly irresponsible behaviour of the Viking Capitalists, which did not always seem to be based on purely business decisions – some of the trophy investments in Copenhagen, for example, which perhaps rather served as a statement that Icelanders were no longer a 'poor nation' subjugated to Denmark, but a modernized equal player in the world of business. After all, they too were children of the Icelandic postcolonial national identity.

This desire for external recognition helps not only to explain the boom but also to understand the defiant response foreign critics of the Icelandic finance-driven Viking economy faced in the mini-crisis of 2006. The criticism directly countered our postcolonial national identity, which can explain why such words of caution were almost categorically dismissed as the ill-willed interference of foreign oppressors. We were living in a financial fairytale told through thick nationalistic rhetoric. The anxiety many Icelanders felt over the misrepresentation abroad after The Crash derives from the same origin.

Interestingly, the national rhetoric has survived all these twists and turns. During the *boom*, the emphasis was on the uniqueness of the Icelandic nation, which was almost destined for greatness; during the *bust*, the emphasis was on defying foreign oppression once again; and when *recovery* was taking hold, Icelanders started to insist on their special achievements in dealing with the crisis – as was articulated by our President after the first referendum on Icesave, when he compared them with the democratic innovations of ancient Greece. Thus, a mixture of neoliberal ideology and our postcolonial national sentiments can, at least partly, explain The Crash.

The Crash, however, not only threatened the viability of the Icelandic Project but also opened up new space to re-examine its foundation. Many initiatives were taken to create what was to be become a reformed Iceland. Our politicians were to be held accountable for their failures leading up to The Crash and the bankers were to be punished for criminal activity. Iceland was to normalize foreign relations by negotiating an agreement over Icesave and then enter into the European Union to underpin a more stable economy by also entering the Eurozone. The political party system, which had been accused of being corrupt, was challenged and the people were to bypass Parliament and directly elect their representatives to write a new constitution. However, as discussed in Chapter 9, these initiatives have not materialized in significant political change. The Icelandic postcolonial project has for the most part survived the crisis without being significantly altered.

The Icelandic crisis, though, still significantly differs from events in many other crisis-ridden European countries, notably the PIIGS. Iceland and Ireland provide for an especially interesting comparison. Both lagged behind the rest of Europe in economic development throughout the 20th century. Both then enjoyed a rapid, finance-driven boom, which resulted in a housing and asset bubble, which burst near the end of the first decade of the new millennium. Ireland, a member of the EU and the EMU, issued a blanket guarantee for its banks' liability while Iceland, an EEA participant with the smallest independent currency in the world, was forced to take its banks into administration. Iceland has more in common with Ireland than with Portugal, Italy, Greece and Spain, which have mostly suffered a debt crisis. Interestingly, neoliberal financialization started in Iceland and in Ireland in the late 1970s and early 1980s, as well as in Greece. The Irish and the Icelandic crises derive from their oversized banking systems. Both landed in an IMF rescue programme. The EU and the ECB backed Ireland while Iceland's emergency money came from the Nordics and Poland. Unlike Iceland, which suffered a blow to purchasing power when the currency plummeted and housing debts peaked, Ireland was able to maintain much greater stability in living standards. However, it can be argued that socializing private debt slowed down growth in Ireland in the wake of the crisis, with the economy slowly suffocating. Iceland was, on the other hand, much faster in generating growth again, but after a much more profound crisis initially.

Iceland's blessing in disguise was that we did not enjoy access to more money leading up to and during The Crash. If Iceland had been able to guarantee the banks' liabilities in the same manner as the Irish, our public debt might have been doubled. Iceland thus accidentally stumbled upon the novel path of not bailing out its banks; until then, it was a commonly held belief that banks should not be allowed to fail in a modern Western economy. In Iceland's case, however, they proved too big to rescue.

Being at the centre of international media attention was new to Icelanders, who often felt frustrated by misreporting. The outside world had little knowledge of the island's internal intrigues and nuances and was prone to make little distinction between bankers, the state and the public. Rather, *Iceland* as a whole was reported to have collectively acted in certain ways. Three main stories were told in the international media about the Icelandic crisis: first, when the crisis hit, that Iceland would be in economic ruin for decades to come; second, in the wake of the Pots and Pans Revolution and the ousting of the government, that the public had sent the bankers to prison while writing their own constitution in a radical revolution; and third, after the 2013 Parliamentary election, that Icelanders had voted back into power those responsible for the crisis. As has been documented here, none of these three commonly told tales is true. As has been discussed at length in this book, the reality of the situation is much more ambiguous.

The parliamentary election in spring 2013 that resulted in a new right-of-centre coalition, replacing the post-crisis left-wing government, marked a paradigm shift away from crisis politics and the continuity of traditional procyclcal economic policies. Promising widespread debt relief to ordinary households and cutting taxes while sponsoring new manufacturing plants in rural areas and simultaneously lowering leasing costs to the fishermen perhaps marked the start of a new economic cycle of boom and bust, which still characterizes Iceland's economy.

Notes

1 Birth of a Nation – A Postcolonical Project

1. Recent research indicates that Iceland was in fact discovered up to 200 years earlier.

2 Coming of Age – Economic History

1. In Icelandic: 'Helmingaskiptareglan'.

3 The Independent State – Foreign Relations

1. Árnason, Tómas. Alþingis Parliamentary Archives: 1968, 08 11.
2. Hannibalsson, Jón Baldvin. Alþingis Parliamentary Archives: 1991, 23 10.
3. Ársælsson, Jóhann. Alþingis Parliamentary Archives: 1992, 03 09.
4. Pétursson, Páll. Alþingis Parliamentary Archives: 1989, 09 03.
5. Guðfinnsson, Einar K. Alþingis Parliamentary Archives: 2000, 08 05.
6. Sigfússon, Steingrímur J. Alþingis Parliamentary Archives: 2000, 08 05.
7. The PP had left a long-standing coalition with the IP in spring 2007.
8. Blöndal, Pétur. Alþingis Parliamentary Archives: 2009, 10 07.
9. Þórhallson, Höskuldur. Alþingis Parliamentary Archives: 2009, 14 07.
10. Daðason, Ásmundur Einar. Alþingis Parliamentary Archives, 2009, 14 07.
11. Ögmundur Jónasson. Alþingis Parliamentary Archives: 2009, 10 07.

4 The Nordic Tiger – Imagined Economic Miracle

1. In its first term (1991–1995), the IP lead a coalition with the Social Democratic Party. In 1995, the IP turned to the Progressive Party, which served as its junior partner for three terms, until 2007 when the IP teamed up with the new Social Democratic Alliance.
2. 1,000 million.
3. In Icelandic: 'Hvernig getur Ísland orðið ríkasta land í heimi?'.

5 Living on the Edge – Hot Air Flaring Up the Economy

1. In Icelandic: 'Tær snilld'.

6 The Crash – Collapse of the Cross-border Banks

1. In Icelandic: 'Birgðu þig upp í Bónus, veldu íslenskt'.
2. In Icelandic: 'Að Haardera'.

7   The Pots and Pans Revolution – and Defiance Abroad

1. The slogan was written in a mixture of Icelandic and English: 'Helvítis, fokking fokk'.
2. The phrase 'My time will come!' (In Icelandic: *'Minn tími mun koma!'*) became popular when Sigurðardóttir shouted it in a defiant speech at the Social Democratic Convention in 1994, after losing a vote for chairman of the party to Mr Hannibalsson.
3. He had previously accepted the first agreement, the one that contained preconditions that the British and the Dutch refused.
4. Harðardóttir, Eygló. Alþingis Parliamentary Archives: 2009, 05.06.
5. Gunnlaugsson, Sigmundur Davíð. Alþingis Parliamentary Archives: 2009, 05.12.
6. Blöndal Pétur. Alþingis Parliamentary Archives: 2009, 10.07.
7. Backman, Þuríður. Alþingis Parliamentary Archives: 2009, 17.07.
8. Tryggvadóttir, Margrét. Alþingis Parliamentary Archives: 2009, 18.06.
9. Benediktsson, Bjarni. Alþingis Parliamentary Archives: 2010, 09.01.

9   Reconstituting Iceland – and the New Critical Order

1. In Icelandic: *'Allskonar fyrir aumingja'*.
2. Interestingly, the Constitutional Convention in Philadelphia in 1776 also had four months to draft the American constitution.

References

25 People to Blame for the Financial Crisis (2009, 02). *Time Magazine*. New York. Retrieved from time.com.

Act on the Office of a Special Prosecutor, Pub. L. No. No. 135, 11 December 2008 (2008). Retrieved from serstakursaksoknari.is.

Adler-Nissen, R. (2008). The Diplomacy of Opting Out: A Bourdieudian Approach to National Integration Strategies. *JCMS: Journal of Common Market Studies*, 46(3), 663–684.

Ægisson, H. (2013, 03). Væntir 75% niðurskrifta [Espects 75% downwriting]. *Morgunblaðið*.

Agreed Guidelines Reached on Deposit Guarantees (2008, 11). *Prime Minister's Office*. Retrieved from eng.forsaetisraduneyti.is.

Aliber, R. Z. (2008). Monetary Turbulence and the Icelandic Economy. lecture, University of Iceland, 5. Retrieved from hi.is.

Alþingi (2011). *Skyrsla fjármálaráðherra um endurreisn viðskiptabankanna* (No. Lögð fyrir Alþingi á 139. löggjafarþingi 2010–2011.). Retrieved from althingi.is.

Anderson, R. (2008, 04). Fears Grow of Baltic States' Addiction to External Capital. *The Financial Express*. Retrieved from thefinancialexpress-bd.com.

Árnason, Ö. (1991). *Á slóð Kolkrabbans; Hverjir eiga Ísland?* [In the Realm of The Octopus. Who Owns Iceland?]. Reykjavik: Skjaldborg.

Árnason, S. (2007, 02). 'Lætur aldrei efast um fjármögnun bankans.' [Never doubts the banks financing]. Reykjavik: *Fréttablaðið*.

Árnason, V., Nordal, S., & Ástgeirsdóttir, K. (2010). *Siðferði og starfshættir í tenglsum við fall íslensku bankanna 2008*. [Ethics relating to the banking collapse]. Reykjavik: Alþingi.

Áskorun til íslenskra stjórnmálamanna (2013). *Snjóhengjan*. [The overhang]. Retrieved from snjohengjan.is.

Ásmundsson, S. (2009, 01). 'Byltingin'. [The revolution]. Reykjavik: *Viðskiptablaðið*.

Axelsson, R. (2011). Comments on the Decision of the Supreme Court to Invalidate the Election to the Constitutional Assembly. University of Iceland. Retrieved from stjornarskrarfelagid.is.

Balakrishnan, A. (2008, 10). UK to Sue Iceland over Any Lost Bank Savings. *The Guardian*. London. Retrieved from guardian.co.uk.

Baldvinsdóttir, H. D. (1998). Networks of Financial Power in Iceland. Retrieved from cfci.org.cn.

Banning, C., & Gerritsen, J. (2008, 11). Dutch and British Block IMF Loan to Iceland. *NRC Handelsblad*.

Banque de France (2000). *The Functions and Organisation of Deposit Guarantee Schemes: The French Experience*. Retrieved from bofs.blog.is.

Bear Stern (2008). *Kazakhstan: A Comparison with Iceland*. Retrieved from 'See' in www.rna.is.

Benediktsdóttir, S., Danielsson, J., & Zoega, G. (2011). Lessons from a Collapse of a Financial System. *Economic Policy*, 26(66), 183–235.

Bergmann, E. (2007). *Opið land: Ísland í samfélagi Þjóðanna*. [Open land]. Reykjavik: Skrudda.

Bergmann, E. (2011a). *Sjálfstæð þjóð – trylltur skríll og landráðalýður*. [Independent nation]. Reykjavik: Veröld.

Bergmann, E. (2011b). *Iceland and the EEA 1994–2011*. Europautredningen. Retrieved from europautredningen.no.

Bergmann, E. (2012). 'Svarti Pétur – breytt staða forseta Íslands og frumvarp Stjórnlagaráðs.' [Black Jack]. Reykjavik: *Skírnir, Vor*.

Bernburg, J. G., Ragnarsdóttir, B. H., & Ólafsdóttir, S. (2010). 'Hverjir tóku þátt í Búsáhaldabyltingunni?' [Who participated in the Pots and Pans revolution?]. In Halldór Sig. Guðmundsson (ed.) *Rannsóknir í félagsvísindum*. Reykjavik: University of Iceland.

Bjarnason, G. Þ. (2013). *Upp með fánann. Baráttan um uppkastið 1908 og sjálfstæðis-barátta Íslendinga*. [Raising the flag]. Reykjavik: Mál og Menning.

Björnsson, P. (2010). Jón Sigurðsson forseti og aðild Íslands and Evrópusambandinu. [President Jón Sigurðsson and membership in the EU]. In Halldór Sig. Guðmundsson (ed.) *Rannsóknir í félagsvísindum*. Reykjavik: University of Iceland

Blöndal, L., & Stefánsson, S. M. (2008, 10). 'Ábyrgð ríkisins á innlánum.' [State guaranties on deposits]. Reykjavik: *Morgunblaðið*.

Blöndal, P. (2008, 12). 'Alþingi samþykkti upprunalega áætlun um Icesave.' [Parliament accepts orginal plan on Icesave]. Reykjavik: *Vísir.is*.

Brown Condems Iceland Over Banks. (2008, 10). *BBC News*. Retrieved from news. bbc.co.uk.

Buiter, W., & Sibert, A. (2008). The Icelandic Banking Crisis and What To Do about It: The Lender of Last Resort Theory of Optimal Currency Areas. *CEPR Policy Insight, 26*, 1–23.

Buiter, Willem (2008, June 2). There Is No Excuse for Britain Not To Join Euro. *Financial Times*. Retrieved from ft.com.

Byrne, E., & Þorsteinsson, H. F. (2012). Iceland: The Accidental Hero. Retrieved from rafhladan.is.

Cailleteau, P. (2008). *Moody's Downgrades Iceland's Ratings to Aa1* (Moody's Investors Service). London: Moody's. Retrieved from bonds.is/assets/files/f. pdf.

Central Bank of Iceland (2008). *Ríkjandi aðstæðu reyna á viðnámsþrótt bankanna*. Reykjavik. Retrieved from sedlabanki.is.

Central Bank of Iceland (2013). *Monetary Bulletin* (No. 2013, 1).

Chartier, D. (2011). *The End of Iceland's Innocence: The Image of Iceland in the Foreign Media During the Crisis*. Ottawa: University of Ottawa Press.

Cold War (2008, 10). *The Daily Mail*. London.

Conway, E. (2010, 17 May). Which Country is the Smuggest of Them All? *Finance – Telegraph Blogs*. Retrieved from blogs.telegraph.co.uk.

Cooper, A. F., & Shaw, T. M. (2009). *The Diplomacies of Small States: Between Vulnerability and Resilience*. Basingstoke: Palgrave Macmillan.

Darling, A. (2008, 10). Extra Help for Icesave Customers. *BBC Online*. London. Retrieved from news.bbc.co.uk.

Davíðsdóttir, S. (2012, 02). The Al-Thani Story behind the Kaupthing Indictment. *Sigrún Davíðsdóttir Icelog*. Retrieved from uti.is.

Detragiache, E., & Demirgüc-Kunt, A. (1998). *Financial Liberalization and Financial Fragility*. International Monetary Fund.

Dómur Landsdóms, No. Nr. 3/2011 (Landsdómur 04 2012). Retrieved from andsdómur.is.

Drainey, N. (2012, 6 April). Cod Wars Payment is 'Too Little, Too Late'. *The Times*. London. Retrieved from thetimes.co.uk.

Duncan, G. (2008, 10). IMF Bailout of Iceland is Delayed until Fate of UK Savers' Frozen Cash is Resolved. *The Times*. London. Retrieved from thetimes.co.uk.

Einarsson, S. (2008, 10). Ísland í dag. [Icelandic TV Show: Iceland today]. Reykjavik: TV Channel 2.

Elkins, Z., Ginsburg, T., & Melton, J. (2012, October 14). A Review of Iceland's Draft Constitution. Constitutional Review. Retrieved from webspace.utexas. edu.

Elster, J. (1995). Forces and Mechanisms in the Constitution-making Process. *Duke LJ*, 45, 364.

Europautredningen (2012). *Utenfor og innenfor: Norges avtaler med EU* (No. 2012:2). Oslo: Europautredningen.

Fagan, H. (2003). Globalised Ireland, or, Contemporary Transformations of National Identity? In Coulter C and Coleman S (eds) *The End of Irish History?*. Manchester University Press. pp. 110–121.

Fanon, F. (1963). *The Wretched of the Earth* (1961). Trans. Constance Farrington. New York: Grove.

Finch, J. (2009, 01). Twenty-five people at the Heart of the Meltdown... *The Guardian*. London. Retrieved from guardian.co.uk.

Finnbogason, G. (1925). Eðlisfar Íslendinga. [Nature of Icelanders]. In Sigurður Nordal (ed.) Reykjavik: Skírnir.

Fitch Ratings (2006). *Fitch Affirms Ratings of Icelandic Banks on Revision of Iceland's Outlook to Negative*. London. Retrieved from bonds.is.

Fitch Ratings (2013). *Iceland: Full Rating Report*.

Flyering, K., Heiðarsson, J., & Stefánsson, S. (2013). *Rannsóknanefnd Alþingis um Íbúðarlánasjóð*. [Parliaments investigative committee on the states housing fund.] Reykjavik: Alþingi.

Foukas, W., & Dimoulas, C. (2013). *Greece, Financialization and the EU*. Basingstoke: Palgrave Macmillan.

Friðriksson, Ó. (2003, 03). Í þessu samtali fólst enginn hálfkæringur. [This was no light discussion]. Reykjavik: *Morgunblaðið*.

Gísladóttir, I. S. (2008a, 09). Gjaldþrot peningahyggjunnar. [Bankruptsy of the Monetary Policy]. Reykjavik: *Samfylkingin.is*.

Gísladóttir, I. S. (2008b, 10). Fyrst IMF og svo ESB. [First IMF and then EU]. Reykjavík: Fréttablaðið.

Gissurarson, H. H. (2000). *Overfishing: The Icelandic Solution*. London: Institute of Economic Affairs. Retrieved from google.com/books.

Gissurarson, H. H. (2001). Hvernig getur Ísland orðið ríkasta land í heimi? [How can Iceland become the richest country in the world]. Reykavik: Nýja bókafélagið.

Gissurarson, H. H. (2004, 29.01). Miracle on Iceland. *Wall Street Journal*.

Give Us Our Money Back (2008, 10). *The Daily Telegraph*. London.

Graham, N. (2008, 12). Who's the World's Worst Banker? *Huffington Post*. Retrieved from hhuffingtonpost.com.

Griffin, P. (2011). Poststructuralism in/and IPE. In *Critical International Political Economy: Dialogue, Debate and Dissensus*. Basingstoke: Palgrave Macmillan. Retrieved from academia.edu.

Grímsson, Ó. R. (1978). *Icelandic Nationalism: A Dissolution Force in the Danish Kingdom and a Fundamental Cleavage in Icelandic Politics: A Draft Framework for Historical Analysis*. Háskóli Íslands: félagsvísindadeild.

Grímsson, Ó. R. (2000, 05). *Speech by the President of Iceland Ólafur Ragnar Grímsson at the Icelandic American Chamber of Commerce's Lunch Los Angeles 5 May 2000*. Retrieved from forseti.is.

Grímsson, Ó. R. (2005). How to Succeed in Modern Business: Lessons from The Icelandic Voyage. *Speech at The Walbrook Club, London*, 3. Retrieved from forseti.is.

Grímsson, Ó. R. (2010, 03). Þjóðaratkvæðagreiðslan styrkir lýðræðisþróun – viðtal við forseta Íslands. [The referendum supports democratic development. Reykjavík: Icelands Channel 2.

Gros, D. (2008). Iceland on the Brink? Options for a Small, Financially Active Economy in the Current Financial Crisis Environment. CEPS Policy Briefs No. 157, 7 April. Retrieved from aei.pitt.edu.

Guðmundsson, M. (2013, 02). *Iceland's Crisis and Recovery and Current Challenges*. Presented at Conference organised by the French-Icelandic Chamber of Commerce, Paris. Retrieved from bis.org.

Gunnarsdóttir, Þ. K. (2008, 07). TV news interview.

Gunnarsson, G. (1987). *Upp er boðið Ísaland. Einokunarverslun og íslenskt samfélag 1602–1787*. [Auctioning Iceland]. Reykjavik: Örn og Örlygur.

Gunnarsson, S. (2009). *Umsátrið*. [Under siege]. Reykjavík: Veröld

Gunnarsson, S. (2004). Davíð Oddsson. In Ólafur Teitur Guðnason ed. *Forsætisráðherrar Íslands – ráðherrar Íslands og forsætisráðherrar í 100 ár*. Reykjavik: Bókaútgáfan Hólar.

Gunnlaugsson, S. D. (2013, 6). *Ávarp forsætisráðherra, Sigmundar Davíðs Gunnlaugssonar, á Austurvelli 17. júní 2013*. [PMs address]. Reykjavik. Retrieved from forsaetisraduneyti.is.

Gylfason, T. (2006). Institutions, Human Capital, and Diversification of Rentier Economies. Retrieved from notendur.hi.is/~gylfason.

Gylfason, T. (2012). From Collapse to Constitution: The Case of Iceland. Retrieved from papers.ssrn.com.

Haarde, G. (2008, 10). Ávarp forsætisráðherra vegna sérstakra aðstæðna á fjármálamarkaði. *Ávarp forsætisráðherra*. Reykjavik: Sjónvarpið.

Hálfdanardóttir, G. (2008, 11). ESB hefði jafnvel sagt upp EES-samningnum við Ísland. [The EU could even have cancelled the EEA agreement]. Reykjavik: mbl.is.

Hálfdanarson, G. (2001). *Íslenska þjóðríkið : uppruni og endimörk*. [The Icelandic nation state]. Reykajvik: Hið íslenska bókmenntafélag.

Halldórsson, Ó. G., & Zoega, G. (2010). Iceland's Financial Crisis in an International Perspective. Retrieved from rafhladan.is.

Hansen, L., & Wæver, O. (2002). *European Integration and National Identity: The Challenge of the Nordic States*. Oxford: Routledge.

Hart, M. (2008, 11). Iceland's Next Saga: The Wounded Tiger's Tale. *The Globe and Mail*. Retrieved from theglobeandmail.com.

Helgason, A., & Palsson, G. (1997). Contested Commodities: The Moral Landscape of Modernist Regimes. *Journal of the Royal Anthropological Institute*, 3(3), September 1997, 451–471.

Hermannsson, B. (2005). Understanding Nationalism. *Studies in Icelandic Nationalism 1800–2000*, 91–7155.

Higgins, A. (2013, 02). Iceland, Fervent Prosecutor of Bankers, Sees Meager Returns. *The New York Times*. New York.

Hirst, E. (2012). Stétt með stétt: og nokkur grundvallaratriði í stefnu Sjálfstæðisflokksins. [Class with class]. In Jakob F. Ásgeirsson. Reykjavik: Þjóðmál.

Hooper, M. (2008, 3). Catch of the Day: Sigur Ros Take Charge. *Guardian*. Retrieved from guardian.co.uk.

House of Commons Treasury Committee (2009). *Banking Crisis: The Impact of the Failure of the Icelandic Banks* (Fifth Report of Session 2008–09). London. Retrieved from publications.parliament.uk.

Hreinsson, P., Gunnarsson, T., & Benediktsdóttir, S. (2010). Report of the Special Investigation Commission 2008. Rannsóknarnefnd Alþingis. Retrieved from rna.is.

Hreyfingin vill ekki norrænan sáttasemjara (2010, 01). *visir.is*. Retrieved from visir.is.

Hussain, A. (2006, 10). Icesave Looks Like a Hot Deal. *The Sunday Times*. London. Retrieved from thesundaytimes.co.uk.

Huyssen, A. (2000). Present Pasts: Media, Politics, Amnesia. *Public Culture*, Winter 2000 12(1): 21–38.

Ibson, D. (2008, 08). Icelandic Banks' Results Calm Fears. *Financial Times*. London. Retrieved from ft.com.

Icelandic Chamber of Commerce (2006). *Ísland 2015*. Reykjavik. Retrieved from vi.is.

InDefence (n.d.). *Wikipedia*. Retrieved from wikipedia.org.

Ineke, J., & Borgstrom, E. (2008). *Iceland – Unsustainable* (Morgan Stanley Research). London. Retrieved from bonds.is.

Ingebritsen, C. (2000). *The Nordic States and European Unity*. Cornell University Press.

Ingimundarson, V. (1996). *Í eldlínu kalda stríðsins: Samskipti Íslands og Bandaríkjanna, 1945–1960*. [In the Cold Wars line of fire]. Reykjavik: Vaka-Helgafell.

International Monetary Fund (2006). *Iceland: 2006 Article IV Consultation—Staff Report; Staff Statement; and Public Information Notice on the Executive Board Discussion* (No. IMF Country Report No. 06/296). Washington. Retrieved from imf.org.

International Monetary Fund (2011). *Iceland: Sixth Review Under the SBA and Proposal for Post-Program Monitoring— Staff Report; Staff Statement; Press Release on the Executive Board Discussion; and Statement by the Executive Director for Iceland*. (No. 11/263). Retrieved from imf.org.

International Monetary Fund (2012). *Iceland: Second Post-Program Monitoring Discussion* (No. 12/309).

Ísland fyrir Íslendinga (1907). *Ísafold*.

Ísland, best í heimi? Alþjóðlegt oðrspor og ímynd (2007, 02). [Iceland, best in the world.] Viðskiparáð. Retrieved from vi.is.

Íslandsbanki (2012). *Íslenski sjávarútvegurinn.* [Icelandic fisheries industry]. Reykjavik. Retrieved from islandsbanki.is.

Jackson, R. (2008, 11). Letter from Iceland. *The Financial Times.* London. Retrieved from ft.com.

Jessop, B. (2004). Critical Semiotic Analysis and Cultural Political Economy. *Critical Discourse Studies,* 1(2), 159–174.

Jóhannesson, B. (2002, 09). Götustrákurinn og keisarinn. [The street hooligan and the Keizer.] *Vísbending.*

Jóhannesson, G. T. (2009). *Hrunið: Ísland á barmi gjaldþrots og upplausnar.* [The Crash]. Reykjavik: JPV útgáfa.

Jóhannesson, Guðni Th. (2006). *Þorskastríðin þrjú. Saga landhelgismálsins 1948–1976.* [The three cod wars]. Reykjavik: Hafréttarstofnun Íslands.

Jóhannesson, Guðni Th. (2011). Tjaldað til einnar nætur : uppruni bráða-birgðastjórnarskrárinnar. [Camping for only one night]. Reykjavik: *Icelandic Review of Politics and Administration.*

Jóhannesson, J. Á. (2008, 09). Ísland í dag. [TV show]. Icelands Channel 2.

Jónsson, A. (2009). *Why Iceland?: How One of the World's Smallest Countries Became the Meltdown's Biggest Casualty.* NY: McGraw-Hill.

Jónsson Aðils, J. (1903). *Íslenskt þjóðerni.* [Icelandic nationality]. Reykjavik: Félagsprentsmiðjan.

Jónsson, I. (1991). *Hegemonic Politics and Accumulation Strategies in Iceland, 1944–1990: Longwaves in the World Economy, Regimes of Accumulation and Uneven Development: Small States, Microstates and Problems of World Market Adjustment.* University of Sussex. Retrieved from ethos.bl.uk.

Jónsson, K. (2000, 05). Vinsælasa ráðið. [The most popular advice]. *Morgunblaðið.* Reykjavik.

Jósepsson, L. (1973). History of the Cod Wars Part 3. Retrieved from youtube.com.

Judgment of the Court 28 January 2013 in Case E-16/11 (2013, 01). EFTA Court. Retrieved from eftacourt.int.

Júlíusson, Þ. S. (2009, 02). Eftirlitin skoðuðu flutninga á fjármagni til Kaupþings. [The supervisory authorities examined money transfers to Kaupthing]. Reykjavik: *Morgunblaðið.* Retrieved from mbl.is.

Kaminsky, G. L., & Reinhart, C. M. (1999). The Twin Crises: The Causes of Banking and Balance-of-payments Problems. *American Economic Review,* 89(3), June 1999, 473–500.

Karlsson, G. (2000). *Iceland's 1,100 Years: The History of a Marginal Society.* C. Hurst.

Katzenstein, P. J. (1985). *Small States in World Markets: Industrial Policy in Europe.* Ithaca, NY: Cornell University Press.

Kaupthing Bank. (2005). Series: Fixed Income Credit Research. Investment Grade. The Royal Bank of Scotland.

Kaupthing Best Bank in the Nordic Region and Iceland. Euromoney Recently Announced the Winners of its Awards for Excellence – The Most Prestigious Awards in the Global Banking Industry (2007, 07). *PRWeb.* Retrieved from prweb.com.

Kirby, P. (2010). *Celtic Tiger in Collapse: Explaining the Weaknesses of the Irish Model.* Basingstoke: Palgrave Macmillan.

Kristinsson, G. H. (2006). *Íslenska stjórnkerfið.* [Icelandic governmental system]. Reykjavik: Háskólaútgáfan.

Kristjánsdóttir, R. (2008). *Nýtt fólk: þjóðerni og íslensk verkalýðsstjórnmál 1901–1944*. [New people]. Reykjavik: Háskólaútgáfan.

Kristjánsson, S. (1977). *Corporatism in Iceland?* Reykjavik: Félagsvísindadeild.

Kristjánsson, S. (2012). Frá nýsköpun lýðræðis til óhefts flokkavalds: Fjórir forsetar Íslands 1944–1996. [Four Presidents]. Reykjavik: *Skírnir*, (Vor).

Krugman, P. (2008, 09). The $850 Billion Bailout. *krugman.blogs.nytimes.com*. Retrieved from krugman.blogs.nytimes.com.

Krugman, P. (2009, 04). Erin Go Broke. *The New York Times*. New York. Retrieved from nytimes.com.

Krugman, P. (2013, 01). Inequality and Recovery. *The Conscience of a Liberal*. Retrieved from krugman.blogs.nytimes.com.

Laffer, A. B., Moore, S., & Williams, J. (2007). *Rich States, Poor States: ALEC-Laffer State Economic Competitiveness Index*. ALEC. Retrieved from google.com/books.

Lán Seðlabankans vegna FIH er tapað (2012). [CBs FIH loan is lost]. *Viðskiptablaðið*. Retrieved from vb.is.

Lewis, M. (2009, 14). Wall Street on the Tundra. *Vanity Fair*. New York.

LEX (2008, 10). World on the Edge. *Economist*. London. Retrieved from economist.com

Loftsdóttir, K. (2010). The Loss of Innocence: The Icelandic Fnancial Crisis and Colonial Past. *Anthropology Today*, 26(6), 9–13.

Loftsdóttir, K. (2011). Negotiating White Icelandic Identity: Multiculturalism and Colonial Identity Formations. *Social Identities*, 17(1), 11–25.

Loftsdóttir, K. (2012). The Place McDonald's Rejected: The Embrace of Desire and Anxieties in a Global Crisis. Work shop paper. Crisis and Nordic Identities. Reykjavik: Universtiy of Iceland.

Lyall, S. (2008, 11). Iceland, Mired in Debt, Blames Britain for Woes. *The New York Times*. Retrieved from nytimes.com.

Macheda, F. (2012). The Role of Pension Funds in the Financialisation of the Icelandic Economy. *Capital & Class*, 36(3), 433–473.

Magnússon, G. (2008, 12). Landstjórinn. [The covernor]. *Eyjan*. Retrieved from blog.pressan.is.

Magnússon, M. Á. (2011). *The Engagement of Iceland and Malta with European Integration: Economic Incentives and Political Constraints*. University of Iceland, Faculty of Political Science.

Mamou (2008, 10). De la difficulté d'anticiper les crises, Économie. *Le Monde*. Paris.

Matthiasson, T. (2008). Spinning out of Control, Iceland in Crisis. *Nordic Journal of Political Economy*, 34(3), 1–19.

McVeigh, T. (2008, 10). The Party's Over for Iceland, the Island that Tried to Buy the World. *The Observer*. London. Retrieved from guardian.co.uk.

Meuwse, A. (2012). Popular Constitution-Making: The Case of Iceland. *Tilburg Law School*, (Working paper).

Ministry of Finance and Economic Affairs. (2013). *Pre-accession Economic Programme 2013* (Government Report). Reykjavik.

Mishkin, F. S., & Herbertsson, T. T. (2006). *Financial Stability in Iceland*. Iceland Chamber of Commerce. Retrieved from verslunarrad.is.

Mjøset, L. (1987). Nordic Economic Policies in the 1970s and 1980s. *International Organization*, 41(3), 403–456.

Montgomery, A. (2008, 10). Identica hit by Icesave collapse. *Design Week*. London. Retrieved from designweek.co.uk.

Moody's (2007). *Credit Opinion: Iceland, Government of* (Global Credit Research). Retrieved from bonds.is.

Moody's (2013). *Moody's Changes Outlook on Iceland's Baa3 Rating to Stable from Negative* (Investors Service). Retrieved from moodys.com.

Morris, H. (2012, 10). Crowdsourcing Iceland's Constitution. *International Herald Tribune*. New York.

Murphy, P. (2008a). Reykjavik-on-Thames. *Financial Times*. Retrieved from ftalphaville.ft.com.

Murphy, P. (2008b, 10). Who Will Stand up for Iceland? We Will. *Financial Times*. London. Retrieved from ftalphaville.ft.com.

Neumann, I. B. (2002). This Little Piggy Stayed at Home: Why Norway is not a Member of the EU. *European Integration and National Identity: The Challenge of the Nordic States*, 88–129.

Niðurstöðum þjóðaratkvæðagreiðslunnar lýst. (2012, 10). [Announcing referendum results]. *Landskjörstjórn*. Official website of the National Electoral Commission of Iceland. Retrieved from landskjor.is.

Nielsen Germaud, A.-S. (2010). The Vikings are Coming! A Modern Icelandic Self-image in the Light of the Economic Crisis. *NORDERUOPAforum*, 20.

Nielsson, U., & Torfason, B. K. (2012). Iceland's Economic Eruption and Meltdown. *Scandinavian Economic History Review*, 60(1), 3–30.

Oddsson, D. (2008, 10). [TV interview]. Kastljós. RÚV.

Ólafsson, J. (2012). An Experiment in Iceland: Crowdsourcing a Constitution. *Bifrost University*,(Working paper).

Ólafsson, S. (2005). 12 Normative Foundations of the Icelandic Welfare State. *The Normative Foundations of the Welfare State: The Nordic Experience*, 7, 214.

Ólafsson, S. (2008, 11). *Útrás íslenskra fyrirtækja*. [Outvation of Icelandic companies]. University of Iceland. Retrieved from ll.is.

Ólafsson, Stefán, & Kristjánsson, A. S. (2012). *Umfang kreppunnar og afkoma ólíkra hópa*. [The scope of the crisis]. Reykjavik: Þjóðmálastofnun. Retrieved from thjodmalastofnun.hi.is.

Overbeek, H. (2004). *Global Governance, Class, Hegemony: A Historical Materialist Perspective*. Amsterdam: Free University of Amsterdam. Retrieved from fsw.vu.nl.

Pálsson, G., & Durrenberger, E. P. (1992). Icelandic Dialogues: Individual Differences in Indigenous Discourse. *Journal of Anthropological Research*, 301–316.

Pettinger, T. (2013, 02). Iceland's Recovery. *Economics Help*. Retrieved from economicshelp.org.

Pilkington, E. (2008, 11). Gordon Brown heralds progress at G20 financial crisis talks. *The Guardian*. London. Retrieved from guardian.co.uk.

Portes, R., & Baldursson, F. M. (2007). *The Internationalisation of Iceland's Financial Sector*. Iceland Chamber of Commerce. Retrieved from faculty.london.edu.

Prime Minister's Office (2006). *Alþjóðleg fjármálastarfsemi á Íslandi: Nefnd forsætisráðherra um alþjóðlega fjármálastarfsemi* (Report). Reykjavik. Retrieved from forsaetisraduneyti.is.

Rozwadowski, F. (2013, 01). Jákvæð áhrif á lánshæfismatið. [Possitive effect on creditworthiness]. Reykjavik: *Fréttablaðið*.

Samtal Árna og Darlings (2008, 10). [Árni and Darlings discussions]. *Morgunblaðið*. Reykjavik. Retrieved from mbl.is.

Samtök Iðnaðarins (2013). *Viðhorf almennings til ESB*. [Public opinion for EU membership]. Reykjavik: Federation of Icelandic Industries.

Scrutton, A. (2013, 02). *Analysis: Icelanders Question their Lauded Economic Recovery*. Reuters.

Shields, S., Bruff, I., & Macartney, H. (2011). *Critical International Political Economy: Dialoge, Debate and Dissensus*. Basingstoke: Palgrave Macmillan. Retrieved from us.macmillan.com.

Sigurjónsson, N. (2011, 08). *Framing the Revolution: The Polyrhytmic Organization of the 2009 Protests in Iceland*. Presented at the Den femte nordiska konferensen för kulturpolitisk forskning, Norrköping.

Skarphéðinsson, Ö. (2008, 10). Fundum vin í Austri. [Finding a friend in the east]. Reykjavik: *Fréttablaðið*.

Smith, A. D. (1993). *National Identity*. Reno, Nevada: University of Nevada Press. Retrieved from google.com/books.

Stiglitz, J. (2013, 01). Inequality Is Holding Back the Recovery. *The New York Times*. Retrieved from opinionator.blogs.nytimes.com.

Sveinsson, S. G. (2013). *Búsáhaldabyltingin*. Reykjavik: Almenna bókafélagið.

Sverrisdóttir, V. (2006, 02). Endalok íslenskrar útrásar. [End of Icelands outvation]. Kópavogur: *Blaðið*.

Teather, D. (2008). Iceland Government Seizes Control of Landsbanki. *The Guardian*. Retrieved from guardian.co.uk.

Teubner, G. (2011). A Constitutional Moment – The Logics of 'Hit the Bottom'. In Poul Kjaer and Gunther Teubner (eds) *The Financial Crisis in Constitutional Perspective: The Dark Side of Functional Differentiation*. Oxford: Hart. Retrieved from papers.ssrn.com.

The Hague Threatens Iceland's EU Bid over Lost Savings (2009, 07). *NRC Handelsblad*. Retrieved from vorige.nrc.nl.

The Landsbanki Freezing Order 2008, Pub. L. No. 2008 No. 2668 (2008). Retrieved from legislation.gov.uk.

The Main Conclusions of the National Forum 2010 (2010, 07). Þjóðfundur 2010. Retrieved from thjodfundur2010.is.

Thomas, R. (2006). *Icelandic Banks. Not What You Are Thinking*. Merrill Lynch. Retrieved from bonds.is.

Thomsen, P. (2011, 10). How Iceland Recovered from Its Near-Death Experience. *IMFdirect*. Retrieved from blog-imfdirect.imf.org.

Thorhallsson, B. (2000). *The Role of Small States in the European Union*. Ashgate Aldershot. Retrieved from lavoisier.fr.

Thorhallsson, B. (2009). Can Small States Choose their own Size? The Case of a Nordic State – Iceland. In *The Diplomacies of Small States, Between Vulnerability and Resilience*. Palgrave Macmillan.

Thorvaldsson, A. (2011). *Frozen Assets: How I Lived Iceland's Boom and Bust*. Wiley.

Tíu aflóga nýlenduveldi ráða lögum og lofum í Evrópusambandinu (2012, 07). [Ten obsolete colonial powers control the EU]. *Fullveldi*. Retrieved from fullveldi.blog.is.

Transcript of Press Briefing by David Hawley, Senior Advisor, External Relations Department (2008, 11). *International Monetary Fund*. Retrieved from imf.org.

Tveir þriðju hlynntir mótmælum (2009, 01). [Two thirds support the protests]. *Fréttablaðið*. Reykjavik. Retrieved from timarit.is.

United Nations (2008). *Human Development Indices*. Retrieved from hdr.undp. org.

Valgreen, C., & Christensen, L. (2006). *Iceland: Geyser Crisis*. Copenhagen: Den Danske Bank.

Wade, R. H., & Sigurgeirsdottir, S. (2012). Iceland's Rise, Fall, Stabilisation and Beyond. *Cambridge Journal of Economics*, 36(1), 127–144.

Welding, L. (2008, 09). Silfur Egils. [TV show.] Reykajvk: RUV

Westwood, M. (2008, 1). Made to Mingle with Electricity. *The Australian*. Retrieved 30 May, 2013, from theaustralian.com.au.

Þorláksson, I. (2013, 04). Uppdiktuð skattbyrði. [Made up tax burden]þ *Eyjan website*. Retrieved from blog.pressan.is.

Index

CPI Antony Rowe
Chippenham, UK
2018-01-31 21:51